PEASANTS AND KING
IN BURGUNDY

CALIFORNIA SERIES ON SOCIAL CHOICE
AND POLITICAL ECONOMY

Edited by Brian Barry, Robert H. Bates,
and Samuel L. Popkin

PEASANTS AND KING IN BURGUNDY

Agrarian Foundations of French Absolutism

HILTON L. ROOT

UNIVERSITY OF CALIFORNIA PRESS
Berkeley   Los Angeles   London

University of California Press
Berkeley and Los Angeles, California

University of California Press, Ltd.
London, England

© 1987 by
The Regents of the University of California

First Paperback Printing 1992

Library of Congress Cataloging-in-Publication Data

Root, Hilton L.
  Peasants and king in Burgundy

(California series on social choice and political
economy)
    1. Peasantry—France—Burgundy—History. 2. Land
tenure—France—Burgundy—History. 3. France—Politics
and government. I. Title. II. Series.
HD1536.F8R66 1987   305.5′63   86-1064
ISBN 0-520-08097-1

Printed in the United States of America

1 2 3 4 5 6 7 8 9

For Nancy

Contents

Acknowledgments

In the course of writing this book I have acquired many debts. Special thanks are due to Keith Baker, Robert Bates, Harold Cook, Robert Forster, Philip Hoffman, Lynn Hunt, David Lux, Samuel Popkin, Jacob Price, Sylvia Thrupp, Charles Tilly, and James Vann. Their readings and criticisms improved the manuscript immeasurably. David Bien provided direction and advice at every stage, especially when this study was taking shape as a dissertation. In France, Jean Bart, Pierre Deyon, François Furet, Emmanuel Le Roy Ladurie, and Albert Soboul gave unstintingly of their time and expertise. I would like to express my deepest gratitude to Jean Rigault and Françoise Vignier and to their staff at the Archives Départementales of the Côte-d'Or in Dijon for their assistance and cooperation. The manuscript also benefited greatly from comments by the anonymous readers of the Press and from the editing of Lydia Duncan. I thank them all.

The Fulbright-Hayes Foundation and the Department of History of the University of Michigan provided fellowships for two years (1978–1980) of research in France. The Horace Rackham School of Graduate Studies and the Department of History generously supported the three years of dissertation writing that followed. A summer stipend from the National Endowment for the Humanities (1984) allowed me to complete my research. The California Institute of Technology provided stimulation and the

Andrew W. Mellon Foundation provided funds for the two invaluable years (1983–1985) during which the dissertation became a book.

Very special thanks are due to my family for patiently enduring my early enthusiasm for travel and study in Europe. And to my wife, Nancy, who made it all possible, I dedicate this book.

Abbreviations

AD	Archives Départementales du Côte-d'Or, Dijon
AN	Archives Nationales, Paris
Annales E.S.C.	*Annales: Economies, sociétés, civilisations*
BM	Bibliothèque Municipale, Dijon
MSHDB	*Mémoires de la société pour l'histoire du droit et des institutions des anciens pays bourguignons, comtois, et romands*

Introduction:
The State, the Peasantry,
and the Revolution

In the thinking of historians about France in the eighteenth century, or indeed any century since the tenth, it is axiomatic that the power of the central state grew. Probably none would disagree. But a corollary to that proposition—one might call it the Tocqueville corollary, though it has been advanced by others—is perhaps more doubtful. This is the view that all growth in the power of the center had to be accomplished at the expense of power exercised locally; that is, centralization necessarily undermined the autonomy of long-established corporations such as the villages. It is to test the validity of that corollary that this book was written. Its subject is villages in eighteenth-century Burgundy and their relations with the state, but it was not intended as a comprehensive history of the peasantry, agriculture, or local administration. However, this study will perhaps have implications for broader issues and will, I hope, at least call into question certain important assumptions about social, economic, and institutional development, as well as the background of rural revolution.

Historians and social scientists usually discuss the state's relationship to the village in the following terms. Organized to protect the peasant's welfare, the villages were bastions of the precapitalist culture. Village institutions were designed to provide insurance from destitution and even subsistence for the inhabitants; they reflected the peasantry's archaic preference for equality and self-sufficiency. But in the eighteenth century, the state, to modernize and to prepare for the transition to capitalism, laid siege to the precapitalist organization of the village. State officials, collaborating with capitalists, attacked the village's communal lands and practices and attempted to dismantle the age-old, corporate villages. The peasants protested this attempt to destroy their ancient communal culture; their protests culminated in revolution.

It is this view of the relationship between the French state and the villages that I seek to reinterpret. I wish to suggest that instead of dismantling these communities, the increasingly active state actually strengthened them. In Burgundy, communal property rights were upheld and communal tax collection and self-governance were encouraged by agents of the state. Royal officials concerned with administrative control and efficient tax collection had reasons to protect communal institutions. The consequences of that protection would be great.

Questions concerning the relationship of the peasantry to markets and to capitalism are not central to the thesis of this book. Nevertheless, because the debate about the origins of capitalism has become a reference point for most discussions of the peasantry under the Old Regime, I will attempt to situate this study within that broader debate.[1] In the analysis of a number of influential scholars, state building and capitalism are linked to the decline of communities, and commercial agriculture is assumed to have expanded at the expense of communal property, thus threatening the peasants' general welfare. In Burgundy, however, village institutions did not level social inequalities, nor did they insulate the village from the external market economy. The preservation of common rights did not result in a redistribution of wealth, but rather maintained and increased inequality and social

1. By capitalism I mean an economic system that includes (1) market exchange of both products and factors of production, with private markets for land and labor; and (2) capital accumulation to secure, reproduce, and expand the means of production.

stratification.[2] Moreover, there was not an implicit contradiction between communal property and production for the market. The commercialization of communal lands during the eighteenth century seems to have contributed to the strength of the village.[3] State officials favored more commercial and market-oriented villages in Burgundy as well as stronger corporate and communal rights. Nevertheless, an economic price was paid for the preservation of common rights. Communal agriculture could accommodate commercialization and capital accumulation, but it retarded the application of new, more efficient technologies and methodologies. French agriculture did not realize its full potential in the eighteenth century because of political arrangements that reinforced communal property rights.

The experience of Burgundian peasants also has implications for the study of rural revolution. Peasant unrest in Burgundy left little evidence of a confrontation between a collectivist peasant community and a rival culture of bourgeois individualism. Nor do Burgundian records support the thesis that the state became the object of rural protest because it had unleashed the forces of capitalism. On the contrary, state officials encouraged peasants to improve their economic condition by disputing in court the legal basis of feudal dues they owed to their lords. Peasants were not acting to prevent the development of the market economy in bringing those suits. They were using a state-sanctioned form of protest, the court case, to escape the power of the seigneurs and

2. AN, H-1486/284. Responding to an administrative inquiry concerned with the possibility of abolishing communal property rights, the *procureur général* of Provence wrote: "One often argues that common pasture rights were established for the benefit of the poor who do not own enough pasture to feed their animals. It is absolutely false in Provence. Common pasture rights were established principally in favor of the rich who can buy and maintain large flocks and who could not feed them if they were kept on their own lands, given the infinite division of our land into a multitude of small properties." This administrator's argument may have been implausible, but the important point is that communal rights did not result in a redistribution of wealth, but rather served the interests of wealthy farmers. Ripert Montclar to M. Parent, *premier commis* of controller general Bertin, 10 July 1766.

3. Efforts to prevent those properties from falling into the hands of seigneurial agents did nevertheless provide a basis for cooperation between rich and poor in the village. On cooperation, see Chapter 5. See also Robert Axelrod, *The Evolution of Cooperation* (New York, 1984); and Michael Taylor, *Community, Anarchy, and Liberty* (Cambridge, 1982). Russell Hardin, in *Collective Action* (Baltimore, 1982), examines the incentives that motivate groups to take action.

to enable themselves to compete more fairly for the benefits of the market. Before presenting my argument in detail, I shall examine some other interpretations of the state's relationship to the peasantry.

OTHER INTERPRETATIONS

Tocqueville is one of the scholars who have made an essential contribution to an understanding of the relationship between the central state and local communities under the Old Regime. He postulated what is still the generally held opinion that centralization undermined local autonomy, although today few sympathize with his fear that in France more democracy would mean more domination of society by the centralizing state. Tocqueville argued that the village assemblies, once the arbiters of local government, became in the eighteenth century "an empty show of freedom; [they] had no real power." After reading the records of village meetings in the district surrounding Tours, he remarked:

It will be noted that this parish assembly was a mere administrative inquiry, in the same form and as costly as judicial inquiries; that it never led to a vote or other clear expression of the will of the parish; that it was merely an expression of individual opinions, and constituted no check upon government. Many other documents indicate that the only object of parish assemblies was to afford information to the intendant, and not to influence his decision even in cases where no other interest but that of the parish was concerned. . . . The government preponderates, acts, controls, undertakes everything, provides for everything, knows far more about the subject's business than he does himself.

Tocqueville was persuaded that centralization was equivalent to sterilization.

Tocqueville was concerned that in the transition from an aristocratic to a democratic society, local autonomy would be sacrificed. "How could it be otherwise? Noblemen take no concern for anything; the bourgeois live in towns; and the community is represented by a rude peasant." Centralization, because it removed the nobility from the countryside, left the peasants defenseless against the bureaucratic tyranny of the state. "Since most of the wealthier or more cultivated residents had migrated to the city, . . . the [country] population was little more than a horde of ignorant, uneducated peasants, quite incapable of administering local affairs." Tocqueville concluded that the tradition of local government, dating back to the Middle Ages, was lost in the eighteenth century.[4]

In interpreting the Revolution, historians since Tocqueville have continued to concentrate on the peasantry's relationship to the state under the Old Regime, but they have added a further consideration—capitalism. More concerned than Tocqueville with the economically determined structure of society, many of them have argued that peasants acted in the Revolution to protect their precapitalist culture and the village organization from the capitalism foisted upon them by the centralizing state. France's foremost historian of the Revolution, Georges Lefebvre, was the first to advance that proposition. He argued that during the Revolution, which marked the coming to power of the bourgeoisie, there was an autonomous peasant revolution that was anticapitalist and traditionalist, aimed at preserving an "economic and social world that was precapitalist." The peasants, Lefebvre argued, were opposed to the capitalism for which the French Revolution had cleared the way, and they responded defensively to the triumph of the bourgeoisie. They acted to prevent capitalism from destroying traditional communal institutions. During that revolution, the peasants "opposed with all their force the capitalist transformation of agriculture. In their spirit there was much more conservatism and routine than zeal for change. It was with elements from their past that they wanted to construct their social ideal." The peasants had a keen sense of social rights and social justice. In contrast to the bourgeois assertion of the inviolability of private property, they claimed that "superior to the rights of property are the just needs of the community in which all the inhabitants have a right to live."

The precapitalist organization of the village was not socialist,

4. Alexis de Tocqueville, *The Old Regime and the French Revolution*, translated by Stuart Gilbert (New York, 1954), pp. 45–51, 252, 255. The Burgundian evidence reveals that, just as Tocqueville had suspected, royal officials encouraged village democracy as a means to increase their control over local politics. Although he accurately predicted how democratic forms of government might facilitate greater bureaucratic supervision, Tocqueville underestimated the vitality of peasant politics during the Old Regime. Making village government more bureaucratic had unexpected results. The problem of villagers' participation in governance is discussed at length in Chapter 3.

Lefebvre insisted, because the peasants did not constitute a class; they possessed divergent economic interests. In addition, the peasantry was more concerned with the distribution of wealth than with organizing a system of production. "They dreamed of enclosing themselves in their time-honored routines and stopping the progress of capitalism. It was the division not the production of wealth that interested them." Rather than socializing the means of production, such as tools, livestock, or land, the peasants "wanted only enough land, in property or lease, to provide for their families." Lefebvre nevertheless asserted that modern socialism owes much to the peasants' commitment to social justice. The notion that socialism can be traced to these rural communities has been unquestioned since Lefebvre. His claim that the institutions of the precapitalist village were morally superior to those of modern capitalism has also gone largely unchallenged.[5]

Albert Soboul, Lefebvre's successor as France's foremost historian of the French Revolution, carried the latter's interpretation one step further and posited the existence of a direct connection between peasant culture and socialism. He integrated the history of the French peasantry directly into a larger debate concerning the transition from feudalism to capitalism. However, his interpretation differed from that of Lefebvre in one important way. Soboul perceived the community as a "natural" premarket economy that feudalism could accommodate, whereas it could not accommodate capitalism. Capitalism required cheap proletarian labor, which in turn required the elimination of the communal practices that sustained the peasant small holding. Soboul claimed that a fundamental antagonism existed between capitalism and the community. The traditional community had to be suppressed so that an essential distinction could be made between labor and capital in order for the transition from feudalism to capitalism to occur.[6]

5. Georges Lefebvre, "La Révolution française et les paysans," in his *Etudes sur la Révolution française* (Paris, 1963), pp. 338–68. This article is the most complete statement of Lefebvre's philosophy. In it he implies that by bringing their communal tradition to the cities, peasant immigrants contributed to the growth of socialism in nineteenth-century France (p. 349).

6. Albert Soboul, "The French Rural Community in the Eighteenth and Nineteenth Centuries," *Past and Present* 10 (Nov. 1956):78–96.

Soboul's principal concern was the relationship of feudalism to capitalism. That the state assaulted the communal traditions of the village to facilitate that transition is a notion that has been discussed most explicitly by American sociologists. Charles Tilly in particular has explored the state's collaboration with the capitalists during the eighteenth century to bring about the demise of communities.[7] To establish the primacy of capitalist relations of production, the crown "generally acted to promote [the land's] transformation into disposable property, to strengthen the rights of owners, to discourage multiple-use rights on the same land. Customary hunting became poaching. Customary gleaning and gathering became trespassing. Customary scratching out a corner of the wasteland became squatting." Thus, "for France's ordinary people, the eighteenth century fused the costs of statemaking with the burdens of capitalism." Tilly found support for this view in royal edicts that "favor the shipment of local supplies wherever merchants could get the highest price, a strenuous effort to break monopolies of workers over local employment, an encouragement of bourgeois property in land—all features of government action that forwarded the interests of capitalism." The most articulate government spokesman for the emerging capitalist order was Turgot, since "he self-consciously advocated the accumulation of capital, the elimination of small farmers, and the spread of wage labor in agriculture and industry." In the process, "all French governments of the later eighteenth century trampled the interests of ordinary people." The state played the capitalist game, Tilly reminds us, for fiscal reasons—"to maintain the crown's sources of credit and to generate new taxable income." In this zero-sum game, what was of benefit to the capitalists was harmful to everyone else.

Charles Tilly's emphasis on the growth of markets and on the impact of state formation has opened new areas for scholars to research and has produced new theories to be tested in future studies. For Tilly, even more than for Lefebvre, rural protest was

7. For an alternative view of France by a scholar of historical sociology, see Theda Skocpol, *States and Social Revolutions* (Cambridge, 1979). Skocpol argues that the state can be autonomous of the dominant class. It can be a partner or a competitor but always acts to perpetuate itself. Thus, in her model, states are actors who are as important as classes.

a defense against capitalism. Social revolutions commonly follow the introduction of capitalism. The peasants protested when
noncapitalist property relations were threatened. They clung to
communal traditions and resisted capitalism because it would
lead to the loss of communal property, to expropriation, and to
proletarianization. "Holders of small capital fought off their ma-
nipulation by holders of large capital, workers struggled with
capitalists, and—most of all—people whose lives depended on
communal or other noncapitalist property relationships battled
others who tried to extend capitalist property into their do-
mains." As the state's commitment to the capitalist program
increased, so did the opposition. Alliances between capitalists
and state officials aroused the opposition of the common people,
who wanted "food at a feasible price, equitable and moderate
taxation, checks on speculators, and guarantees of employment." Nevertheless, economic expansion continued by under-
mining communal rights and the consumer-oriented economic
regulation upon which these people depended for their survival.
"France's government did not cause these evils on their own;
the capitalists were the real offenders. By collaborating with
those capitalists and authorizing their profit-taking, the French
monarchy took on the stigmas of their misdeeds. King Louis and
his agents paid the price."[8]

Barrington Moore has also argued that in 1789, the precapitalist peasantry wanted to prevent France's transition to a modern
capitalist democracy. Like the other scholars discussed here,
Moore believed that in the eighteenth century "the modernization of French society took place through [efforts of] the crown."
Those efforts to modernize were hindered, however, by the emphasis on peasant property rights, which was a carry-over from
earlier state policies. Beginning in the Middle Ages, the kings of
France had attempted to consolidate their political authority by
protecting peasant property rights. The crown reinforced those

8. Charles Tilly, "Statemaking, Capitalism, and Revolution in Five Provinces
of Eighteenth-Century France," Center for Research on Social Organization
Working Paper no. 281, pp. 14, 15, 15, 15, 8, 18, 52; now collected in The
Contentious French (Cambridge, Mass., 1985). See also Tilly's introduction to
The Formation of National States in Western Europe (Princeton, N.J., 1975).

rights to establish a counterweight to seigneurial authority. Later, with its property rights firmly established, the peasantry
wielded enough power to determine how far the Revolutionary
government would go in the direction of capitalism. Moore
argued, as Lefebvre and Tilly had, that the peasants opposed the
Revolution because "as a pre-capitalist group, peasants frequently display anticapitalist tendencies."[9]

To summarize, there is a convergence of opinion between
French Marxists and American sociologists on the subject of the
role of the peasantry during the French Revolution. The ideas of
Lefebvre, Soboul, and Tilly overlap. All three asserted that the
peasants wanted to protect traditional values from the disruptive
influences of capitalism. Tilly made explicit the implication of
Soboul and Lefebvre that the state was an agent of class exploitation. Lefebvre's interpretation was a point of departure for Barrington Moore, but Moore's principal concern was the kind of
political regime that results when agrarian societies become
modern industrial ones. Tocqueville concentrated on the politically determined structure of society under the Old Regime.
That the royal administration destroyed aristocratic institutions
was his greatest regret. Tocqueville linked the excesses of the
Revolution, and of France's movement toward democracy in
general, to abolition of the nobility's role as intermediary between the king and the nation.

What is common to all these interpretations of long-term political change is the belief that the state was the winner and
communities were the losers: The progressive, modernizing

9. Barrington Moore, Jr., "Evolution and Revolution in France," in *Social
Origins of Dictatorship and Democracy: Lord and Peasant in the Making of the
Modern World* (Boston, 1966), pp. 40–108. Moore's analysis of the relationship of
the Old Regime state to the peasantry differs from the one presented in this
book. He emphasizes that the monarchy built its political base in alliance with
individual peasant proprietors. The point made here is that the state did not have
the administrative capacity to work with individual peasants. That is why it
dealt with the community instead. Robert Brenner, in his study of the agrarian
class structure of the French state ("Agrarian Class Structure and Economic
Development in Pre-Industrial Europe," *Past and Present* 70 [Feb. 1976]:30–75),
also emphasizes an alliance between the crown and the peasants as individual
producers. In this study I argue that it was not the strength of peasant proprietors
but the strength of village communities that hindered agricultural development
in France.

state gained authority by eliminating the traditional communal institutions. In this book I provide an alternative view of the impact of state formation on village organization during the Old Regime.

THE BURGUNDIAN EXAMPLE

The documents from Burgundian villages do not support the theory that precapitalist villages were destroyed by the forces of state building and capitalism. In Burgundy, the corporate structure of the village was more developed in the eighteenth century than it had ever been. Royal administrators had promoted collective ownership of property and collective responsibility for debts in order to extract goods and services from the peasantry. As a result of this state policy, the corporate village became a vital component of the centralized state structure.[10]

The experience of Burgundian peasants raises doubts that communal institutions provided more security for the average peasant than did capitalist institutions. In Burgundy, collective agriculture, collective tax responsibility, and egalitarian participation in village assemblies seem not to have ensured the redistribution of wealth or the leveling of inequalities; nor did they guarantee subsistence. Communal property relations were not predicated upon preference for subsistence over market production. Peasants actually exploited collective rights so that they could produce more effectively for the market. Thus, there seems to have been no fundamental conflict between village customs and capitalist practices.[11]

Historians have described the French state and its bureaucracy as agents of modernization. Under the Old Regime, the state took great efforts to identify itself and its policies with the

10. In this book "the state" is synonymous with the interests of the king as defined by his council. The term is interchangeable with king or crown and does not include provincial estates or parlements. They are viewed as representatives of the society.

11. Even the poorest peasants were able to find important commercial uses for common rights. Land-poor peasants might use their rights to the commons to pasture sheep for town butchers. The butchers provided the livestock and the peasants kept a percentage of the profits. See Françoise Fortunet, *Charité ingénieuse et pauvre misère: Les baux à cheptel simple en Auxois aux XVIIIème et XIXème siècles* (Dijon, 1985).

most modern ideas regarding economic development. It supported academies, funded competitions for new ideas on how to reform the economy, and provided employment within the administration for the advocates of new ideas. In the twenty years that preceded the Revolution, the crown issued extensive legislation that incorporated the ideas of the reformers. In policy statements, the king reiterated a commitment to transforming the society and the economy. Beyond the governmental pronouncements, however, lay a different reality. The state had to conduct an extensive publicity campaign to persuade opponents that its intention was to modernize precisely because bureaucratic practice differed radically from the rhetoric.

In this study, I attempt to determine what this reality was—that is, how provincial administrators exerted their control over the villages. I will examine the mechanisms developed by the crown to monitor village tax collection, the monarchy's dependence upon credit operations, and the village's importance to the kingdom's credit structure. When the royal budget was finally made public a few years before the Revolution, many contemporaries were shocked by the magnitude of the state debt and by the fact that more than 50 percent of current revenues was being used to finance that debt. I will argue that the size of the royal debt and the survival of the villages were closely related.

I chose Burgundy as the focus of this study, first, because its judicial and administrative archives on communities under the Old Regime are more extensive than those of the other provinces, and second, because another historian, Pierre de Saint-Jacob, had already completed a comprehensive analysis of the province's population, economic situation, and seigneurial system—one of the most oppressive in the kingdom. Publication of this pioneering study of the eighteenth-century Burgundian peasantry, based on his thorough analysis of notarial archives, fiscal rolls, and seigneurial accounts, allowed me to concentrate on pursuing an institutional and political analysis by researching the administrative and judicial archives. Though it was not his primary focus, Saint-Jacob considered the role of the intendant. His conclusions parallel the findings presented here. He also found that the intendant's policies contributed to the survival of the community and that the communities increasingly initiated litigation against the lords.[12]

Agriculture in eighteenth-century Burgundy consisted primarily of grain growing in the open fields of the Northeast; wine growing south of Dijon; and cattle rearing in the South. This study concentrates on the villages in the northeast—in what is presently the department of the Côte-d'Or. It is not concerned with the wine-growing area south of Dijon or with the Brionnais (southeastern Burgundy), which was then converting to cattle production to supply markets in Lyon. The distinction of economic variations in Burgundy, and in France itself, is not within the scope of this study. When more is known about the state-community relationship that existed in other parts of the country during this period, we will perhaps be able to generalize that certain kinds of agriculture generated certain forms of communal organization. In the absence of such information, this book can only present some conclusions about eighteenth-century France, based on the correspondence of the Burgundian intendancy and the court records of Burgundian villages. Nevertheless, such a regional study does enable us to distinguish the main processes and structures that have shaped both the past and the present.[13]

This study confirms Tocqueville's argument that the central government had replaced the seigneur as the primary political force. However, unlike Tocqueville, I have concluded that establishment of a strong central government actually increased the power of the community. Tocqueville claimed that the power of the community, like that of the seigneur, was declining. One reason for these different conclusions could be that an extensive collection of administrative archives on Burgundian communities has survived. Tocqueville consulted the administrative archives of Tours, where village records had all but disappeared.

12. Pierre de Saint-Jacob, *Les paysans de la Bourgogne du nord au dernier siècle de l'Ancien Régime* (Dijon, 1960). "It must be said that the policies of the intendant promoted the survival of these ideas [referring to the peasantry's "attachment to collective customs and properties"] by maintaining intact his old mission of protecting village communities. He fought against their dissolution until the end" (pp. 517–18).

13. Charles Tilly makes a similar point about regional monographs in *Big Structures, Large Processes, Huge Comparisons* (New York, 1984).

There is also evidence that the crown's authority was strongest in Burgundy. At the end of the Old Regime, Burgundy had thirty-four royal subdelegates—more than any other province.

Royal officials were adept at concealing their administrative weakness and the extent of the king's debts. I found no document that explains the state's credit structure or the involvement of the province in the national financial networks. Nor does the correspondence of administrators include statements of general principles. I have attempted to reconstruct these networks by analyzing thousands of decisions made at the local level.

Royal Administration in Burgundy

Fiscal pressures in the seventeenth century led royal officials to encourage corporate methods of tax collection, stimulate broad participation in village meetings, and protect collective property. Since these administrators had to operate with a limited number of personnel, they concluded that enforcing collective liability was the most efficient way to collect taxes. Although they claimed to have the power of coercion, the crown's representatives did not possess the means by which to measure, monitor, or enforce compliance with royal policies.[14] Administrators sought to avoid the costs that attended direct supervision of individual taxpayers. In the eighteenth century, the state's administrative capacity had not increased sufficiently for local royal officials to abandon the old policies of collective coercion. Therefore, collective restraints remained the crown's only method to compel compliance with its tax policies and to avoid incurring these costs. Collective responsibility helped cut the costs of tax collection in an additional way. Fiscal authorities could estimate the income of a village more accurately than they could the income of any particular taxpayer in the village. To over-

14. See Margaret Levi, "The Predatory Theory of Rule," *Politics and Society* 10 (1981): 431–65. Reprinted in Michael Hechter, ed., *The Microfoundations of Macrosociology* (Philadelphia, 1983). Margaret Levi attempts to construct a theory of the state to explain why different revenue-raising policies are generated by different political economies. She treats the ruler as a decision maker and views the evolution of institutions as an outcome of bargaining between rulers and private agents.

come the difficulties they faced because of their inadequate means of monitoring compliance, royal administrators persisted in using methods that political economists of the eighteenth century considered retrograde.[15]

The Burgundian evidence suggests that the structure and development of the state financial system prompted state officials to uphold communal property rights in the seventeenth century and to resist agrarian reform in the eighteenth century. If modernization means the creation of a society based on competition and individualism, on the destruction of corporate bodies, and on the institution of private property, then the state of the Old Regime did not play a modernizing role. The state at that time depended on the financial and political support of corporate bodies, such as the village.[16] If royal policies had not been predicated on fiscal needs, the corporate characteristics of the village might have disappeared before the eighteenth century.

Most historians argue that peasants organized communities to protect themselves from oppression, and that communal organization was an expression of an immemorial peasant culture. Furthermore, they point out that communities existed before either the seigneurie or the crown became a political force in the countryside. Communal rights may have evolved, in part, as the peasantry attempted to defend itself against predatory feudal lords, tax officials, and capitalist merchants. Seigneurial and, later, royal officials nevertheless had their own reasons to uphold communal property rights. By upholding those rights, authorities could more easily extract goods and services from the peasantry. Long before the commune was recognized by the crown, feudal lords had insisted on the collective organization of the village, for such a system simplified estate management and tax collection. Only later did the commune make its appearance

15. Robert H. Bates, "Some Conventional Orthodoxies in the Study of Agrarian Change," World Politics 36 (Jan. 1984):234–54. Using examples from colonial Africa, Bates argues that many of the communal characteristics of African villages were a result of the encounter with agents of capitalism.

16. David Bien claims that the early modern state was not in effect a precursor of the modern state but a distinct historical and cultural entity whose institutions and imperatives originated in its baroque structure and heritage. See his "The Secrétaires du Roi: Absolutism, Corps, and Privilege under the Ancien Régime," in E. Hinrichs, ed., De l'Ancien Régime à la Révolution française (Göttingen, 1978), pp. 153–67.

in royal jurisprudence, because the crown used it to counterbalance local seigneurial authority.

In eighteenth-century Burgundy, the crown attempted to restrain seigneurial power by restricting the lords' supervision of village assemblies. To do so, the king needed the support of strong communities. An instance in which the state decided a conflict between a lord and his village over the right to choose a village school rector is discussed in Chapter 2. Once the state had successfully eliminated seigneurial supervision of village assemblies, all that remained of the lord's authority was the collection of feudal dues. State officials wanted this function eliminated as well because it competed with the collection of royal taxes.[17] To achieve its fiscal aims and to eliminate this last vestige of feudalism, the state once again relied on the communities to resist seigneurial authority.

Communal Institutions and Peasant Welfare

During the eighteenth century, village institutions did not guarantee the majority of Burgundian peasants equality, or provide them with subsistence or insurance against calamity.[18] Membership in the village was carefully restricted to ensure that communal rights were not extended to outsiders. Court cases that sought to enjoin outsiders from enjoying village rights were common. The system of collective tax responsibility, in which the wealthy inhabitants were held personally responsible when the village defaulted, did not redistribute income since the rich, in turn, sued the village to reclaim their confiscated property. Rather, it was a method that enabled the state to promise tax

17. For an example of and discussion of this competition, see Pierre Chaunu, "L'Etat," in Fernand Braudel and Erneste Labrousse, eds., *Histoire économique et sociale de la France*, vol. 1 (Paris, 1970).

18. Samuel L. Popkin, *The Rational Peasant* (Berkeley and Los Angeles, 1979). Popkin did not analyze Burgundian evidence, but in the first two chapters he notes that the existence of collective institutions need not imply a collective rationality. He argues that in colonial and premodern European societies, villages were often organized to serve the interest of the state rather than that of the peasants. In proposing an alternative to the moral economy model of the premodern village, Popkin argues that markets do not necessarily make peasants economically worse off.

collectors that the village would pay its taxes. Gleaning rights provided subsistence to the poor but also made subsidized labor available to the rich. This practice kept the poor in the villages where their labor could be employed by the wealthy during the harvest.[19] When times were hard, many of the poor left the countryside for the cities, where they hoped to find the subsistence guarantees they could not find in the villages. Political authorities in urban areas at least provided cheap bread to avoid riots that might weaken the stability of the government.[20]

The welfare value of village membership varied in reverse proportion to needs; the wealthy benefited most.[21] Wealthy inhabitants had the greatest use for the undivided common fields and common grazing rights because they had the largest herds. In Burgundy, therefore, the poor generally advocated division of the common lands, whereas the wealthy championed their preservation.[22] Efforts to deny the local seigneur village forest rights in the late eighteenth century also indicate that the sense of community benefited the wealthy. Beginning in 1750, those rights were assigned in proportion to tax payments (thus unequally); consequently, villagers who paid the most taxes began to monopolize wood allotments. Thereafter, opposition to seigneurial forest rights increased substantially.[23]

19. Gleaning was done after the harvest and did not compete with harvest work. Thus, village laborers received an additional margin of subsistence at no direct cost to property owners. In this sense, gleaning rights helped reduce the costs of village labor to the well-to-do. The community as a whole, not the individual property owners, bore the cost of this welfare mechanism.

20. See Steven L. Kaplan, *Provisioning Paris* (Ithaca, N.Y., 1984).

21. Kathryn Norberg provided evidence regarding the tendency of wealthy inhabitants to dominate communal resources in "The Struggle over the Commons," paper presented at the 12th Annual Meeting of the Western Society for French History, Albuquerque, New Mexico, 1984. For a more general discussion of why village elites might prefer open fields as a means to realize scale economies in the use of pasture, see Carl Dahlman, *The Open Field System and Beyond: A Property Rights Study of an Economic Institution* (Cambridge, 1980).

22. See Alfred Cobban, *The Social Interpretation of the French Revolution* (Cambridge, 1964), pp. 113–19. Cobban's research confirms that the tendency for the better-to-do peasant farmers to defend common rights existed throughout France. This study owes much to the criticism of traditional interpretations launched by Cobban.

23. Court cases to dispute seigneurial forest rights (*triage*) proliferated when the rules governing village forest rights were changed. Traditionally, wood had been divided equally among all inhabitants, but in the eighteenth century officials began to insist that the rights be distributed in proportion to tax payments—see Chapter 4.

The thesis that peasants revolted to restore the justice that had existed in the precapitalist community and to protect village institutions from commercialization, and more generally from capitalism, can be disputed on several grounds. First, there is little evidence to suggest that the peasants' general welfare was better served in closed corporate villages than in capitalist society. I have already noted that village institutions were not efficient in their attempts to provide subsistence, or to restrain involvement with external markets.[24] Second, long before the eighteenth century, French peasants were familiar with the market exchange of both the products and the factors of production; they were aware of the existence of private markets for labor; and they knew that capital accumulation was necessary to secure, reproduce, and expand the means of production.[25] Moreover, French peasants became landowners, and gained their freedoms, because access to the market allowed them to buy land and freedom. They became citizens of the king's nation by paying his taxes. In short, the peasantry had bought its entitlement to property, liberty, and citizenship. In court cases they brought against their lords during the eighteenth century, peasants demanded freedom from feudalism, not capitalism. Perhaps a number of them wanted to escape from, rather than to restore, institutions that prevented capital accumulation. Finally, in the eighteenth century, as a result of bureaucratic intervention, the growth of the market and of capitalism actually resulted in stronger, more independent peasant communities and more clearly defined communal property rights. If indeed those communal property rights were precapitalist, it was the bureaucracy, not the peasantry, that was restraining capitalist expansion.

24. Jonathan Dewald notes in *Pont-St-Pierre, 1398–1789: Lordship, Community, and Capitalism in Early Modern France* (Berkeley and Los Angeles, 1987) that "the pace of land sales during the late Middle Ages seems not to have been qualitatively different from that in the late eighteenth century" (chapter 2). As further confirmation of the thesis being presented here, Dewald points out that during the Revolution "it was the village, not the market town, that had accepted the free market economy, in both its possibilities for profit and its difficulties" (chapter 4).

25. A new trend in Marxism is emerging that also emphasizes the capitalist orientation of the poorest peasants. See Albert Soboul, "A propos d'une thèse récente sur le mouvement paysan dans la Révolution française," *Annales historiques de la Révolution française* 211 (1973):85–101. See also Florence Gauthier, *La voie paysanne dans la Révolution française* (Paris, 1976).

Burgundian documents reveal no fundamental incompatibility between communal rights and commercial agriculture in the eighteenth century. Communities found that they could lease communal property to the highest bidder to gain additional revenue. By auctioning rights to use communal property, the village forced its wealthiest inhabitants to pay for the use of property that they might otherwise have used at no cost. That royal officials encouraged such auctions is further evidence that the state protected communal properties. Villages could borrow funds on the basis of the revenues they anticipated from leasing collective property. The villages' involvement with the market and with national financial networks increased the value of communal properties, and the commercialization of communal lands provided the villages with needed income and credit. Thus, commercial agriculture and common rights were not incompatible and might have complemented each other. By the same token, administrators never saw themselves as having to choose between purely fiscal and social improvement explanations of their policies.

Supporters of the "precapitalist" argument assert that on August 4, 1789, the Constituent Assembly eliminated feudal dues in response to peasant protests and that the Revolutionary government acted to ensure peasant welfare. But the records of the debates in the Constituent Assembly and the correspondence between Paris and the provinces suggest that the administrators had other worries. Most of their correspondence concerns tax collection and provisioning the cities. Abolition of feudal dues was a way to reduce bread prices in cities and to make it easier for peasants to pay state taxes.[26] By 1794, the leaders of the Revolution had turned their backs on reforms that had earlier been instituted to promote agrarian capitalism. That too, we are told, represented a concession to peasant welfare brought about by peasant protest. But the administrative correspondence during the Revolution that is concerned with the need to limit agrarian reform focuses on the link between village solvency and

26. AN, AD18^B7. Reports and mémoires from the Constituent Assembly, 18 July to 11 Aug. 1789.

tax collection.[27] Peasant unrest might have had little influence on the course of agrarian reform during the Revolution.

Historians generally claim that the abolition of feudal dues in 1789 and the elimination, in 1794 and 1796, of laws designed to encourage agrarian individualism were concessions made by the national assemblies in response to peasant demands to ensure the communal welfare. Historians beginning with Georges Lefebvre have often asserted that an autonomous peasant movement determined how far the Revolutionary government would go in the direction of capitalism. The administrative correspondence and the records of the debates in the Revolutionary assemblies, however, provide little proof that the peasants had forced the state to yield precipitously to their demands. The same concerns that dominate the correspondence of administrators under the Old Regime (state debt, tax collection, and war) also dominate the correspondence of administrators during the Revolution. The same fiscal weakness that, in 1793, led the Revolutionary government to abandon hopes of transforming agriculture had, under the Old Regime, prevented the state from eliminating communal property. It was the structure of state finance that determined how far the French government would go in the direction of agrarian capitalism, both under the Old Regime and during the Revolution.

The State and the Revolution

Even if attempts at state building did not incite reactionary protests of the peasants against capitalist expansion, they did have the result of involving the peasantry in national politics in new ways. During the eighteenth century, the state codified the decision-making functions of the village assembly. Collective decisions of the village were thenceforward recognized as a legally binding statement of the village's general will, thus making it easier for peasants to organize and to influence governmental decisions. These ad hoc assemblies became an integral part of the nation's political system. The result was that peasants increas-

27. See Chapter 7, "Financing the French Revolution."

ingly asserted their independence from both the seigneurs and the state. One indication was the increase in the number of court cases initiated by peasants against the seigneurs over payment of feudal dues.[28] Recognition of assembly decision making also gave the village greater access to credit. Contractors, creditors, and merchants could count on state officials to guarantee that the village would fulfill commitments noted in village assembly records. By integrating the village assembly into the state's political structure, the crown had also integrated the village economy into the nation's financial structure.

French politics became triangular as a consequence of the growth of the state bureaucracy. Because the peasants were no longer dependent on the lords for representation before the king, politics now consisted of the interaction between three groups: the state, the peasants, and the lords. Integration of the village assemblies into the state's political structure provided peasants with at least the illusion of having a range of political options that they did not have when their primary link with the king was the seigneur.

As the state's intervention in local administrative matters became more frequent, an escape from political isolation by means of coalition politics became possible for the peasantry, as did increased access to external markets, limitation of seigneurial dues, just decisions by the king's courts, and more direct access to national authorities. The promises of benefits were many, but the tangible benefits were few. The parlementary judges under the Old Regime heard the claims of lawyers who promised the peasantry that feudal dues could be abolished by the courts. The judges, however, generally sided with fellow members of the landholding nobility, and the peasants lost case after case. The state's intervention in grain markets continued to be unpredictable and was often prejudicial to rural interests. Export restric-

28. The court cases reveal a striking irony about state making and peasant contention during the Old Regime. The growth of the state provided the peasantry with the capacity for collective action. First, state officials undermined the dependence of the village on the local landlord. Then, to help the community mobilize against seigneurial domination, administrators protected the communal properties. As a result, the community had the revenues it needed to challenge seigneurial dues in court. The crown's agents actually encouraged reluctant communities to sue. In the end, however, the state became a target of the weapons it had provided the village. See Chapter 5, "Challenging the Seigneurie."

tions and price controls resulted in market distortions that benefited the city rather than the country. The peasants' hopes of
escaping from seigneurial domination and overcoming their political inferiority were not fulfilled. By integrating the village
assemblies into the state's political structure, the crown had
aroused among the peasants expectations of better government
that it did not, and could not, satisfy.[29] Thus, the growth of the
state gave the peasantry both the capacity to protest and new
reasons to do so.

29. Robert Forster makes the same point in assessing rural revolution in
Burgundy. "Historians have perhaps overestimated the importance of bread
prices and rising taxes as the twin ingredients of open resistance to the old
establishment." Forster points out that the peasants were called vassals by the
seigneurial agents but citizens by the king. This different treatment "must have
affected the self-esteem of more than one villager. The later appearance of an
equalitarian vocabulary in village cahiers and petitions was not imposed entirely
from 'outside.' " See Robert Forster, *The House of Saulx-Tavanes* (Baltimore,
1971), pp. 207–8.

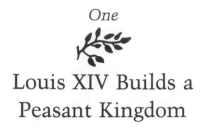

One

Louis XIV Builds a
Peasant Kingdom

The harvest was a disaster in 1661, the year that Louis XIV began his personal reign. In that year and the next, the French endured the worst famine of the seventeenth century. Despite the famine, the king increased taxes in some areas and eliminated long-established exemptions and fiscal privileges in others. The response of his subjects was fierce. In the Boulonnais alone, the king had to send thirty-eight companies of troops to quell the riots of thousands of peasants.[1] Those troops left a trail of blood behind them; they had ordered the hanging of many rioters and sent four hundred to the galleys for life. These disturbances made only a slight impression on the young king. Louis scarcely mentioned famine or riots in his memoirs, written nine years later for the education of his son. He even remarked that in the first years of his reign, there was "no unrest or the fear or appearance of unrest." Nevertheless, between 1661 and 1675, hardly a year went by without popular demonstrations, all of which were rapidly put down by royal troops. Because of such harsh repression, Louis earned a reputation for indifference to the sufferings of the common people. It was a reputation that he

1. Before Louis XIV, the Boulonnais had been exempt from most forms of royal taxation.

did not shun, for he noted in his memoirs that the swift repression of "anything that ever so slightly approached disobedience . . . was the greatest kindness I could do my people."

Louis was also insensitive to the hardships caused by economic depression. The misery endured by the peasantry during the five years following the famines of 1661 and 1662 did not receive mention in the king's memoirs either. Amid economic depression and fiscal disorder, the young king pursued what he regarded as a more important goal: France's preeminence in Europe. Attainment of this goal required money and the vigilant monitoring of fiscal resources, and its quest had led the crown to bankruptcy by 1661. That detail did find a place in Louis's account of those first years.

Louis's ambitions in the realm of foreign policy were territorial, commercial, and dynastic, and they could only be achieved through conflict or war. First, he sought to acquire safe, easily defended borders. Twice during his childhood, Paris had been threatened by enemy troops, and foreign troops had been on French soil frequently during the preceding centuries. Second, Louis desired colonies and a greater share in Europe's growing maritime commerce. Louis, like many in his day, believed that the wealth of Europe was fixed; therefore, France's share could only be increased at its neighbors' expense. For France to be first in commerce, Louis considered it essential to crush Europe's leading commercial nation, Holland. Third, Louis wanted France to succeed Hapsburg Spain as the dominant power in Europe. Shortly after Spain's king died in 1700, leaving no heir, Louis led his exhausted subjects into a thirteen-year war involving all the nations of Europe. There were strong economic incentives for participating in that war, and nothing could have pleased the aging monarch more than to see the heirs of Francis I finally prevail over the descendants of Charles V.

It has been said that when Louis was not at war he was preparing for war. His ambitions involved France in war about one year in every two during his fifty-four-year personal reign. The wars commenced in 1667 when the king invaded the Spanish Netherlands and the Franche-Comté; Holland, England, and Sweden allied against him. In 1672, Louis took the one truly decisive move of his reign when he declared war on Holland.

That year was critical not only because French troops crossed the Rhine but also because expenditures began to exceed revenues and continued to do so for the remainder of his reign. The Dutch War expanded in 1673–1674, when the Hapsburgs and all the nations in their empire entered it. The war ended in 1678; however, Louis continued his policy of expansion by initiating *réunions*, or annexations (such as Strasbourg in 1681). By 1688–1689, France was fighting again on all fronts. This series of wars ended in 1697, but in 1701 France entered the War of the Spanish Succession, which ended in 1713–1714, shortly before the king's death.

Louis's ambitious foreign policy made necessary large-scale military deployments and extensive diplomatic efforts and required inordinate expenditures. It also required an enormous sacrifice by the French people. Peasants were annually conscripted to construct the king's roads that carried supplies and troops; this was only one of the many new demands placed on them. The militia was created in 1688, and by 1702 the crown was conscripting peasants to serve for seven-year terms. By 1715, some 200,000 Frenchmen had been conscripted. No single innovation was more loathsome to the peasantry than conscription, but lodging the king's troops on a campaign—a traditional peasant responsibility—was by far the most odious burden of all.

Despite a stagnant economy, taxes were increased. Many questioned the soundness of such a fiscal policy. In their letters to the king, his agents evoked mortality, mendicity, and famine. But with revenues anticipated for the next several years already spent, there was no hope of easing the tax load. The *taille*, the principal direct tax, was increased by almost a third;[2] that increase was borne by fewer taxpayers, for the population was declining. To further increase revenues, the king introduced many new indirect taxes, so that the *taille* became a much

2. This increase came after 1683. Colbert did not significantly increase the per capita weight of the direct taxes, but he increased the yield substantially. Before Colbert the charges on the revenues were equal to about two-thirds of the *taille*. Enormous progress was made under Colbert in reducing collection costs and lowering interest rates. In effect, he cut interest charges of all kinds by repudiating the debt. That, more than anything else, is what increased net revenues. Colbert tripled the crown's revenues without demanding much more than Richelieu or Mazarin had. See Pierre Chaunu, "L'état," in F. Braudel and C. E. Labrousse, eds., *Histoire économique et sociale de la France* (Paris, 1970), 1:191.

smaller percentage of total income. All kinds of public offices, as well as titles of nobility, were sold, but this did not sufficiently increase revenues. The king then established two new direct taxes, the *capitation* (1695) and the *dixième* (1710). Both were intended to supplement the *taille*. In principle, both new taxes were supposed to tap the income of persons who did not pay the *taille*.[3] They were to be paid in proportion to the income received by French of every class, including the tax-exempt nobility. The nobility soon found ways to buy exemptions, however, so that the onus of paying the new taxes fell on the peasantry. Therefore, the new taxes became, in effect, additions to the *taille*. Louis's subjects paid dearly to support an army that at one point totaled 400,000 men.

Before beginning his quest for victories in the field, Louis undertook to enforce a number of measures calculated to achieve order and ensure obedience at home. Most notable were his measures aimed at domesticating the great families, who had a long tradition of sedition. In 1648, only thirteen years before Louis began his personal reign, a large segment of the nobility and the parlements, led by members of those families, revolted in an effort to control the monarchy. The lessons of four years of civil war had affected the young Louis deeply. He would never forget how in 1649 the royal household had to flee Paris in the middle of the night and how, one month later, the English Parliament sent his uncle Charles to the block. Following a course that had been set by Capetian monarchs in the four preceding centuries, Louis XIV made every possible effort to bring his fractious subjects to heel. But Louis went further than his ancestors in attempting to domesticate the magnates: They were given no important positions in his councils and were denied administrative posts in the provinces—in short, they were offered no role in governing the realm. Only careers in the army and in the domestic service of the king were available to them. To remove the magnates from their provincial seats of power and to divert their attention from local affairs, the king required their continual attendance at court. Not to be seen regularly by the king was to

---

3. The *capitation* was suppressed in 1698 but was reestablished permanently in 1701. The *dixième* was introduced despite famines in 1709 and 1710.

lose any hope of promotion and to forgo all sinecures. In moving the court to Versailles, Louis spared no expense and oversaw all details. The brilliant court life there required borrowing and left some families crippled with debt. At court, the fortunes of the great came increasingly to depend on his majesty's generosity and on their skill in pleasing him. Thereafter, instead of fomenting rebellion in the provinces, the king's gentlemen fought for the honor of handing him his shirt in the morning, or his napkin at dinner.

There was one area, however, in which these men were invited to participate, at least covertly: Louis welcomed their involvement in state finance. As Daniel Dessert has shown, much of the capital raised through borrowing to support the king came from old, landed families. Using financiers as intermediaries, members of these families could secretly invest in short-term loans to the king at high interest rates and obtain substantial quick profits.[4] In the short run, there were significant political advantages for the monarchy in having such families share in fiscal profits. It was an ingenious way for the monarchy to gain access to their wealth without making political concessions to them. In a curious way, the large private fortunes were being linked to those of the regime. Many of the established families thus had an investment in the success of the absolutist state, yet they had no formal or institutional mechanisms for influencing the crown's policies.

Nothing, however, forced the monarchy to keep the faith of creditors whose links to the regime were purely personal, dependent on contacts with or networks around a particular minister. Consequently, investors were extremely vulnerable to a change in ministers. A new king or minister of finance could and generally did repudiate the debts of his predecessors. With no institutional means of exerting their will or of protecting themselves, the king's creditors were subject to constant fleecing. Eventually holders of capital came to resent this vulnerability and demanded political reforms. The monarchy frequently lost the

4. Daniel Dessert, "Finances et société au XVIIe siècle: A propos de la Chambre de Justice de 1661," *Annales E.S.C.*, vol. 29 (July–Aug. 1974); Daniel Dessert and Jean-Louis Journet, "Le lobby Colbert," *Annales E.S.C.*, vol. 30 (Nov.–Dec. 1975).

confidence of lenders and had difficulty raising new funds by borrowing.[5]

The financial arrangements that had long-term effects were, in fact, often designed to deal with short-term emergency situations. One such arrangement had particularly important implications for the nobility. The monarchy had transformed into a permanent right the temporary concession, made by the Estates General in 1439, that permitted the king to tax the peasantry directly without convoking the Estates General.[6] That the king could act independently of this body decisively influenced the form monarchical government was to take in France. This right tended to prevent political participation by the nobility, for the monarchy could raise money without consulting the seigneurs. Thus, lacking opportunities to demand political concessions from the crown, the nobility was reduced to staging futile revolts and committing treason in order to maintain a political role. Tax-exempt nobles had no chips with which to bargain for political representation, and without an institutional body to represent them, they could wrest few real concessions from the king.

The fiscal reforms of Colbert, Louis XIV's minister of finance, are an example of measures that were taken to deal with an immediate financial crisis and that would shape the future. Historians have often judged those reforms by their long-term results and therefore have credited Colbert with wanting to restructure the French economy and system of finance, and to extend permanently the crown's political authority. Such assumptions are pure speculation. We cannot penetrate fully Col-

5. In the late seventeenth century, there were more opportunities to make substantial quick profits from short-term loans to an increasingly bankrupt monarchy than from investments in the depressed land and produce markets. Some might argue that it was because of the appeal of quick and easy profits in state finance that wealth was diverted from long-term investments in agricultural productivity. But as we shall see in Chapter 4, the problem was more complex: technical innovations in agriculture were also blocked by the strength of peasant collective traditions.

6. Because each province had its own privileges and its own special relationship to the crown, and because all provinces paid taxes on a different basis, the Estates General could not effectively negotiate general rates or establish principles of taxation that would have satisfied all provinces. For the same reason, the Estates General could not arrive at a consensus broad enough to enable it to represent the entire nation before the king.

bert's motives. His reforms, however, do make sense from a much narrower perspective. All the measures he took to restructure the kingdom's financial system were necessary to overcome the existing crisis. Colbert had been appointed finance minister of a monarchy on the verge of bankruptcy. To get the funds necessary to rescue the monarchy from financial ruin, Colbert had to assure creditors—the private investors upon whom he depended to finance the public debt and to collect taxes—that the king was a worthy credit risk and that collecting the king's taxes would be sound; consequently, investing in loans to the monarchy would be a lucrative activity. Colbert's rise to power also marked the rise to power of a tightly knit group of financial families and interests—a network of personal clients whose ties often included marriage alliances. These financial families represented a larger clientele of potential investors. On the basis of their personal credit, which was often based on their assets, or projected profits, as the king's tax collectors, they borrowed money for loans to the king. Before they would risk their own fortunes and those of their friends and relatives, financiers needed assurances from the monarchy. Since Colbert's success as the king's finance minister depended on how effectively he could use the resources of such groups, he sought to assure investors that tax collection would proceed in an orderly manner, so that they would be payed both the capital and the interest owed to them.

To develop his financial programs, the king required greater control over local administration. Most important, more thorough royal supervision over tax collection was necessary to restore confidence among lenders. Since the lenders were generally exempt from taxes, they did not personally fear intensified supervision over tax collection. Unable to trust the provincial nobility to carry out his orders and to ensure that villagers could carry the tax burden, Louis needed administrators who were loyal to him alone. The crown took a major step toward increasing fiscal efficiency by assigning an intendant to the already existing units of fiscal administration, called *généralités*. The intendants were to represent the king permanently in the provinces, and all of the *généralités* were to become intendancies.[7]

7. See Marcel Marion, *Dictionnaire des institutions de la France aux XVIIe et XVIIIe siècles* (Paris, 1923), p. 257.

Supervising the collection of taxes was the intendants' first and foremost function.

The use of intendants was not a new idea, for Richelieu had also relied on them. Richelieu's intendants, however, were stationed in the provinces only sporadically and on particular assignments, usually military. Thus Louis XIV had made one of Richelieu's intermittent practices a permanent institution.[8] Unlike the bureaucrats of earlier French kings, the intendants were not *officiers*, that is, they served on a commission basis and did not own their offices.[9] The king could revoke their powers in the provinces at any time. Selection of intendants did not depend on their having a local clientele or a local patronage. The individuals chosen generally had no roots in the provinces where they served, and they could be rotated from one province to another as it pleased the king.

As the crown's representatives, the intendants were armed with royal *arrêts*—orders or decrees issued by the king or in the king's name. The *arrêts* did not need the approval of the parlements or other intermediaries, nor could the *arrêts* be set aside on the basis of provincial custom or law. In this sense, the intendant's authority was not founded on the legal customs of the province where he served; it reflected the will of the sovereign. Moreover, the intendant was not accountable to provincial authorities, since the decrees and sentences he issued could be appealed only in the King's Council.[10]

8. Louis XIV institutionalized and made permanent many of the ideas developed by Richelieu. But the two differed radically in that Richelieu attempted to create a state more in line with the views of the older aristocracy. Louis's policies were aimed at limiting the political authority of the magnates.

9. Intendants did own offices in the King's Council, but not in the intendancy. There was no incentive for the holders of venal offices to remain loyal to the king since no advancement or transfer of the holder was permitted once an office was purchased, and revocation was unlikely since it required reimbursement.

10. As the king's direct representative, the intendant had superiority over all other officeholders in the realm, including the parlementaires. As the *maître des requêtes*, the intendant was a member of the King's Council and could not be summoned before the sovereign courts. Any member of the sovereign courts, however, could be called to appear before the King's Council. Consequently, the installation of the intendant undermined the administrative hierarchy—the parlement could no longer be considered the chief administrative power in the province. Since the intendant's administrative decrees superseded the decisions of the parlement, the royal administrators would henceforth have priority in any public matter over which the king wished to exercise exclusive jurisdiction. All this, the parlement insisted, violated the customary territorial rights that were the basis of the province's attachment to the crown.

Louis had formulated the new arrangements in 1661, just after attaining his majority. He issued a decree ordering the sovereign courts "to defer to the decrees of his councils forbidding [the courts] to take cognizance of affairs and proceedings that his majesty retains and reserves for himself and for his councils." In 1665, to demonstrate further his intention to limit the parlements' participation in affairs of state, Louis began referring to the parlements as *cours supérieures* rather than *cours souveraines*. The king's efforts to establish the supremacy of his council in Burgundy had a direct and practical effect on the work of that court. In Dijon, they led to a new distinction between the parlement's judicial and administrative functions, which had traditionally overlapped. Not merely a law court, the parlement had exercised public authority by enforcing its own *arrêts*, which constituted a body of local administrative law. But as we have seen, with the installation of the provincial intendant, the monarchy began to rule by administrative decrees that took precedence over provincial laws. The parlement was left with undisputed jurisdiction only in cases concerning private law. Henceforth, it could function effectively only as a court.[11] This growing separation of the parlement's judicial and administrative functions was particularly noticeable in the area of village finance.

THE VILLAGE AND THE KING

If we consider how the crown developed ties with the peasantry, the close relationship between bureaucratic growth and state finance will become much clearer. Those ties assumed a new importance as the king increasingly attempted to circumvent the nobility and the parlement. For some time, peasant communities had provided a large part of royal revenues, and because the royal treasury depended on the villages' effectiveness in providing specified sums annually, it was essential for Louis to protect the communal structures that ensured tax collection.

---

11. The division between the parlement's administrative and judicial functions was far from absolute. The parlement still possessed jurisdiction in areas of local administration (road construction, hospitals, and charity), but its authority over municipal and village finance had been assumed by the intendant.

Reinforcing those structures and exerting direct authority over peasant communities became the focus of the crown's drive for more efficient taxation.

The local nobility could not be trusted to supervise communal finances since they would be the first to profit from the village's financial instability, for it would allow them to buy the village's commons and forests. In addition, seigneurs often acted to shield communities from royal taxation, which they viewed as competing with the collection of seigneurial dues. Not surprisingly, protection of the crown's long-established right to tax the peasantry directly became the intendant's task. This responsibility, as we shall see, involved the intendant with the peasant communities but not with the individual peasants. This limitation was initially a source of strength; it allowed for more effective tax collection despite the weakness of the administration and the traditions of the village. Administrators simply did not have the resources to deal with taxpayers on an individual basis, nor was there any precedent or record of the crown attempting to detect or discipline delinquent taxpayers. Furthermore, peasants had always been liable for, and paid, taxes as a community.

To understand the advantages administrators gained from collective responsibility, let us shift the focus from royal to seigneurial administration. Those advantages are explicitly stated in the correspondence, in 1756, between the lord of Etaules (the monastery of Saint-Chapel de Dijon) and an expert on seigneurial administration (a *feudiste*) hired by the monastery to organize and to renew its seigneurial titles. The lord had written to ask the *feudiste* his opinion of a request from the village's wealthiest inhabitant for permission to pay his share of the *cens*, the most substantial feudal due collected at Etaules, directly to the monastery, even though traditionally the village inhabitants paid the *cens* as a collectivity. This arrangement had an obvious advantage for the wealthy inhabitants: they could use their influence to reduce their share so that the poor ended up paying a disproportionate part of the total. However, the arrangement also had an advantage for the collector of the *cens*. If the village defaulted on an undivided *cens*, the lord could sue the wealthiest inhabitants and confiscate the sum from their personal estates. This was why, the *feudiste* pointed out, it was very common for wealthy inhabitants to request release from the solidary unit. To permit wealthy inhabitants to make individual payments was extremely risky, he warned the monastery. Further investigation of this argument will illustrate why the undivided *cens* was common in the eighteenth century, and why, even in an age of individualism, seigneurs insisted on maintaining the unity of the *cens*.

As the *feudiste* reminded the monastery, in the law of the manor all peasants were equal in their relationship to the seigneurie and therefore were subject to the same laws. This meant that if one peasant were liberated from the collective *cens*, all could request to be. As a result, the *cens* would soon be splintered into individual payments, with each inhabitant paying the lord directly. How difficult it would then be for the monastery to adjust the *cens* to each mutation in ownership. Thus, the *feudiste* asserted, by dividing the *cens* into individual portions, "one makes collection even more difficult and more irksome. Although collection is assured when you assess the whole group, . . . when you divide it into individual portions you turn collection into a base task—the lowness of the task will lead to negligence, and as the inconveniences multiply, the yield will be annihilated." The *feudiste* further pointed out that the key to tax collection was that the wealthiest paid for the group in cases of default. "It is always easier to collect the *cens* if there are a number of *censitaires* because one can always hold the wealthiest responsible for the group." In addition, "if all are co-liable the payment will be more certain because each of those who is 'co-liable' has an interest in betraying his fellow villagers in the fear of increasing his own part of the payment by hiding them." Certainly that was a better way to ensure payment than negotiating with households separately. Besides, he added, "it is well known how powerful self-interest is in men, and especially in the country-dwellers, who make it a crime to pay for others."[12] The wisdom of this *feudiste* reveals why the monarchy insisted on maintaining communal responsibility.

12. G-1372, 1756 (unsigned *mémoire*). Division of the *cens* in proportion to what an individual owns is called *égalation*. M. Violet was the inhabitant who requested the *égalation*. He was described as the most "solvent" of Etaule's inhabitants.

Royal officials in the seventeenth and eighteenth centuries insisted upon collective tax responsibility, as seigneurial officials had earlier, for essentially three reasons. First, detecting whether individuals had cheated on their taxes was very costly. Administrators could see the differences in wealth between one village and another, but they could not as easily determine the relative wealth of individuals, since information about individual wealth was hard to procure. The inhabitants, however, knew who owned what. With collective responsibility, if one individual did not pay his share, the burden on the others would be increased, thus providing incentives for the inhabitants to disclose tax evaders. Furthermore, by insisting upon collective tax payments, the crown could avoid the cost of keeping track of changes in individual wealth. Second, collective responsibility allowed authorities to additionally cut the costs of information gathering. Because royal officials were not able to maintain records of individual fortunes, the cheapest way for them to prevent village defaults on loans and contracts was to confiscate the wealth of the richest inhabitants. It was relatively easy to ascertain who belonged to that group. Third, the expense of collecting the assessed sum household by household would inevitably have diminished returns. Bargaining over assessments with each household separately was also time-consuming, and the crown simply did not have the means to do so. In sum, collective responsibility was necessary because of the scarcity of information on individuals and the rudimentary level of administrative specialization. Collecting the same information about individuals that was available on communities would have further increased expenses.[13] The need for administrators to reduce information costs was especially acute in France because French politics made the cheapest solution—trusting the local nobility to collect taxes—impossible.

This communal responsibility was not a vestige of village traditions with regard to redistributing wealth and protecting the village poor. Nor did such communal practices persist because of a "precapitalist" predilection of the peasants to look

13. See Richard A Posner, "A Theory of Primitive Society, with Special Reference to Law," *Journal of Law and Economics* 23 (Oct. 1980):54, for a discussion of such costs of gathering information in premodern societies.

after each other. Rather, collective responsibility persisted because authorities insisted on it. Collective responsibility reduced information costs, as the *feudiste* explained, because peasants were willing to betray each other and provide the tax collector information about their neighbors in order to reduce their own portion.

The importance of the communities' collective responsibility for taxes under the Old Regime is particularly evident in Burgundy. There, by the middle of the seventeenth century, the provincial estates were annually presenting a lump-sum assessment to the village as a corporation. The village in turn chose one of its residents to divide the assessment equally among the individual inhabitants. Thus the villages handled their obligations to the state in much the same way that they handled their day-to-day expenses for such items as church repairs, ditch and road maintenance, public fountains, and court cases. Although these expenses were routine, they were inevitably incurred in emergencies: a flood could destroy existing ditches; passing soldiers might confiscate the church bell to make cannon; a church wall might unexpectedly collapse. Since villages seldom had funds put aside in advance, they needed access to credit.

From the perspective of the crown, these day-to-day expenses were important because they impinged on the village's ability to meet its obligations to the crown. The sums villages needed for emergencies could be enormous; their current expenditures had already stretched their resources to the limit. Villages often had to resort to borrowing. Potential creditors, however, might want assurances in the form of assets that could be entailed before they would lend money. Villages used their collectively owned fields, meadows, and forests as collateral.[14] Once a community lost its collective properties, however, it had to tax individuals the next time it needed emergency funds. Such internal taxes

14. AN, H-193/163, fol. 1. In a *mémoire* on communities (1770), the Estates of Burgundy defined communal properties as follows: "Les biens que possèdent les communautés n'appartiennent pas aux membres qui les composent, considérés comme particuliers. Personne ne peut en distraire aucune portion pour son usage particulier; chacun a seulement un droit de jouissance indivisé sur la totalité par concurrence avec les autres; il n'est pas même permis aux habitants de partager entr'eux les biens communs, ils doivent les user en communauté."

left less for royal tax officials to collect. The monarchy, therefore, did not want communities to lose their collective assets.

When Louis XIV came to power in 1661, the debts of communities were large. In Burgundy, many villages had already lost or
alienated their communal properties. Beginning with the Wars
of Religion in 1562 and continuing through the Thirty Years'
War, almost a century of war was waged on Burgundian soil. On
their way to Germany, campaigning troops wintered in the province and pillaged when they could not buy the supplies they
needed. Since soldiers were seldom paid on time, they often
resorted to living off the land. To feed themselves, they might
decimate entire village herds or force communities to yield their
next harvest's supply of seed. In some instances, soldiers spite-
fully burned entire villages when they found that the inhabitants had hidden grain or cattle.[15] Even when soldiers were not
guilty of theft or other offenses, the cost of billeting troops could
exhaust the resources of a village. To recover from such war-
related burdens, villages often sacrificed communal properties as
collateral for loans, or sold them outright.

Fiscal concerns—chiefly the desire to keep the profits of agriculture in the countryside where they could be taxed directly by
the crown—moved the king to protect peasant properties. Contemporary economic circumstances favored urban interests and
thus made tax collection especially difficult. Large profits were
being made by townsmen who procured supplies for the armies.
Once having made their fortunes in war speculation, however,
they were likely to seek safer, more lasting investments in land,
especially because tax exemptions made land ownership very
profitable for urban dwellers.[16] At a time when the well-being of
the peasantry was at a low ebb, the influx of capital from tax-
exempt townsmen threatened to alter land ownership patterns.

15. Peasants commonly fled to the forests or to the lord's château with their
cattle and grain until the soldiers had passed. In the late seventeenth century,
the intendants restricted the looting and destruction by the private armies that
had previously roamed the countryside, uncontrolled by any governmental
authority.

16. See Philip T. Hoffman, "Taxes and Agrarian Lands in Early Modern
France: Land Sales, 1550–1730," *Journal of Economic History* 46 (March 1986):
37–55. Hoffman argues that on account of tax exemptions, land in the country
was cheaper for town dwellers than for peasants.

The townsmen leased their new properties to peasants but kept some of the profits in the form of rent. The crown wanted to prevent townsmen from expropriating the lands of indebted communities or of individuals because urban investors, unlike the peasants, did not pay direct taxes on their landed income. In short, the takeover of the land by such investors threatened to diminish the crown's tax revenues.

For several reasons, then, the crown launched a campaign to allow villages to recover alienated communal properties. The king, calling himself the protector of communal rights and properties, issued numerous edicts (the first in 1662) to verify all communal debts. The entire verification process and responsibility for subsequent efforts to liquidate debts were placed under the intendant's exclusive jurisdiction. In the 1662 edict, the king ordered the Estates of Burgundy to proceed with "the acknowledgment and verification of debts of towns and communities of the said province, the regulation of ordinary expenditures, the rectification of abuse introduced by the disorders of the war, or otherwise, the listing of the subject for which the said debts were created, and their use."[17] The edict of October 1662 charged the intendant in Burgundy with the verification of all communal debts; a second edict (February 1665) authorized the intendant to oversee the liquidation of those debts. As a result of this legislation, the intendants acquired *tutelle* over communities, that is, they became guardians of communal properties and rights.

The Parlement of Dijon attempted to block the intendant's investigation. It did not believe that royal officials were entitled to this kind of information and insisted that the verification process interfered with its own jurisdiction over communal properties. In several towns there was violent opposition to the investigation, and the intendant accused the parlement of inciting the disturbances. Because the parlement would not cooperate, in 1665 the king permitted the intendants to appoint subdelegates to continue the investigation. In an *arrêt* of August 16, 1666, he detailed how the investigation should be conducted.

17. Printed collections of this royal legislation can be found in AN, H-140, or BM, Fonds Saverot, vol. 47, no. 9.

In 1667 the crown intensified its attack on usurpers of communal property by issuing an edict that forbade "all persons, of whatever quality or condition, from interfering with, or troubling, the inhabitants of the said communities in the whole and entire possession of their common goods, and the said inhabitants from alienating anew their usages and commons."[18] This edict was aimed at tax-exempt parlementaires and noblemen. The monarchy wanted communal lands to produce taxable income. Therefore, it did not want those lands to pass from the peasants, who paid taxes, into the hands of those who could not be taxed. The king further ordered that communities "recover, without any formality of justice, the properties, meadows, pastures, woods, lands, usages, common pasture lands and wastelands, rights, and other common goods sold or mortgaged by them since 1620."[19] He asserted that communal rights were fundamental to the constitution and the governmental structure of the kingdom and that seizure of communal property by individuals was an intolerable violation of communal rights. Those who had acquired communal properties would be reimbursed by the community for their original investment in ten yearly payments. The reimbursement would be "levied on all and each of the inhabitants of the said communities."[20]

On December 12, 1670, Controller General Colbert instructed the intendants that "the settlement of the communities' debts being critical for the succor of the people, there is nothing to which you should give more care and application than to the conclusion of this affair."[21] Still dissatisfied with the progress of the verifications, the king told the Estates of Burgundy in October 1671 that "there still exist some of the said debts to settle, and our intention is that communities be and remain wholly and entirely discharged of all debts of whatever nature and quality."[22] The monarchy again insisted on its right to regulate disposition of, and to intervene in questions concerning, communal property. Despite the commission of 1671, efforts to re-

18. Ibid.
19. Ibid.
20. Ibid.
21. Pierre Clément, ed., *Lettres, instructions, et mémoires de Colbert* (Paris, 1861–1883), 4:50.
22. BM, Fonds Saverot, vol. 47, no. 9.

cover alienated communal properties met with strong resistance. The fiscal pressures of the Dutch War led the king to
issue a general edict in 1677 stating that as a result of the acquisition of common properties by individuals, communities had
been deprived of the "assistance they could derive from their
properties and rights for supporting the charges of the war. It is
very fair that the holders of their lands contribute some part of
the enormous expenses to which we are necessarily obligated in
order to repulse the efforts of our enemies."[23] The edict pertained
to all holders and users of properties that had been given, sold,
alienated, exchanged, usurped, or mortgaged since 1555.[24] It
called for an investigation to distinguish acquirers "in good faith
from those who had seized [properties] without legitimate title."
Possessors lacking legitimate title could hold community lands
for fifteen years, providing they restored to the state the profits,
"fruits [taxes], and revenues of thirty years."[25] At the end of the
fifteen-year period, the lands would be returned to the communities. Those who could not raise the required sum would forfeit
their lands. The edict did not prevent attainment of the crown's
fiscal objectives, but it did delay achievement of the stated goal
of returning alienated properties to communities. Since the acquirers of communal properties were often townspeople or seigneurs, this edict can be viewed as a means to extract money
from those who were exempt from taxes.

Colbert continued to insist on the necessity of the verification
process. In February 1680 he wrote to all the intendants reminding
them that "the principal and most important diligence that his
Majesty desires from you consists in the settlement and payment
of communities' debts in all the generalities of his kingdom; for
that, he does not doubt at all that you work with the care and
industriousness necessary to such a large undertaking—so wished
for by him and so useful for the relief of the people. He orders me to
add that he wants you to examine carefully the means to prevent
communities from becoming indebted in the future."[26]

23. Ibid.
24. Ibid.
25. Ibid.
26. Clément, Lettres, 4:138. Thirteen months earlier, Colbert had written to
the intendant of Rouen: "As for the debts of communities, the king wishes all
intendants to apply themselves to this task in order to deliver communities of

The objectives of the verification program were never realized. Few communities actually received back the communal lands they had lost or alienated. But the edicts did arrest the process of debt accumulation and prevent communities from alienating communal properties in the future. The monarchy achieved several important political and administrative gains as well. With each edict, the intendant further consolidated his authority over communal properties and over the community. In 1683 the intendant was assigned the function of approving all village expenses. In April 1685 and August 1687, the intendant was granted the power to authorize communal lawsuits. In 1691 the intendant was authorized to review and to verify all communal accounts. Thus, the verification process ultimately provided the intendant with almost complete jurisdiction over village finance.

As noted earlier, the reforms, at least initially, had had another goal. Colbert was searching for credit. To keep the war effort going required continuous outlays that only borrowing could sustain. Fiscal reforms and exercise of control through the intendancies were essential for restoring confidence among lenders. The reforms permitted Colbert and his associates to assure investors that royal administrators were armed with the power to prevent villages from accumulating new debts. Village solvency was critical because the crown's credit depended to a large extent upon the security of tax revenues that came from the villages.

Although Colbert's concern was with solving the immediate crisis, the edicts the king issued eventually served as a blueprint for the dramatic assertion of his authority in the provinces. In appointing himself protector of communal rights, the king established two principles that were to become the juridical basis of the intendant's political authority over communities. First, the royal legislation protecting communities from the loss of communal properties established the rural community as *mineur* and the king as its *tuteur*. The earliest expression of the idea that "the communities are considered minors" is found in a

---

this vermin that gnaws at them continually, [so that they will] be able to bear more easily the charges of the state." Georges Bernhard Depping, ed., *Correspondance administrative sous le règne de Louis XIV* (Paris, 1850–1855), 3:279.

royal ordinance of June 22, 1659 (pertaining to the *généralité* of Châlon), which forbade communities to alienate their rights and properties without the king's permission.[27] After 1659, the term *mineur* was applied to all French communities. Second, the monarchy declared that the rights and powers that inhabitants had collectively possessed since medieval times were public rights and powers and therefore subject only to royal jurisdiction. This second principle became the primary justification for the exercise of royal administrative power in the provinces because it enabled the crown, as guarantor of the public weal, to administer a wide range of village affairs. Most important, it allowed the king to dominate the institution responsible for governing peasant communities—the village assembly. Thus, what began as a program to regularize village finance had great, although originally unforeseen, political and administrative significance.[28]

INCREASING IMPORTANCE OF COLLECTIVE RESPONSIBILITY

Those corporate institutions that could serve to guarantee communal solvency were reinforced in the villages. One such institution—*contrainte solidaire*—was critical. *Contrainte solidaire* meant that the community was collectively responsible for the obligations of its individual members, and individuals could be made responsible for the obligations of the entire community. In other words, individual liability and collective liability were merged. *Contrainte solidaire* had a long history; it had been the key to the seigneur's coercive power over the village. By con-

27. In the early 1660s, however, the Parlement of Dijon had begun to dispute openly both the community's reputed *puérilité* and the monarchy's claim that communal goods and rights were public. The parlement asserted that communal goods were neither *biens de mineurs* nor *choses publiques*. They "belonged to the community as a legal person, and just as properties belonging to any person could be sold, leased, or willed, properties belonging to communities could be alienated" (see AD, B-11600/37, 11600/38). The Estates of Burgundy, which were responsible for paying the province's taxes and dividing the yearly assessment among the villages, did not object as strongly as the parlement to the intendant. (In fact, they welcomed the intendant's assistance in tax matters.) For this reason, they lost to the Parlement of Dijon their traditional reputation as principal defenders of provincial liberty.

28. Copies of the legislation can be found in *Code rurale ou maximes et règlements concernant les biens de campagne* (Paris, 1762), 2:708–14.

sidering the village as having a single will, the seigneur eliminated the necessity of making difficult and time-consuming
settlements with individuals. Thus, he protected himself against
rebellion and evasions of seigneurial dues and regulations. If the
village failed to pay its dues or to meet other contractual obligations, the seigneur could confiscate the property of the four leading inhabitants, and they would have to recover their loss from
the community as a whole.[29] Beginning in the mid-seventeenth
century, the *solidité* once so valuable to seigneurial authority
became equally valuable to royal authorities. In 1650, and again
in 1666, the Parlement of Dijon agreed that the monarchy had
the right to enforce *contrainte solidaire* when villages failed to
pay royal taxes. Communities, formerly collectively responsible
for seigneurial dues, were now held collectively responsible for
royal taxes.

The importance of *contrainte solidaire* for the future became
particularly clear in 1683 when, as part of a broader program
designed to prevent communities from falling back into financial disorder, the monarchy began to prohibit villages from
selling, leasing, or mortgaging their communal goods and properties.[30] According to the new royal legislation, communities
could raise funds only by taxing themselves or by using the
revenues from communal properties. Henceforth, communities
should no longer count on using their communal goods and properties as surety for loans, or on selling their properties or assigning the revenues anticipated from them. Since communal goods
and properties were declared inalienable, communities had to
find another way to secure loans. In the future, the surety for
communal loans would be the collective liability of the community's inhabitants. *Contrainte solidaire* was a guarantee to creditors that a community would pay its debts. Thus, the ancient

29. *Contrainte solidaire* is mentioned in the earliest seigneurial documents;
therefore, its practice must have antedated such documents. The idea was referred to in seventeenth-century jurisprudence as *solidité*. In his codification of
Burgundian custom (*Coutumes générales du pays et duché de Bourgogne* [Dijon,
1698]), Taisand stated it simply: "L'action du cens est solidaire." The notion of
solidité was applied not only to the payment of seigneurial dues but to payments
for the charters of enfranchisement as well. Generally, in Burgundy, the village
negotiated such charters in common and all inhabitants were bound to fulfill the
established obligations.

30. Edict of April 1683; see BM, Fonds Saverot, vol. 47, no. 9.

practice acquired a renewed importance. Creditors could now do what royal and seigneurial authorities had done. *Contrainte solidaire* also contributed to an increase in the intendant's control over communities. Only the intendant could authorize a creditor to entail the property of the community's four leading inhabitants when that community defaulted on a loan. No other authority could sanction the application of *contrainte solidaire*.

Although the monarchy did not acquire the right to enforce *contrainte solidaire* as part of the campaign to verify debts, restoring the credit and solvency of communities would have been much more difficult without *contrainte solidaire*. *Contrainte solidaire* was an effective way for the intendant to safeguard communal properties. Finding another mechanism to guarantee that communities would reimburse their creditors would not have been easy, considering the limited means of coercion and supervision available to the intendant.

CONCLUSION

Most of the powers exercised by the Burgundian intendant before the Revolution can be traced to the campaign to verify debts. In 1683 Intendant Harlay (1683–1689) explained: "There are few affairs [for the intendant] in this province, fewer than in any other. The royal *tailles* and the reimbursement of post houses, as well as the repair of the king's roads, are in the hands of the estates. At present, the principal affair of this province's intendancy is what remains of the verification of debts."[31]

In 1743 the monarchy stopped renewing the commissions to verify debts, which it had done every year since 1662. But that cessation did not mean that the crown had lost interest in the matter, or its power to act. It meant that the commissions were no longer necessary because administrative routines were now firmly established. When, in 1764, the controller general asked the intendant, Joly de Fleury, if renewal of the commissions would be useful, Fleury responded that there was no need for them. "The intendant's authority and rights being so well estab-

31. 20 Sept. 1683. A. de Boislisle, ed., *Correspondance des contrôleurs généraux de finances avec les intendants des provinces* (Paris, 1874–1897), 1:1.

lished in the Provinces, a special commission would add nothing. In fact, the intendants continue to exercise the powers, which consist of verifying communal debts."[32]

By that time, the rights assigned to the intendant by the commission were no longer vulnerable. The Estates of Burgundy, in 1764, could declare: "The competence of the intendant is clearly demonstrated and easy to know. It is based on this principle: the interests of communities are only to be expressed [*stipulé*] under his authority."[33] In 1785 the intendant, Amelot, reported to the controller general, Calonne, that "the work of the Burgundian intendant can be reduced to the surveillance and administration of communities and communal rights."[34]

In 1787 a lawyer, M. de Goron, proposed to the Estates of Burgundy that he write a history of administration in Burgundy. Goron identified the intendant's public power in Burgundy as control of all matters that could be termed "collective." He wrote that "the administration of communal goods and business is attributed directly to the intendant; it is he who authorizes and sanctions all acts that are collective in nature."[35] Burgundian intendants never interfered in matters concerning relations between individuals or attempted to resolve questions of private property. Even as late as 1789, when two inhabitants of the village of Senailly petitioned the intendant to arbitrate a conflict over the distribution of the barley that they had jointly harvested on communal properties, the intendant refused to act; he reminded them that "it is an affair that concerns only individuals." Since the affair involved private and not collective property, the intendant concluded that "it is not within the competence of my office."[36] But collective affairs were quite another matter.

Louis XIV's relationship with the peasantry is one of the great

32. AN, H-200/173, fol. 8: Projet de travail de M. Amelot, intendant de Bourgogne, avec M. de Calonne, contrôleur général. 17 Dec. 1785. This document refers to correspondence of 1764 and summarizes earlier reports and correspondence from the intendants. See also AN, H-140, for additional reviews of intendants' correspondence.

33. AD, C-4401: Reported in the *mémoire* of M. de Goron, 1787, p. 2.

34. AN, H-200/173, fol. 6

35. AD, C-4401: *Mémoire* of M. de Goron, p. 1.

36. AD, C-1402, Senailly, 14 Nov. 1788 to 13 Aug. 1789: Procès-verbal; correspondence between subdelegate and intendant.

ironies in the history of the French nation. The king openly and
willfully pursued policies that were detrimental to the peasantry's well-being. He made it known by his actions that he
would not sacrifice his reputation, his *gloire*, for his subjects'
happiness. And yet the survival of the villages was a result of
Louis's policies. In creating the position of intendant and establishing the commission to verify debts, Louis provided the peasant community with a source of protection. Although not always benevolent, the intendant could help communities resist
the exactions and abuses of seigneurs, tax collectors, and campaigning troops. True, Louis acted to protect his share of what
the peasantry produced. But the long-term effect was to prevent
the further decline of the peasant community. Inadvertently,
Louis linked the fate of the French monarchy to the collective
traditions of the village.

Two

Two

A Bureaucratic State
in the Making

In 1756 a Burgundian seigneur, Loppin de Gemeaux, was engaged in a bitter and protracted struggle with the provincial intendant, Joly de Fleury. At issue was the seigneurial prerogative entitling Loppin to convoke, and preside over, meetings of the village assembly in Gemeaux. But as we shall see in this chapter, Loppin was defending much more than a procedural detail. At stake was the essence of lordship, which, in Loppin's view, combined the ownership of land with the exercise of public authority.

The struggle began when Loppin threatened to take legal action against his villagers because they had met without his consent to select the new village schoolmaster. On the grounds that the village assembly could not meet without his approval, Loppin rejected the selection. Loppin, an influential man, *avocat général honoraire de Dijon* and "lord of high justice in Gemeaux," sent his grievance directly to the King's Council—but in vain. The council refused to consider the case and referred it to the intendant, who supported the peasantry's initiative and warned Loppin

An earlier version of this chapter, entitled "En Bourgogne. L'état et la communauté rurale, 1661–1789," appeared in *Annales: Economies, Sociétés, Civilisations* 37 (March–April 1982):288–302.

that he would lose the case even if it were to pass through all the levels of provincial justice. The King's Council, the intendant said, would reverse any decision that might prohibit the village assembly from meeting without the lord's consent. Loppin, however, was determined to resist the intendant's contention, which he viewed as a clear threat to the prerogatives of local seigneurs with regard to governing. But even Loppin's position as a parlementaire and his family's ancient name and prestige were not sufficient to protect him from the loss of what he described as "the most precious right of my land [le plus beau droit de ma terre],"[1] or what his lawyer described as "the most precious rights of high justice."[2]

Loppin had good reason to think he would win his case. After all, his rights as a "lord of high justice" were firmly established in provincial law. According to Burgundian custom, villagers who were subject to high justice (gens de poëté) could not meet "without the permission of lords of high justice or their officers."[3] In addition, Loppin's terrier (a survey or collection of all the contractual relations and obligations between peasant and lord) stated that the inhabitants could not meet "without the authority and permission of the lord and his officers" or "outside their presence."[4] He saw this issue as an important challenge to seigneurial authority and wrote to the intendant that it was crucial that his peasants not be able to "escape this mark of their submission and their subjection to high justice."[5] Moreover, Loppin said, the peasantry's successful appeal to the intendant would establish a second dangerous precedent: the right of community members to appeal to a "superior tribunal for [resolution of disputes concerning] their ordinary and individual affairs."[6] By recognizing that right, the King's Council would undermine the peasantry's loyalty to their seigneur and would inevitably lead his peasants "to defy their lord and to scorn him."[7]

---

1. AD, C-1256, 12 Jan. 1756: Dossier on the Loppin affair.
2. Ibid.
3. P. Taisand, Coutumes générales du pays et duché de Bourgogne (Dijon, 1698), pp. 762–64.
4. AD, C-1256.
5. Ibid.
6. Ibid.
7. Ibid.

The case of Loppin de Gemeaux raises new questions about the triangular relationship between seigneur, state, and peasantry during the Old Regime. In his now classic work on the Burgundian peasantry, Pierre de Saint-Jacob hypothesized that the Burgundian peasantry faced "an agricultural regime where the seigneurie and state conspired against it."[8] But the intendant's confrontation with the seigneur of Gemeaux in 1756 suggests another interpretation. For we find the monarchy not working in alliance with the nobility but instead joining with the peasant community to curtail the local administrative authority of seigneurs. The state in this instance was not a simple coalition of "class" interests uniting monarchy and nobility in the use of state power against the peasantry. Loppin de Gemeaux's case suggests that the state under the Old Regime extended its power as a distinct and independent entity, acting in its own interest.

Important changes were taking place in the mid-eighteenth century—changes that involved the definition of sovereignty and the distribution of public authority. Today we can easily separate public authority from private property rights, and lordship from ownership, but these distinctions were less clear in the eighteenth century. For Loppin and his contemporaries, lordship was more than the possession of land and the proprietary right to collect seigneurial dues. Lordship was also, and fundamentally, a kind of property that included jurisdiction and some aspects of what we would define as public authority. Citing Charles Loyseau, eighteenth-century defenders of seigneurial rights considered inseparable the lord's possession of administrative rights and his ownership of land.[9] By attacking an important function of the lord's public authority, the monarchy seemed to attack the institution of property. Contemporaries of Loppin may well have feared that an assault on one element of seigneurial property—jurisdiction—could be extended to an attack on feudal dues. In the end, the intendant's position with regard to Loppin's right to convoke and preside over village assemblies might imply that the

8. Pierre de Saint-Jacob, *Les paysans de la Bourgogne du nord au dernier siècle de l'Ancien Régime* (Dijon, 1960), p. 139.
9. See Charles Loyseau, "Traité des seigneuries," in *Oeuvres complètes* (Paris, 1640).

economic privilege of lordship (which was what would remain after the lord had been divested of his public rights and functions) was a mere honor, and hence difficult to defend.

Loppin's case was followed by other successful attacks by the monarchy on the administrative functions of the Burgundian seigneurie. They were clearly part of the monarchy's long-term campaign to absorb the principal administrative functions of the seigneurie and to put the village under the direct administrative authority of the intendant. An analysis of the long-term development of monarchical policy, then, is needed before we can fully understand the meaning of Loppin's case. The monarchy's efforts to take over the public rights and functions of local seigneurs were a principal feature of state building in France.

The first inroads into the seigneur's local authority were made in matters of taxation. As noted earlier, toward the end of the Hundred Years' War the monarchy began to tax the peasantry directly. By the seventeenth century, it had been clearly established that the village assembly could meet without the lord's permission to decide questions concerning the "interests of the Prince," that is, concerning taxation. In his codification of Burgundian custom, Taisand stated that, since the province's union with the crown, provincial custom recognized that even "*gens de poëté* . . . could assemble without the permission of their lord to discuss the subject of royal taxes [*tailles*] and those [taxes] of Messieurs the Elus of the province . . . this imposition [the *taille*] being undertaken by the authority of the King, which overrides that of lords."[10] This communal privilege, which had been established in both royal and provincial jurisprudence, was rarely exercised, however, because royal taxes were generally collected under the supervision of a seigneurial judge—a right that was often established in the seigneur's *terrier*.[11]

The first explicit statement of the monarchy's intent to curtail seigneurial participation in village assemblies throughout the kingdom was contained in the *Code Michaud* of January 1619, in which the king forbade "all governors, gentlemen, or others of whatever quality that they be, from providing any ob-

---

10. Taisand, *Coutumes générales*, pp. 762–63.
11. AD, B-10856: Archives of seigneurial justice.

stacle to the distribution of justice, from intervening in the portioning out of our taxes, from disturbing or hindering the inhabitants of the parishes in the free nomination of their *syndics*, assessors, and collectors, or from insulting them while performing the said charges."[12] Although the Code was never fully implemented, it was the harbinger of similar legislation. A further step toward limiting the Burgundian lord's local administrative authority was taken in 1645, when the King's Council authorized villages that did not have a seigneurial judge to name officers responsible for supervising accounts and taxation.[13]

Nevertheless, it was not until the personal reign of Louis XIV that seigneurs began to experience serious competition from the royal administration. Louis XIV began his personal reign by issuing legislation that allowed his provincial representatives to bypass local seigneurs and to establish direct administrative ties with the village. We saw earlier that the intendant, as the king's permanent representative in the province, was the principal instrument for extending royal control into the provinces. The edicts concerned with the liquidation of communal debts (discussed in Chapter 1) considerably extended the intendant's authority by assigning to him public functions that had traditionally been performed by the seigneur or the Burgundian parlement.

Beginning in 1683, another series of edicts consolidated those powers. The first gave the intendant the right to approve all communal expenditures. As noted in Chapter 1, edicts issued in April 1685 and August 1687 forbade communities, or their *syndics*, to begin any court action or to arrange any deputation in the community's name without a signed declaration of a village assembly accompanied by the intendant's written authorization. Now the intendant, not the seigneurial or parlementary authori-

12. Isambert, Jourdan, and Decrusy, eds., *Recueil général des anciennes lois françaises depuis l'an 420 jusqu'à la Révolution de 1789*, 29 vols. (Paris, 1821–1833), 16:282.

13. AD, C-3519: "Arrêt du conseil, 1645, qui authorise les habitants des villages dépourvus de justice seigneuriale à nommer des commissaires pour contrôler les rôles des greffiers des tailles." J. Garnier claimed that among the archives for the year 1659 of the seigneurial court at Molême, reference is made to a royal commission decreeing that when there was no seigneur or seigneurial agent on the premises, communities could annually elect *syndics* to execute the orders of the government. See J. Garnier and E. Champeaux, *Chartes de communes et d'affranchissements en Bourgogne*, 4 vols. (Dijon, 1867), 1:351.

ties, could authorize communal loans and the lease or sale of communal property. In 1691 an edict assigned to the intendant the right to review and to verify all communal accounts, a function previously exercised by seigneurial officers. In April 1695, the intendant received the right to approve and supervise the renovation of churches, presbyteries, and cemeteries. Thus by the early eighteenth century, village officers were accountable to the intendant alone for the disposition of all matters concerning village finance. Royal edicts had charged the intendant with overseeing village expenditures, the construction and repair of communal buildings, and the leasing of communal properties.[14] The only important power he lacked was the authority to prevent the seigneur's convoking of and surveillance over village assembly meetings. Clearly the monarchy was moving in that direction, for by 1756 the Burgundian intendant could write to Loppin de Gemeaux that "without speaking of the general orders which strictly prohibit it, there are several regulations specific to Burgundy that [prevent] seigneurial judges from exercising authority in communities and interfering in their affairs."[15]

Although the royal edicts gave the intendant the rights to intervene in a wide range of quotidian affairs, these rights were for the most part highly theoretical.[16] The actual powers wielded by the intendant were acquired in an ad hoc manner and differed in their exercise from one province to the next. The intendant's effectiveness depended on his ability to adapt royal policy to local circumstances and customs. The civil archives (intendancy) of the Departmental Archives of the Côte-d'Or provide evidence that the intendant, within the framework of Burgundian traditions, intervened in local cases and established precedents that would increase intendants' control over village communities. In 1702, for example, the intendant permitted the community of

14. These edicts can be found in their entirety either in AN, H-140, or in BM, Fonds Saverot, vol. 47, no. 9.

15. AD, C-1256. A royal decree deprived the seigneurs in Champagne of the right to convoke village assemblies, but no such edict was issued pertaining to the kingdom in general, or to Burgundy in particular. This decree was mentioned in a resolution of the inhabitants of Grancey-le-Château, who had met to "demander la création d'une chambre composée de 17 notables du pays à l'effet d'administrer les affaires de la communauté": AD, C-2035.

16. Royal edicts are best understood as general statements of policy, defining principles of action.

Villiers-le-Duc to meet without the consent of its seigneur. The seigneurial officers there had forbidden such a meeting, but the intendant, Ferrand, intervened on behalf of the community and ruled that seigneurial officers could not prevent it from meeting (although at this stage seigneurial officers were still permitted to be present at community meetings).[17] The intendant's ruling demonstrated clearly that the community's right to assemble did not depend on seigneurial authorization. This was an isolated example, but the ruling set an important precedent.

In the same year, the royal administration created the office of *syndic perpétuel*. This official represented the king within the village and replaced, for a time, the annually elected village *syndics*. By creating this venal office, the king recognized the new village *syndic* as the community's exclusive formal representative and extended to him "the care and administration of affairs."[18] This was one of many offices that Controller General

17. AD, C-2923, 3 Feb. 1702: Ordinance of Intendant Ferrand.
18. AN, AD[1]-611, 20 March 1702: "Edit du Roy, portant création des syndics perpétuels." The *syndic*, who was elected by the community for a term of one year, filled a traditional role associated with village membership. In the administrative language of the Old Regime, the position of *syndic* cannot be described as an office, for under the Old Regime no one was elected to an office. Offices were bought and sold; they were a form of property held by individuals. The *syndic's* rights and duties varied from one community to another. However, all *syndics* had the right to convoke village assemblies, were guardians of the village archives, and supervised the collection of village and national taxes and the utilization of village funds. They were also charged with drawing up the lottery for recruitment of the militia, overseeing road maintenance, managing the *corvée royale* (for repair of the king's roads), making a regular census of village studs, and notifying authorities of fire and outbreaks of epizootic diseases and epidemics. Perhaps their most unpleasant task was arranging the lodging and provisioning of troops—the most burdensome of the community's official obligations. The village *syndic* became the last link in the bureaucratic chain. The royal edict of 1702 commissioning the sale of the position of *syndic perpétuel* increased the importance of that position by rendering the *syndic* directly accountable to the intendant and by establishing the position throughout the realm. The *syndic* was not exempt from the *taille*, nor could he evade the task of lodging troops. As a token compensation for a position generally viewed as more onerous than profitable (for there was no formal recompense), the *syndic's* personal share of the *taille* was generally not augmented during his incumbency (AD, C-3519). Lacking police powers or other formal means to enforce his authority, the *syndic* was entirely dependent upon the cooperation of the village inhabitants. He was exposed to pressures not only from the community but from the seigneur and the intendant. "In person and property," the *syndic* was accountable to the central administration for everything occurring in the community. The community could not disavow a *syndic's* actions that had led to costly or disastrous legal proceedings; however, it could countersue to reclaim damages from the *syndic's* estate, and such an action could conceivably result in his ruin.

Ponchartrain had created to meet the massive financial demands of the military buildup for war. But creation of the office of *syndic perpétuel* was more than a fiscal expedient; it was consistent with the crown's long-term political aim of circumscribing seigneurial administration. The edict of 1702 extended to village communities the rights and powers of local administration already given to cities in an edict of August 1692. It prohibited "all the lords of towns and officers from disturbing the said mayors in the above functions, and from interposing themselves in order to preside at the said elections and nominations, or from receiving the oath of office from the said *échevins [syndics]*, *capitouls, jurats, consuls*, and other similar officers."[19] The edict of 1702 created "maires et assesseurs perpétuels" in all villages and restricted the seigneur's role in the election of village officials. The village *syndic*, theoretically at least, became the crown's representative in the community.

The Estates of Burgundy bought the offices of *syndic perpétuel* en masse from the monarchy. By dealing directly with the estates rather than with each town and village, the monarchy could promptly receive a lump sum on behalf of the entire province. There is no evidence that the estates then sold the offices to particular villages; what was done with them is not clear. The office was abolished in 1717[20] but re-created by an edict in 1722. The estates' accounts for that year reveal that all parishes regardless of size bought the office.[21] Like the edict of 1702, that of 1722 was aimed at weakening the power of seigneurial judges in Burgundy by reaffirming the rights and powers given to elected municipal and communal officials in 1692. In buying the offices of *syndic*, villages literally bought the right to exclude seigneurial

19. Isambert, Jourdan, and Decrusy, *Recueil général*, 20:161.
20. AD, C-3516: "Arrêt du Conseil pour la liquidation des offices."
21. AD, C-3517: "Rôle arrêtée au Conseil d'Etat, des sommes fixées pour la finance des offices de syndics des paroisses créés par l'edit d'août 1722 et rachetés par les Etats." Ahuy was the first to buy; its office was evaluated at 18 livres. Arceau was second and bought an office that was evaluated at 5 livres. The sum for the province was 1,143,750 livres. The roll was headed: "Rolle des sommes que le Roy ordonne estre payées pour la Finance des offices de syndics de Paroisses de la Généralité de Bourgogne créez & rétablis par l'Edit du mois d'Aoust 1722, pour jouir par les Pourvus desdits offices dans les Paroisses de leurs établissements de Droits Privilèges & Exemptions à eux attribuéz par Edit du mois de Mars 1702, ensemble de gages à raison du denier cinquante de leurs finances dont l'imposition sera fait conjointement au marc la livre de la Taille."

officials from participating in the election of village officials and from convoking or presiding over village assembly meetings.[22]

Nonethcless, the 1722 edict does not seem to have contributed immediately to changes in local administration. There are no instances in which communities cited that edict in disputes over seigneurial administrative prerogatives. The lord's *terrier* (which was backed by the authority of the parlement and was grounded in provincial custom), not royal proclamations, continued for a time to govern relations between lord and peasant. Most villages bought the office of *syndic perpétuel* collectively but continued, as in the past, to elect village officers annually. During the last half of the eighteenth century, the intendant attempted to eliminate the few offices, such as the one at Sombernon, that had actually been bought by individuals. The edict of 1722 is significant because it recreated the office of *syndic* in all Burgundian villages.

With creation of the office in 1702, royal legislation was enacted rendering village *syndics* directly responsible "in their own and private names" to the intendant for the fulfillment of duties and for the execution of the intendant's orders. Additional royal legislation in 1710 made the *syndic* personally responsible for the resolutions and actions taken by the community. He now reported to the intendant on "contracts regarding construction, repairs, or improvements" of churches or other public places, as well as on all legal actions undertaken in the community's name.[23] The king had never been able to hold a seigneurial judge personally responsible for the acts of a community; however, this legislation increased royal control of village administration. The village *syndic* became the bottom rung in the royal administrative ladder.[24]

22. That the estates bought the offices from the monarchy and sold them to the villages seemed to run counter to seigneurial interests. The estates were selling an office that weakened seigneurial power in the village. This and other actions by the estates suggest that collecting taxes had become far more important to those bodies than merely protecting seigneurial rights.

23. AD, C-2931: "Jugement rendu par l'Intendant Trudain qui porte défense aux officiers municipaux des villes et communautés de passer marchés de construction ou de réparation d'édifices sans authorisation préalable de l'Intendant; comme aussi d'intenter aucune action judiciaire"; issued 30 July 1710.

24. Intendants issued numerous injunctions reaffirming the *syndic*'s direct and personal responsibility to the intendant for decisions made by the community. For example, the intendant issued the following injunction with regard to

These edicts would seem to indicate that royal control was expanding rapidly, but in practice, changes occurred gradually. In the early eighteenth century, local courts ruled on business over which royal legislation had given the intendant exclusive jurisdiction. For example, although royal legislation stipulated that communities could not sell communal properties without the permission of the king's administrative officers, the village of Agencourt in 1712 obtained the approval of the *bailliage* court (the level of jurisdiction between the seigneurial court and the provincial *parlement*) before selling a portion of its communal forest. The sale was annulled by the intendant, but only because it had been prohibited by the Maîtrise des Eaux et Forêts. In that same decision, the intendant prohibited *bailliage* judges from approving sales of communal properties.[25] In the same year, an intendant issued an order to the magistrates of Cuiseau to suspend the harvesting of the communal woods, begun without the intendant's written permission.[26] Two years later, the intendant renewed "the prohibition against all *bailliage* officers taking cognizance of requests for the acquisition, construction, or repair of churches or presbyteries."[27] Substantial evidence indicates, however, that having obtained the approval of local judicial officials, communities continued to commission constructions and repairs without seeking the intendant's permission in spite of the royal legislation.

Many rights claimed by the intendant with regard to rural communities were within the customary jurisdiction of the *parlement* and of its local subordinates: the *bailliage* court and

---

Epoissottes: "We enjoin the said *échevin* or *syndic* during the time of his office to take all the actions necessary for the administration and business proceedings of the community under penalty of being held personally responsible for the damage and interest which could result."

25. AD, C-2932: "Jugement rendu par l'Intendant de la Briffe qui casse une délibération de la communauté d'Agencourt, qui mettait en vente une coupe de bois, annule l'adjudication qui en avait été faite à la maîtrise avec défense aux communautés de Bourgogne de mettre leur bois en vente sans autorisation préalable et aux officiers des maîtrises de les mettre en délivrance sans être revêtus de cette approbation."

26. AD, C-2932: "Injonction aux magistrats de Cuiseau de suspendre l'exploitation des bois communaux qu'ils ont commencée sans authorisation."

27. AD, C-2936: "Jugement de l'Intendant qui renouvelle la défense aux officiers des bailliages de connaître des questions de demandes en acquisitions, constructions, ou réparations d'églises ou presbytères."

the seigneurial judge. The intendant, it should be remembered, had increased his control over rural communities by placing under his authority many of the civil functions of parlementary and seigneurial justice. And, because seigneurial judges were responsible to the *bailliage* courts and not to the intendant, the continued importance of both seigneurial judges and *bailliage* courts compromised the royal administration's effectiveness. Thus, limiting the *bailliage* courts' civil or administrative functions, and the kinds of cases that came before them, was an important element of the crown's efforts to extend royal power. But in the early eighteenth century, royal administrators did not yet possess the resources to directly supervise village officers or assemblies; therefore, they continued for a time to depend on seigneurial officials.

Before analyzing the Loppin case in more detail, let us examine an earlier, but similar, conflict between the seigneur of St. Mesmin and his peasantry. In 1722 the community of St. Mesmin "chose a school rector without the permission of the lord." The seigneur rejected the community's choice and pleaded his case before a *bailliage* court, claiming that the community's decision was invalid because the inhabitants had chosen the rector in an assembly convoked without the lord's permission. The seigneur also claimed that "the said inhabitants cannot assemble without my permission. I alone have the right to name the said schoolmaster."[28] The *bailliage* court upheld the lord's claims, and the case did not reach the parlement or the intendant.

The claims made by the seigneur of St. Mesmin against his peasantry were exactly the same claims that, thirty-four years later, Loppin de Gemeaux, an even more powerful seigneur, would make against the villagers of Gemeaux. In 1756, however, Loppin lost. The administrative documents of this period are seldom extensive enough to demonstrate intent. In their communications, administrators usually treated specific problems, not long-range strategies, because they assumed that readers of such communications would have a familiarity with general principles. But the documentation of Loppin's conflict with the intendant, Fleury, provides an unusual opportunity to discern

28. AD, E-807: Archives for community of Saint-Mesmin.

the overriding goals of administrative policy. Loppin's case was not considered by a *bailliage* court because the intendant intervened on the side of the peasant community. The intendant not only upheld the community's right to choose a school rector without seigneurial consent but challenged Loppin's right to convoke, or even to be present at, meetings of the village assembly.[29]

Loppin opposed his community's choice of schoolmaster solely on the grounds that the community had assembled to decide that question without the lord's permission. The intendant, Fleury, insisted that a seigneur could not block a community's decision merely because a seigneurial agent had not been present during the deliberations of the assembly. Moreover, the intendant reminded Loppin that appointing a village schoolmaster was a community financial matter and involved expenses that the seigneur did not help to defray. Thus, according to royal decrees, the issue was entirely outside seigneurial jurisdiction. But the intendant's opposition had an even broader implication, for it established a precedent. Loppin had bypassed the intendant by writing directly to the King's Council, which angered Fleury. The council supported Fleury, refused to consider Loppin's request, and referred his case to the intendant. Backed by the King's Council, Fleury was assured that in the future, Loppin and his peers would know why there was an intendant in the province.

In the same year, the intendant received a request from the community of Gemeaux for permission to challenge explicitly the seigneur's claim that the community had to have his con-

29. The earliest injunction forbidding seigneurial officers to preside over or be present at village assemblies was issued, probably by the intendant, in 1749 for the village of Saulx-le-Duc: AD, C-1286. The injunction permitted the inhabitants to choose, "for writing up their acts, anyone they think appropriate." The precedent was mentioned on 24 June 1776, when "les habitants de cette communauté se plaignent des vexations, et des chicanes qu'ils éprouvèrent, surtout depuis un an, de la part de leurs officiers de justice." Evidently the seigneurial judge and the "fermier de la dixme du curé" both forbade the village notary to "rediger les actes d'assemblée des habitans." This, the village claimed, was "au mépris du droit qu'ont les dits habitans." Moreover, the lord's officials declared that the inhabitants could "convoquer aucune assemblée sans son consentement." The lord put the village *syndic* in prison when he opposed this order. The members of the community wrote to "reclamer la protection de Monsieur l'intendant pour les faire jouir d'une faculté qui ne leur aurois point contestée."

sent to meet. The claims of both sides were now in the hands of the local royal official most interested in limiting seigneurial rights with regard to village assemblies. The intendant issued the following response to the community: "The claim of the seigneur appears peculiar to me . . . [it is] contrary to the rights of the community to assemble without the permission of the seigneur and outside the presence of his officers."[30]

Loppin's claims were supported by his *terrier* of 1728, which stated that "the inhabitants cannot, without the authority or license of their seigneur or officers and outside their presence, assemble to name anyone charged with any public function for the said community, give any procuration, or do generally anything else."[31] As the contractual basis of the lord's authority, a *terrier* was generally acceptable as evidence of the validity of a point or principle of law. The intendant, however, found other administrative rulings from local cases to support his decision against Loppin. That decision was particularly threatening to the Burgundian parlement, because the intendant was asserting his right to conduct community business according to procedures established by administrative decrees that were outside the parlement's jurisdiction.

At first, Loppin attempted to overawe the intendant. In his first letter to the intendant, a supercilious Loppin wrote, "We have here, Sir, an important matter for me, as much, perhaps, for the annoyance of seeing the triumph of a troop of agitators as for the loss of one of the most precious rights of my land."[32] He then threatened to take legal action against his peasants. In a second letter, Loppin did not accuse the intendant directly but accused the intendant's secretary of collaborating with the peasants and of yielding to the "ideas of a handful of factious subalterns in whose presence he should have kept his mouth shut, but he supports them and has doubtless promised them such good results from their scheming that they are bragging about it publicly."[33] Loppin was not reluctant to write the intendant, telling

30. AD, C-1256, Jan. 1756: Report on the Loppin affair, signed by Ranfer and Beruchot.
31. Ibid.
32. Ibid.
33. Ibid.: Loppin de Gemeaux to the intendant (12 Jan. 1756), p. 2.

him how much he had suffered from this insubordination and
that he suspected the intendant's complicity in it: "You are
aware, Monsieur, how painful it is for me to be exposed to the
talk of such people, to see them congratulating themselves for
their triumph and defying me openly."[34] He warned again that he
was ready to take legal action.

When it became clear that the intendant would continue to
support the peasant community, Loppin sent him a third letter,
detailing his position and reaffirming his willingness to go to
court. He added now a threat to use his influence in the parlement to undermine support for legislation that was of great interest to the intendant. In the intendant's words, Loppin threatened
to "have destroyed in the parlement an order I rendered 20 July
1753 which prohibits seigneurial judges from participating in the
presentation of accounts, except as [ordinary] inhabitants."[35]

Loppin's lawyers, described by him as "men of weight [*gens
de poids*]," drew up a point-by-point explanation of Loppin's
case, which Loppin sent to the intendant. "I have the honor," he
began, "of enclosing the following reply to your letter":

First of all, the right that I have to prevent my inhabitants from assem-
bling *without my permission* for the internal affairs of the community,
a right established on an immemorial usage by my *terrier* and by the
very text of Burgundy custom vis-à-vis the *gens de poëté*, is as solidly as
it is clearly explained in the brief that I have the honor of sending you.

Second, I have never heard that the exercise of my right prevented
M. the Intendant from permitting my inhabitants to assemble for all
the affairs in which this superior and respectable authority ought to be
claimed. But in the ordinary affairs of these inhabitants, they must not,
by scorn and by a kind of rebellion, shake the yoke of subjection that is
imposed on them. Do I not have reason to complain, Monsieur, that in
the affair of the school rector where they had absolutely no reason or
pretext to call you in, and where they should have requested *my permission*, they nevertheless applied to you in order to elude the subjec-

34. Ibid., p. 4.
35. Ibid. The provincial estates had already approved legislation that "ex-
pressly inhibits and prohibits *échevins, syndics,* assessors, collectors, and all
other inhabitants of the said communities to make a third double or copy of
the said roll to be placed at the seigneurial justice's secretary's office." This
arrêt formally deprived seigneurial authorities of all involvement in, or
knowledge of, tax-collecting procedures. The parlement and estates, however,
had competing jurisdictions and often created conflicting legislation. Similar
legislation approved by the parlement, that "bastion of aristocratic privilege,"
was particularly interesting to the intendant.

tion to me to which they are held, and for the reprehensible motives that I have had the honor to explain to you and that I will not repeat?

Third, I observe that this recourse to M. the Intendant of the province every time *gens de poëté* would be obligated to assemble for their affairs would become a charge for communities, as much by the expense of making a request as by the trip of the *syndics* responsible for delivering it.

Fourth, even in the cases that require recourse to the permission of messieurs the intendants, it would be proper, for the maintenance of the rights of seigneurs and to hold the inhabitants to the submission they owe them [seigneurs], to order that these assemblies be held in the presence of seigneurial judges. The sovereign authority given to messieurs the intendants would suffer no injury and the rights of seigneurs would be preserved.[36]

The intendant's response to all of Loppin's claims and counterclaims was unequivocal: "I insist that this affair does not involve you at all, and that one cannot force the choice of a schoolmaster on a community; it alone pays him and this seigneur does not contribute to his salary. I assure you that during the ten years that I have had the honor of being intendant of the province, I have never seen a seigneur meddle in a similar matter."[37] The intendant further stated that the inhabitants could nominate their *échevins* without seigneurial consent, and that the seigneur "will not be able to harm or prejudice the rights of the community to meet without the seigneur's permission and outside the presence of his officers."[38]

The intendant knew that he had the backing of the King's Council and only feared, at this point, that the community, discouraged by the prospect of an expensive court case against a powerful seigneur, might abandon its claims. The peasant community had no reason to be confident of the administration's support and little trust in the administration's intentions. Fleury's main concern was to prevent the seigneur from intimidating the community. The dossier includes a note by the intendant stating that the lord's case

could be destroyed by the path of appeal, but the community would incur considerable costs, it would be obligated to try three levels of

36. AD, C-1256, 2 Feb. 1756: Loppin de Gemeaux to the intendant.
37. Ibid.
38. Ibid.

jurisdiction [seigneurial court, *bailliage* court, and finally the parlement], and during the length of the trial this community would find itself exposed to the caprice and to the vexation of seigneurial judges. Finally, it can be feared that the inhabitants, discouraged by having to advance the money, may decide to abandon their lawsuit, and I think that such an example would have dangerous consequences.[39]

The intendant's motives in this affair are clearly spelled out in his correspondence with Paris. He explained "of what great interest it is to prevent seigneurial judges from taking authority in communities and from meddling in their affairs."[40] His affirmation of the principle of seigneurial nonintervention in village decision-making procedures significantly reinforced royal authority.

In this affair, the fates of the intendancy and the peasant community were intertwined. The success of administrative policy depended on the resolve of the peasant community. If the community withdrew, the intendant would suffer an important setback. The conflict between Loppin de Gemeaux and his peasants is a well-documented example of how intendant and community worked together to contest the traditional authority of parlement and seigneur.

In the end, Loppin de Gemeaux abandoned his claims and did not bring his case to court. The intendant had succeeded in proving to Loppin what had been clear from the beginning: the King's Council would have reversed any decision in his favor. After 1756 Loppin's officers no longer presided over meetings of the village assembly.

Beginning in 1756, numerous similar confrontations took place between intendant and seigneur. They generally reveal the same pattern: the royal administration's success in challenging local seigneurial authority depended on the determination of the peasant community.[41] Each time the seigneur withdrew his

39. Ibid.
40. Ibid.
41. The village assembly archives of Epoissottes are better preserved than those of other villages and provide particularly valuable examples of the collaboration between administration and peasantry to prevent the seigneur from convoking and attending village assemblies. The seigneur of Epoisses, unlike most Burgundian seigneurs, lived at his château and directly oversaw the management

claim. After 1770 it was rare to find a seigneurial officer at a village assembly in Burgundy. For example, the assembly records of Brazey-sur-Plaine are extensive for the years 1744–1746 and 1778–1789. They reveal that after 1778 the meetings were convoked by the village *échevin* and not by the seigneur's agents.[42] Already in 1768, the intendant could report that the article of Burgundian custom [article 6, title 30] stipulating that " '*gens de poëté* cannot assemble, nor make an imposition or collection, nor make or pass a procuration without the authority or permission of their lord of high-justice' has fallen into disuse in practically the whole province."[43]

The contrary view, that the seigneurie increased its control over the village in the last half of the eighteenth century, has frequently been asserted by a number of historians of Burgundy. Citing the growing importance of the *cours d'assises*, they claim that seigneurial justice increased in effectiveness and in scope

---

of his estate, which included the village of Epoissottes. The village assembly archives reveal that the seigneurial officers were present at, and maintained surveillance over, all village assembly meetings, even those concerned with the most trivial village transactions. The seigneur ignored the intendant's injunction of 3 July 1766 that forbade "Poulen [seigneurial official] and all others except the *échevin* or *syndic* of Epoissottes to function in the capacity of special procurator with regard to the community's affairs" (AD, C-1690). On 17 Aug. 1766, the inhabitants of the community took matters into their own hands and refused to nominate a "harvest warden" (*sergent garandier*) chosen by the seigneur: "Jean Liquard, one of the *syndics* of the said community, was opposed and did not want the said Angely [seigneurial judge] to take the votes of the inhabitants and even took the paper out of the said Angely's hands." The seigneur was powerless. The intendant's decrees gave the community the confidence to confront their ever-vigilant seigneur. After 1770 seigneurial supervision of village assembly meetings was effectively curtailed. AD, B²-583: Meeting of 17 Aug. 1766, presided over by the *syndic*, Jean Liquard.

42. AD, F-621, Brazey-sur-Plaine: Village assembly deliberations. These records reveal that the village strongly adhered to communal customs. It refused to consider enclosures or partition of the commons. There were numerous prosecutions of individuals accused of usurping communal lands. Even Pierre Phillipon, merchant and *fermier* (farmer, or collector, of seigneurial revenues), whose *taille* was 550 livres in 1789, was prosecuted by the village for usurping communal properties. This village's efforts to prevent usurpations and to conserve its communal properties were unending; according to these deliberations, the usurpations occurred constantly.

43. AD, C-940, 1768: Report from Subdelegate Adrien to the intendant. After 1774 village assemblies in Nolay were convoked by the *syndic*; there was no longer any mention of seigneurial officers presiding at those meetings.

during this period, thereby making communities more dependent on seigneurial authority.[44] But closer examination of village archives reveals that the trend was toward a decline in seigneurial authority, as exemplified by Loppin's conflict with Intendant Fleury. The *cours d'assises* (also called the Grands Jours) was a court presided over by a seigneurial judge before whom all inhabitants of a community were summoned to appear. The court's jurisdiction was not clearly defined, and comprised a wide range of social, economic, religious, and even moral issues that included hygiene, sanitation, industry, agriculture, and church attendance. It set standards for the maintenance of ditches, chimneys, and roads and regulated pasture usage, assignment of gleaning rights, and harvesting procedures. The Grands Jours also provided an opportunity for the seigneur to confirm his customary monopoly of hunting and fishing rights. The court, as the guardian of public morality, intervened in the private lives of a community's inhabitants; for example, it established regulations forbidding swearing, invocation of the devil, and work on holy days; proscribed fights and the bearing of arms; and limited cabaret attendance. The Grands Jours generally began with a public recitation of the seigneurial, parlementary, and royal regulations within the court's jurisdiction (referred to in the documents as "La déclaration de règlement de police rurale et de comportement personnel"). New *ordonnances, dispositions,* or *arrêts* adding to the police powers of the court were then presented and explained, the schedule of fines was recalled or amended, and offenses were tried. The Grands Jours were above all an occasion for the community to publicly reaffirm its submission to the lord's justice.

In 1768 the Parlement of Dijon issued a *règlement* that required seigneurs to hold the Grands Jours once a year; it also required that communal officers (*messiers, collecteurs, asses-*

---

44. In *Villages du Lyonnais sous la monarchie (XVIe–XVIIIe siècles)* (Lyon, 1978), Jean-Pierre Gutton discussed Burgundy's *cours d'assises:* "The assize courts, while keeping their role of judicial assembly, became above all organs of local administration" (p. 96). Gutton viewed the *règlement* of 1768, issued by the Parlement of Dijon, as "simply a manifestation of the will of the Parlement of Dijon to keep its control over agrarian life" (p. 97). He claimed that, as a result of this *arrêt,* "the *cours d'assises* gained importance at the end of the eighteenth century at the expense of the village assembly" (p. 96).

seurs, syndics) be "sworn in during the *cours d'assises.*"[45] The legislation also required that the accounts of the church warden be presented and examined. Legal historians often cite the *règlement* of 1768 as proof of the continuing strength of the *cours d'assises* in Burgundy.[46] But the actual *règlement* has never been found and indirect references to it in other documents are the only proof of its existence.[47] Because of the *règlement*'s importance in Burgundian historiography on the seigneurial reaction, more direct evidence on the *cours d'assises* merits examination.

Seigneurial court records provide ample evidence that the institution had begun to decline by 1768 and that the *règlement* was merely an effort to revive a largely moribund practice. Functional Grands Jours were seldom found in those seigneuries where responsibility for tax collection was farmed out. The lord's revenue collector, or *fermier*, often found that the expenses of holding the Grands Jours exceeded his profits from upholding justice. The cost of hiring highly trained judges increased, while the yield from fines stagnated. Long before 1768, the courts were held no more than once every three years, in accordance with seigneurial custom.[48] "La déclaration de règlement de police rurale et de comportement personnel" was much less extensive at the end of the eighteenth century than at the beginning. *Règlements* about game playing, swearing, and observing the Sabbath were increasingly infrequent. Although inhabitants were

45. Ibid., p. 96.
46. Cf. Pierre de Saint-Jacob, *Les paysans de la Bourgogne du nord au dernier siècle de l'Ancien Régime* (Dijon, 1960), pp. 522–24.
47. AD, C-1764. The *arrêt* is mentioned in a procès-verbal in which the inhabitants of Pagny-le-Château asked the intendant to resolve a disputed election of the village *échevin*: AD, C-1764, 13 March to 30 March 1775. The intendant refused to intervene, citing the parlement's *arrêt* of 1768. He claimed that "la connoissance de cette affaire appartient aux off. de la justice." The subdelegate, however, reminded the intendant that "dans l'usage ordinaire de ces cantons . . . les habitants s'assemblent entre eux pour nommer leurs collecteurs ou échevins" (23 March 1775). The community had appealed to the intendant because these matters were not discussed during the Grands Jours—in part because the Grands Jours were held irregularly. That a provincewide *arrêt* was needed to support a right traditionally established in the lord's *terrier* is indicative of that right's decline.
48. AD, Chambre de Notaire, Dijon, no. 1447, 3 May 1711.

supposed to nominate village officers during the Grands Jours, they seldom did; moreover, it is clear that sessions of the *cours d'assises* rarely coincided with village elections. Elected village officials took their oaths of office before seigneurial judges, often months after the officials had taken office. The procès-verbaux of the *cours d'assises* became briefer in the 1770s and seem to have been a mere formality. (Those of Magny and Aubigny-en-Plaine are good examples.) These records indicate that in the 1780s, the courts' activities were few and insignificant. The courts' effectiveness had been undermined by an apparent increase in peasant insubordination, which probably began with their refusal to pay fines and ended with the court in disorder. The parlementary *arrêt* of 1768 did not increase the community's dependence on seigneurial authority but rather reflects an attempt to save a declining institution from inevitable demise.[49]

The principal fault of the argument citing the increasing importance of the *cours d'assises* as evidence of the seigneurie's increasing control over the community is that the village assembly was the essential element of local administration; the *cours d'assises* were not. The management of communal properties and communal finance, and decisions to spend communal revenues, to initiate a legal action, or to commission public works were all the responsibility of the village assembly. Even if the seigneur could have increased his control over the administration of local justice, that would not have replaced his loss of control over the village assembly. Struggles between the monarchy and the landed nobility to dominate the village centered on control of the village assembly.

CONCLUSION

Loppin de Gemeaux's unsuccessful defense of his seigneurial rights demonstrates how both the lord's customary authority, established in his *terrier*, and his political authority—his control over village assemblies and over the administration of local justice—were being eroded as a result of the growth of the royal

49. AD, B¹-703. The same tendencies on the functioning of Grands Jours can be found in AD, B²-696, -703, -784, -796, -1024. All are *Registres des jours et amendes*.

bureaucracy. By the mid-eighteenth century, the seigneurie as a local governing authority was on the defensive. The lord's right to exercise sovereignty, as a form of property, was under attack as well. Thus, the seigneurie was losing the judicial and administrative justifications of its economic rights and privileges. One of the underlying justifications of the manorial system and of seigneurial privilege—that the lord's possession of land carried with it the right and the duty to govern and to protect the village—was being challenged by the monarchy.

The example of Loppin de Gemeaux is but one among many that show that as the royal administration expanded its local power, the lord was being replaced by the intendant as the intermediary between king and community. As a result of the centralizing process in Burgundy, and no doubt elsewhere in France, possession of a seigneurie became no more than a lucrative privilege. As a local governing authority, the seigneurie was becoming an anachronism.

In general, the interests of the state were not always those of the dominant classes. The case of Loppin de Gemeaux does not support the conclusion of Saint-Jacob and others that the state of the Old Regime can be characterized as an alignment of seigneurie and monarchy against the peasantry. In Gemeaux, crown and peasantry worked together to curtail seigneurial powers.[50] Clearly, Loppin de Gemeaux's confrontation with Fleury reveals a fundamental conflict between the interests of the state and the interests of the seigneurial nobility. The outcome of Loppin's case suggests that the French state did not acquire its power merely as an instrument of the seigneurial nobility, nor did it function to increase that group's power over the peasantry. It shows, instead, that the state of the Old Regime extended its power by subordinating society, pitting one social group against the other, and standing above all. In its movement toward absolutism, the monarchy interposed its justice, its taxes, and its bureaucracy between lord and peasant.

50. I found no cases in the archives that did not support this conclusion.

Three

Village Assemblies and
the General Will

In *The Age of the Democratic Revolution*, R. R. Palmer argued that the government set up in France after 1789 was "incomparably more democratic" than any that had preceded it.[1] Not everyone in eighteenth-century France, however, would have shared that belief. Although there may have been more citizen participation in national policymaking through elected representatives after the French Revolution, participation in local government was more limited in many provinces after 1789. In Burgundy, the heads of village households had assembled to discuss and to settle matters of village administration since the Middle Ages. After 1789, however, fewer persons were entitled to vote and to participate in village government. Therefore, the notion that a more democratic government was what separated the society created by the Revolution from the society that preceded it merits further consideration. A second and related point to consider is whether the spirit of egalitarian democracy was the real challenge to the habits and institutions of the Old Regime. Although scholars of history have generally held this to be the case, the movement toward revolution appears to have been

1. Robert R. Palmer, *The Age of the Democratic Revolution*, 2 vols. (Princeton, N.J., 1959–1964), 1:501.

more complicated. The chief obstacle to a definitive conclusion is the evidence that some of those who were clearly revolutionary and who most strongly opposed Bourbon absolutism were able simultaneously to attack democracy when they found it expressed in rural tradition. It was the crown, surprisingly, that upheld traditions of rural egalitarian participation; groups opposing the crown associated rural democracy with absolutist practices. These groups wanted to abolish the age-old assemblies and replace them with village councils, participation in which would be limited to the wealthier inhabitants, on the ground that such councils might act as a buffer against absolutist control. The debates between eighteenth-century Frenchmen over how villages should be governed suggest that there was an unexpected lineup of forces in 1789.

ROUSSEAU'S *SOCIAL CONTRACT* AND THE GENERAL WILL

In arguing his point about democracy, R. R. Palmer claimed that "if we were to name the one book in which the revolutionary aspirations of the period from 1760 to 1800 were most compactly embodied, it would be *The Social Contract*."[2] Peasants deliberating in their village assemblies figure prominently in that work. Rousseau tells us that "the peasants are among the happiest people in the world regulating the affairs of state under an oak tree."[3] At these meetings, "the simple and upright peasants" were happy because the "general will" of the entire community was being expressed and was so "manifestly evident that only common sense is needed to discern it."[4] Rousseau's notion of the general will is the key to his concept of a democratic society, but was Rousseau's formulation the gospel of revolutionary democracy?

Rousseau explains that to arrive at the general will, individuals must submerge their desires and submit "to the free suf-

2. Ibid., p. 119.
3. Jean-Jacques Rousseau, *The Social Contract*, trans. Maurice Cranston (New York, 1968), p. 149.
4. Ibid.

frage of the people."[5] But a numerical majority may not necessarily represent the "general will." He notes that "there is a great difference between the will of all [what all individuals want] and the general will; the general will reflects only the common interests where the will of all reflects private interests, and is indeed no more than the sum of individual desires."[6] Thus, it is the interpretation of the general will that is binding; numbers of votes are not decisive. The "blind spirit of faction" is the great enemy of the general will. Rousseau warns that "if groups, or sectional associations, are formed at the expense of the larger associations, the will of each of these groups becomes general in relation to its own members but private in relation to the state."[7] The majority opinion may actually express a private and sectional rather than general will because "when one of these groups becomes so large that it can dominate the rest, the result is no longer the sum of many small differences, but one great divisive difference; then there ceases to be a general will, and the opinion which prevails is no more than a private opinion."[8]

Palmer has instructed us that the best way to understand the revolutionary value of Rousseau's book is to contrast "its doctrine with the attitudes prevailing at the time it was written."[9] But in so doing we find that intendants of eighteenth-century Burgundy understood the term "general will" and applied it in precisely the manner prescribed by Rousseau. The language in the bureaucratic documents pertaining to Burgundy is so much like that of *The Social Contract* that local officials would seem to have had a copy of Rousseau when writing their reports from the field. This consistency of administrative practice with Rousseau's general will raises doubts about Palmer's claim that "*The Social Contract* remains the great book of the political revolution"—especially since the Revolution was precipitated by the political demands of groups that opposed the model of participation proposed by Rousseau and idealized by the intendants. Rousseau's idea of the general will helps us to understand not

5. Ibid., p. 86.
6. Ibid., p. 72.
7. Ibid., p. 73.
8. Ibid.
9. Palmer, *Democratic Revolution*, p. 120.

the postrevolutionary governments but that of Old Regime France.

By appointing themselves arbiters of the general will, the administrators of the eighteenth century were able to ensure and extend the sovereignty of the king over the local community. Only the intendant could distinguish the authentic general will from the number of voices claiming to speak for a community. Thus the general will was a powerful tool in the hands of centralizers, who used it as a method of bureaucratic surveillance.

THE INTENDANTS AND THE VILLAGE

In Burgundy, the village assembly was an essential agency of village administration. Both seigneurial and royal officials recognized the will of the community in assembly decisions. Moreover, those decisions were the personal responsibility of each inhabitant. In the eighteenth century, for which the evidence is abundant, the assembly routinely handled all matters concerning the collective financial liability of the community. The assembly was responsible for the collection of seigneurial dues, the collection of municipal and royal taxes, and the mortgaging or leasing of communal properties. Decisions concerning the village's rights and the use of the village's collective property were made in the assembly. Most village assemblies also supervised the numerous collective tasks required by the system of open-field agriculture: fixing the first day of harvest, scheduling crop rotations, allocating strips in the open fields, regulating the utilization of common and fallow lands, and managing the village herd. It was in the assemblies, as well, that a community agreed to initiate a legal proceeding or to undertake public works. The most important official elected by the village assembly was the *syndic*, or *échevin*.[10] The assembly also elected tax assessors and collectors,[11] the village shepherd, and often two

10. See footnote 18, Chapter 2, for a description of the *syndic*'s functions.
11. Villages sometimes appointed lawyers to help with village financial problems; for example, they ensured that taxes were accurately assessed.

messiers who oversaw the upkeep of the village's woods and fields.[12]

The assembly's role in governing the community was not new in the eighteenth century. The earliest surviving seigneurial *terriers* contain regulations governing village assemblies. These regulations suggest that seigneurial officials wanted the heads of all households to participate, a requirement that would also be imposed by royal administrators.[13] For example, the fifteenth-century *terrier* of Saint-Seine stipulates that all household heads should participate to avoid "intrigues, monopolies, and cabals" (*brigues, monopoles, et cabales*).[14] This early emphasis on political equality is also evident in the phrase "those of most sound judgment and the largest number" (*la plus saine et majeure partie*), which was the almost universal description of the attendance requirement well into the eighteenth century. The meaning of this phrase is vague and its interpretation may have differed from manor to manor. However, some generalizations can be made concerning its meaning and intent, based largely on later application of the phrase. The aim of the prescription *majeure partie* was probably to limit factionalism by guaranteeing that a majority of inhabitants would vote in the assembly. Seigneurial officials might have wanted to prevent the interests of cliques from being wrongly presented as those of the entire village. Wide participation might have been a way to prevent the assemblies from becoming vehicles for the realization of wealthy inhabitants' ambitions. The required presence of *la plus saine* indicates a concern that the wealthy and best educated not be excluded, in order to prevent a majority of inhabitants from making decisions that would jeopardize the interests and rights of the few prosperous inhabitants. In short, the probable intent of *la plus saine et*

12. *Messiers* could fine inhabitants for damages caused to communal properties and, to this end, they could confiscate carts, horses, or harnesses. They could keep half of the fines collected, but like most village officers, *messiers* were personally responsible for any damages to communal properties during their tenure. Similarly, the village shepherd was held personally responsible for any damages caused by communal herds.

13. *Terriers* generally included mention of the seigneur's right to preside at these assembly meetings.

14. AD, C-1201: *Terrier* of 1497.

majeure partie was to balance the interests of the wealthier peasants with the general interests of the community, thus preventing abuse by interested majorities or minorities.[15] It is unlikely that the authorities wanted the phrase to have too precise a meaning.[16] A vague phrase could be applied as they saw fit.

There is also some indication of the early emphasis on the political equality of all inhabitants in the Burgundian charters of enfranchisement. Some of the wealthiest inhabitants are listed as paying no more for their freedom than the poorest. The charters thus imply that the rights, duties, and obligations of liberty were equal for all inhabitants regardless of their economic status and suggest the belief that in the best of possible worlds, all peasants should be equal.[17] We can speculate that this political equality was useful to the seigneur's officials, who did not want to compete with powerful inhabitants for leadership of the village.[18]

Nevertheless, little direct evidence survives to indicate the level of participation in village assemblies before 1660. No early village assembly archives or administrative reports that could document who participated have been uncovered. Because a tradition of participation had not clearly been established, seigneurial officials no doubt dealt with cases on a day-to-day basis. This

15. We can assume, as well, that inhabitants who did not pay taxes did not have a voice at the assemblies. In Burgundy, however, that group was rarely a majority.

16. Even if the phrase *la plus saine et majeure partie* had at some time meant "the better sort," that is not how administrators of the late eighteenth century interpreted and applied it.

17. J. Garnier and E. Champeaux, *Chartes de communes et d'affranchissements en Bourgogne*, 4 vols. (Dijon, 1867). See also Maurice Clément, "Etude sur les communautés d'habitants dans les provinces du Berry," *Revue du centre* (1891–1893). In the charters of enfranchisement, the inhabitants of Berry are listed as paying the same amount for their freedom, regardless of their economic standing.

18. In *Histoire de la civilisation en France* (Paris, 1859), François Guizot claimed that the monarchy was the source of France's egalitarian traditions. Equality, he argued, was a product of the monarchy's efforts to unify the nation. The emphasis on political equality in Burgundian charters of enfranchisement, however, seems to indicate that equality was not introduced by the monarchy but by the seigneurie. Equality was a product of the peasantry's submission to seigneurial authority long before it became a result of the nation's submission to the supreme public authority of the monarchy.

would mean that who participated varied from seigneurie to seigneurie and depended on who the seigneurial judge was, as well as on the specifics of the matter at hand. But when the king's officials took over surveillance of the village assemblies from the seigneurs, they could not risk being so informal. Since they could not be at every meeting, they imposed fixed rules and established routines for all meetings and all villages. These bureaucrats became progressively more insistent that their rules be followed systematically. Participation was one area where the bureaucrats could not afford to be haphazard. Failure of some community members to attend an assembly meeting was often suspected as being the work of a cabal.

No Burgundian source originating during the reign of Louis XIV specifies the level of or the rules governing village participation. In the administrative correspondence of Burgundy's first six intendants (1654–1712), the only references to assembly organization are routine, such as the recommendation that the village should meet in the "accustomed manner" or that *la plus saine et majeure partie* should meet to decide a particular matter. This correspondence implies not only the existence of village assemblies, but also that *la plus saine et majeure partie* of the village participated in them. The earliest specific indication that the intendant interpreted this phrase to mean participation by the heads of all households appears in orders issued by an intendant in 1711 and 1712 requiring all the inhabitants of Talant, Is-sur-Tille, Saint Laurent-les-Châlon, and Mirebeau to attend meetings of the general assembly.[19] The issuance of those explicit orders suggests that there was a tendency for a number of inhabitants not to attend, or to be excluded. It is not possible to trace the origins of the rules that stipulate full participation; however, the sources are richer for the eighteenth century, when the crown preferred and actively pursued a policy of full participation.

Colbert's well-documented policies with regard to the New World colony of Quebec early in Louis XIV's reign provide an

19. AD, C-2931: Talant, 4 Dec. 1711, order signed by Intendant Trudane, "qui enjoint aux habitants de Talant d'assister aux assemblées de la communauté sous peine de 5 livres d'amende"; Is-sur-Tille, procès-verbal, includes order from Intendant Trudane and "Extrait des registres du Greffe de la mairie d'Is-sur-Tille." AD, C-2932, Mirebeau, 10 June 1712: Order "qui enjoint aux habitants de Mirebeau d'assister aux assemblées générales."

insight into the royal administration's insistence on full participation in village government. In Quebec, bureaucrats could create the local governing structures of their choice unhindered by tradition. Colbert instructed the intendant of Quebec to prohibit the creation of any elective village offices, including that of village syndic. The finance minister did not trust elected village officers, who were, he thought, too easily influenced by cliques. He insisted instead upon the participation of all heads of households in general assemblies, where each would speak for himself only and no one could speak for all.[20] The crown implemented a similar policy in eighteenth-century Burgundy, instructing intendants to insist upon the full participation of all inhabitants in village assemblies.

Although Burgundian officials called for the full and direct participation of all inhabitants, it is clear from their subsequent practices that they did not mean all inhabitants but rather all heads of households. Women (unless they were widows) and unmarried children were clearly not expected to attend. The documents did not spell this out for the obvious reason that it was perfectly understood by contemporaries.

But the rules could and did change. The sources suggest that during the reign of Louis XIV, the Burgundian intendants consistently favored the practice of having village decisions made by *la plus saine et majeure partie*. However, shortly after the king's death, Burgundian intendants began to approve petitions from wealthy inhabitants asking for the creation of Councils of Notables. Although no evidence exists that similar petitions were approved during the fifty-five years of Louis XIV's personal rule, what survives of the intendant's archives for 1719–1733 reveals that the intendant approved ten petitions for the creation of Councils of Notables during that period.[21] The petition in 1724 of Cuisery illustrates how leading inhabitants justified the establishment of such councils:

20. See Sigmund Diamond, "Le Canada français au XVIIe siècle. Une société préfabriquée," *Annales E.S.C.* 16 (March–April 1961):317–54.

21. AD, C-2944, Chaussin, Cuiseaux, Saint-Genoux, 1719; AD, C-2946, Frense, 1721; AD, C-2950, Cuisery, 1724; AD, C 2951, Gemeaux, Jancigny, Saint-Seine-sur-Vingeanne, 1725; AD, C-2955, Faye-Billot, 1729; AD, C-2956, Fontaine-Française, 1730.

This community being too large, it is as difficult to have regular assemblies as it is to write up the minutes—a required formality—for if the number of assembled inhabitants is not sufficient, deliberation is impossible, and if they all assemble, they are too numerous; the diversity of opinions causes such an uproar and confusion that it prevents the minutes from being written up, or at least delays them considerably.[22]

In a similar petition in 1729, the wealthier inhabitants of Fontaine-Française insisted that a Council of Notables was necessary

because most of those who go [to assemblies] are illiterate, without any knowledge of affairs. They allow themselves to be swayed by the slightest word; therefore, it is impossible to form decisions advantageous for the community, which has resulted in an infinity of legal proceedings that the said community of Fontaine-Française has lost. . . . Today the community is actually overburdened with charges and impositions of considerable sums.[23]

No document has been found that precisely explains the reasons for the royal administration's decision to allow notables to play a role in local government after 1719. Perhaps the best explanation lies in the monarchy's long-term effort to deprive local seigneurs of their authority over the village. Royal administrators may have viewed the councils as a means for bypassing the seigneur, who was still exercising considerable administrative control over the village in 1719. The seigneur, who traditionally had the right to preside over and to supervise the village assemblies, did not possess this same prerogative in the new councils.

The crown's new policy of supporting the establishment of Councils of Notables was temporary, however. The last instance of an intendant approving a petition for the formation of a Council of Notables was in 1733.[24] The correspondence of Intendant de la Briffe between 1733 and 1740 (his last year in office) provides no explanation of this reversal of policy, and most of the administrative correspondence for the years 1740–1749 has been

22. AD, C-2950: Judgment of Intendant de la Briffe, approving a petition from the inhabitants of Cuisery for creation of a committee of six or seven to administer that village.

23. AD, C-2959, 1729: Judgment of Intendant de la Briffe approving a petition from the inhabitants of Fontaine-Française for establishment of a council of twelve notables to administer the commune.

24. AD, C-2956, Chaussin. (Chaussin had its Council of Notables reduced from sixteen to twelve members.)

lost.[25] To understand the change of policy, then, we must bypass direct statements, and attempt to draw some inferences about the administration of village affairs after 1750.

DETERMINING THE GENERAL WILL

Clearly, one of the most important forces within the community was the demand for delegation of political responsibility to representative councils, but after 1770 those demands came from an additional source. Wealthy peasants still wanted increased local powers, and more than ever they bound together to push for a council in which they would control village affairs. Their motive was very narrow: they simply wanted institutional mechanisms through which to exert their social and economic dominance. But they were joined by a new group of supporters for councils. This time it was not the intendants but enlightened reformers, concerned with developing a representative government for the nation, who argued for creating standing committees of wealthy elites. These committees would manage village affairs but would have an added role. In a hierarchy of national assemblies, the councils would represent villages before the king. The goal was to reform the monarchy in order to restrain arbitrary government. There was no obvious relationship between the programs of political reformers and the desires of wealthy peasants: they were parallel but distinct developments. In the remainder of this chapter, I shall analyze from several angles the complex and contradictory forces supporting and opposing village councils.

What is immediately clear from the numerous documents that began to be collected in the mid-eighteenth century is that a return to the policy of full participation had occurred and the intendant was routinely rejecting all petitions for the creation of Councils of Notables.[26] Those councils that had been formed

25. In the archives of the Bureau des Finances, which included the intendant's archives until 1749, for the period 1712–1740, under the title "Suite des jugements de l'Intendant," there are 300 to 400 pages per year (AD, C-2932 to C-2965). But for the period 1740–1749, there are only 19 pages per year (AD, C-2966).

26. It seems that after 1750, the intendant required that the villages maintain archives, and they did so until the Revolution. The archives were organized by village and cataloged by subdelegation (C-418 to C-1829).

were either abandoned or suppressed. The intendant required that communal business be treated in meetings of the village assembly, with all inhabitants attending and with each speaking for himself. Voting was to be public and oral so that intrigues and cabals could be more easily detected.[27] For an act of the assembly to be valid, the participation of all household heads had to be attested. The village had to provide documented proof that its decisions represented the will of the entire community and not the desires of a few interested parties. In the words of one subdelegate, the new policy required that one "know the will of most of the inhabitants." He added that "we believe that the only course to take is to keep tumults and cabals out of the assembly."[28] To this end, the subdelegate sometimes imposed order simply "by his presence," as at Mont-Saint Jean.[29]

The increase in the authority of the intendant toward 1750 explains these policies and made possible their implementation. One sign of that increase was the expansion of the system of subdelegates, who were the intendants' official field representatives. Burgundy's first intendant, Bouchu (1654–1683), had many informal agents to provide him with information, but he had only a few subdelegates to help him with large administrative tasks, such as liquidating the debts of Burgundy's more than one thousand communities.[30] Colbert had little confidence in subdelegates. He feared that local officials would become enmeshed in local patronage networks and would not be reliable agents of central authority. For this reason, he preferred that subdelegates receive no powers beyond those necessary to execute specific assignments. The finance minister was so mistrustful of subdelegates that in 1680, to prevent their proliferation, he formally ordered the revocation of the commissions of any existing subdélégués perpétuels.[31] Colbert's successors, however, encour-

27. When the village of Laignes attempted to substitute vote by secret ballot for public and oral voting in 1758, the intendant forbade it (AD, C-1974).

28. AD, C-1651, Missery, 1775: Procès-verbal; correspondence between Subdelegate Merle and the intendant.

29. AD, C-1652, Mont-Saint Jean, March 1786.

30. AN, G-7: Letter of Intendant Harlay, 5 Aug. 1683. Bouchu's subdelegates were described by his successor as "de simples correspondants qu'il entretenait dans tous les bailliages et principaux lieux de l'étendue de son départ."

31. Pierre Clément, ed., Lettres, instructions, et mémoires de Colbert (Paris, 1861–1883). See also Henri Moreau, "Le subdélégué en Bourgogne," MSHDB (1947).

aged intendants to appoint permanent subdelegates and to divide their *généralités* into subdelegations. In contrast to Bouchu, Amelot, Burgundy's last intendant, had no less than thirty-four permanent subdelegates and thus could exercise more direct supervision over communities.

There are other indications of the continuing growth and institutional consolidation of the intendant's power. Before 1752 neither the intendant nor his subdelegates had any regular source of income. The intendancy financed itself by collecting a fee for each transaction. Beginning in 1752, however, the intendant could count on an annual income from the Estates of Burgundy. In 1770, to adjust for inflation, the estates raised the intendant's salary from 9,000 to 15,000 livres per year,[32] and by the 1780s, the intendant's annual income was 26,791 livres.[33] His income had not only kept up with inflation but in real terms had increased considerably from what it had been in 1752.[34] The increased salary reflected his increased authority; the increased budget enabled him to exert it.

The significance for village government of the growth in the intendant's authority became clear when the intendant began to limit the seigneur's traditional right to supervise village assemblies. We have seen, in Chapter 2, how the crown launched a campaign in the 1750s to deprive the seigneur of that right. By the 1770s, that campaign was enjoying success in Burgundy. At last, with his increased funds and manpower, the intendant could replace the seigneur as supervisor of the assemblies. The

32. AD, C-3366, 16 Dec. 1784. Of this increase, 3,000 livres came from the king and 3,000 livres came from the province, bringing the province's share to 12,000 livres. The intendant claimed that "cette nouvelle concession eut pour motif la multiplicité des affaires" (from "Lettre écrite par MM. les Elus Généraux en réponse à celle de M. de Calonne, au sujet de l'augmentation du nombre et du traitement des commis des bureaux de l'intendance"). On 13 Dec. 1784, the intendant wrote to the controller general, Calonne, asking for an additional 6,000 livres because "les affaires se sont considérablement multipliées" (AD, C-3366).

33. AN, H-185, p. 111: "Etat des fonds qui servent à l'entretien des Bureaux de l'Intendance de Bourgogne." These figures do not accurately represent the costs to society of maintaining the bureaucracy, because the subdelegates received a fee for each transaction. By stepping up their activity, they could increase their revenues without having such increases show up in government accounts.

34. Budgets, correspondence, and reports on the costs of the bureaucracy can be found in AN, H-185; and AD, C-3366.

intendancy seems no longer to have needed the Councils of Notables to bypass the seigneur in controlling the village assembly. The administrative correspondence after 1750 suggests that Councils of Notables ultimately presented an obstacle to the goal of bringing all communal business under the direct supervision of the intendant. In their correspondence, administrators suggested that such councils could easily evade the intendant's supervision and would also allow abuses of power by factions in the village. Village assemblies, on the other hand, provided the officials with the means to limit factionalism. A majority vote in a full village assembly could be used to control dissidents, whether majorities, minorities, or individuals.

To understand how the intendant supervised village assemblies, we must understand how he defined community and participation. His definition of those terms differed from the one that emerged in the nineteenth century and that seems usual to us. Then, many supported universal suffrage and the secret ballot in the belief that when all opinion was registered, the extremes would cancel each other out, and the opinion that was common to the majority would be in the community's interest. The intendant in the eighteenth century was not so confident of such a result and thought that the extremes should not be represented in the voting. Although in the abstract, he favored the fullest possible participation of the village's inhabitants in governance, he reserved the right to exclude from participation those inhabitants who, on account of their interests, views, or behavior, could be identified as opposing the common interest. To protect the community's interests, individuals supposed to have interests that differed from what the intendant defined as the "general will" (such as the lord's revenue collector, beggars, and those described as "mutinous" or "republican") could be excluded, or their vote disqualified.

In *The Social Contract*, Rousseau wrote that "every authentic act of the general will binds or favors all citizens equally, so that the sovereign recognizes only the whole body of the nation and makes no distinction between any of the members who compose it."[35] In supervising the village assembly, the intendants fol-

35. Rousseau, *The Social Contract*, p. 76.

lowed similar principles. The wealthy village inhabitants posed the most formidable obstacle to the expression of the general will. Intendants found that the exercise of direct authority was one way to limit abuses by the wealthy peasants, as the following example indicates. In 1775 the intendant received a petition from two inhabitants of Châteauneuf claiming that, due to irregularities, the village had sold its *regain* (the second harvest of hay from the communal meadows) at a price far below its real value of 200 livres. The intendant annulled the first sale and ordered a second auction, at which the *regain* was sold for 129 livres, even less than the first price. The intendant annulled the second sale as well and ordered his subdelegate to supervise a third auction, at which no less than 200 livres should be accepted. The intendant was distressed that the subdelegate had not taken measures on his own to ensure that the village auction would not be affected by the intrigues of a few wealthy inhabitants, who evidently wanted the *regain* sold at a low price because they hoped to be the buyers. The intendant wrote to the subdelegate: "I am shocked that you were not careful about this at the time. I cannot recommend to you too strongly to apply more care to the objects which concern the administration of communities. . . . I cannot recommend to you too strongly to watch that they [the interests of the community] not be given over to the crude cupidity of the well-to-do inhabitants."[36]

The village assembly archives contain numerous examples of how the supervision or investigation of assembly decision making by a subdelegate permitted the royal administration to curtail abuses by the wealthy inhabitants. Consider Pagny-la-Ville, where a bare majority of thirty-two (of sixty-two) inhabitants elected M. Léger as tax collector. The seigneurial judge then intervened, charging irregularities, and called for another election. A different inhabitant, Guichard, having promised that he would assess the inhabitants at lower rates than could his rival, was then elected with thirty-four votes. The intendant suspected foul play. First of all, he surmised that Guichard, who had contracted to collect seigneurial revenues as the lord's *fermier*,

36. AD, C-649, July 1775 to Jan. 1776: Procès-verbal, includes correspondence between the intendant and Subdelegate Rondot.

might want to use the money collected as village taxes to pay
what he owed the seigneur. Second, few of the thirty-two inhabitants who had originally elected Léger were present when the
thirty-four elected Guichard. Third, Guichard was one of a group
of inhabitants who were suing the village in a disagreement over
the previous year's tax assessment. In an attempt to clear up the
matter, the intendant wrote to the subdelegate, insisting that
any decision of the voters must be truly general. "Each party has
its man and each nomination appears to be the fruit of a cabal.
Both parties want to plead the case of the community and that
cannot be. A general deliberation held before the subdelegate
will clear away the fog and prevent one part of the inhabitants
from litigating against the other." The subdelegate therefore
ordered that another meeting of the village assembly be held and
that all inhabitants lacking a legitimate excuse had to be present
to give their "opinion each separately, without confusion or tumult." The meeting revealed that Guichard's nomination had
been the result of pressures exerted by five of the community's
principal inhabitants and that these five inhabitants had also
persuaded the seigneurial judge to call for a second election. In a
third election, supervised by the subdelegate, Léger was elected
once more, fifty-one to ten.[37]

In another case, the inhabitants of Flagey petitioned the intendant in 1769 to permit the community to reimburse one of its
inhabitants, Monsieur Mussot, for "a horse that while crossing a
bridge belonging to the community injured its foot so seriously
that it died a few days later." The petition stated that "most of
the inhabitants of Flagey" wished to levy a *taille négotialle* to
reimburse Mussot for his loss. The intendant was suspicious and
asked the subdelegate to investigate. The subdelegate found that
"most of the inhabitants of Flagey are relatives of the said Mussot, and the richest members of the community convoked an
assembly and by their intrigues engaged other individuals."
Mussot, apparently dissatisfied with his horse, had exaggerated
what was in reality a minor injury in order to buy another one.
The subdelegate concluded that the community's opinion did

---

37. AD, C-1762, Pagny-la-Ville, June 1781. Includes the subdelegate's observations and correspondence, as well as an ordinance from the intendant.

not reflect the "general will of the community but rather [that of] a few of the principal inhabitants who brought others over to their own side."[38]

In still another case, abuse by the leading inhabitants of Montmançon was prevented by the subdelegate. He discovered that village meetings were being held at the home of the *syndic* and that only several leading inhabitants were present. To give the impression that the meetings constituted a general assembly, they had the record of the deliberations sent from door to door for signature by the other inhabitants.[39]

Although subdelegates intervened most frequently to prevent the villages' wealthy inhabitants from misrepresenting the communal will, abuse came from many sources. Factions formed along lines that often had nothing to do with wealth. In 1766 a subdelegate, Daubenton, arrived in Fontaine-les-Sèches, hoping that his presence would bring to reason the "rebellious minority" responsible for that community's refusal to permit the intendant to review its accounts. The village *échevins* claimed the accounts had been rendered to a village assembly, "and that was sufficient."[40] During a year-long investigation, the subdelegate met separately with several different groups of leading inhabitants and village officials, each with a different set of facts, each opposed to the other, and each describing itself as the *"principaux et Notables habitans de la communauté."* After a year of mutual recriminations, the community's accounts were still being withheld, and it became clear that the chief problem was to prevent the minority factions in the village from multiplying. The subdelegate finally decided to require an "authentic act that will make known the will of the community" and convened a meeting of the village assembly, "for one is needed to contain a community that is divided."[41] Such a meeting at which each inhabitant would speak was, he concluded, the only possible way to overcome the factionalism that was blocking his investi-

38. AD, C-758, Flagey, 20 March 1769 to 12 Aug. 1769: Procès-verbal.
39. AD, C-800, Montmançon, 1779: Letter from the subdelegate to the intendant.
40. AD, C-1361, Fontaine-les-Sèches, 23 April 1766: Subdelegate Daubenton to the intendant.
41. Ibid., 13 July 1776.

gation.[42] In all of these interventions, the intendant was guided by the notion that "whenever a private grievance is created . . . the sovereign's power is no longer complete."[43]

The seigneur represented another special interest that had to be watched, controlled, and eliminated. For example, the intendant sent a subdelegate to Gissey-sur-Ouche to supervise a meeting of the village assembly called to discuss the seigneur's request for permission to enclose a *chenièvre* (hemp field) within the walls surrounding his château. In return for that permission, the seigneur offered to cancel fines owed him by the village. In his letter to the subdelegate, the intendant advised taking precautions: "I ask you to take the necessary measures so that the inhabitants' voting be not at all influenced, so they may express themselves freely on the lord's proposals."[44] In 1777 the intendant asked a subdelegate to visit Echirey to verify that in making its decision, the village had not been intimidated by the illegal presence of a seigneurial lieutenant. As the intendant put it, "it is possible that the deliberations were constrained by the pressures of a local seigneurial judge."[45] Seigneurial abuse was again the issue when a subdelegate discovered, while supervising a meeting of the village assembly, that the seigneur of Sainte-Sabine was hoping to prevent that community from suing him by negotiating a separate settlement with each inhabitant. In his report the subdelegate noted that "the seigneur has the greatest interest in dividing the community and he has put great pressure on those who depend on him not to go along with the suit."[46]

42. A community's refusal to cooperate with authorities was not always the work of a group of rebellious individuals. Nor could cabals or intrigues easily be traced to the machinations of a few wealthy conspirators. This was especially true in Burgundy. Burgundian peasant society generally comprised a significant percentage of self-sufficient families whose income was not very stable. An ecological disaster or the untimely death of the family breadwinner could cause the family's fortunes to vary dramatically from one generation to the next. For this reason, poor and rich villagers sometimes had overlapping kinship ties.

43. Rousseau, *The Social Contract*, p. 77.

44. AD, C-658, Gissey-sur-Ouche, May 1789: Procès-verbal, includes intendant's instructions to the subdelegate.

45. AD, C-578, March 1777: Ordinance of the intendant and instructions to the subdelegate.

46. AD, C-679, Sainte-Sabine, 20 April 1777: Procès-verbal. Of the thirty-two inhabitants who attended the assembly convened by the subdelegate, twenty claimed they were neutral in the dispute, that is, they were not against the suit. The subdelegate was writing to the intendant asking what to do next, since the meeting did not produce a majority decision.

As a further measure to limit seigneurial influence in the assemblies, the intendant made efforts to prevent the lord's *fermier* from attending assembly meetings. In Remilly-sur-Tille, the *fermier* was banned from assembly meetings on the grounds that he "has often made himself master of the deliberations and has, on several occasions, abused his standing and influence as the lord's *fermier*, and his higher intelligence, over the other inhabitants. His stature, strength, and threats have rendered him tyrannical and a dangerous (*redoubtable*) opponent."[47]

Another measure commonly employed to curtail seigneurial influence in the assemblies was to exclude those who were in debt to the seigneur. In the eighteenth century, intendants issued numerous injunctions to specific villages for this purpose. In Missery, even the majority of villagers was banned from participating when it was shown that the seigneur was their creditor. A group of inhabitants had asked the intendant for permission to question in court several clauses in the seigneurial *terrier*. Before giving his permission, the intendant had the subdelegate determine whether the "general will" of the community was represented in this request, and whether the community's lawyers might have been "mistaken" in sustaining the inhabitants' claims. The community was basing its case on titles that dated from 1660. Because these titles were not very old, the subdelegate sought to determine whether the community possessed earlier titles that it was hiding. To verify that the community had a case, he called a meeting of the village assembly, explaining that "it is essential that each inhabitant be questioned about this . . . separately in order to discover the truth and to uncover the true interests of the community of Missery." At that meeting, the heads of only nineteen of the community's forty-four households voted in favor of going ahead with the suit. The subdelegate found, however, that these nineteen inhabitants "have given a much more exact account of the affair and expressed themselves with less confusion [*avec moins de détours*] than the individuals of the opposite opinion." He added that those "nineteen individuals who are of the opinion to maintain the claim against the

47. AD, C-575, 31 Aug. 1773: Ordinance of the intendant excluding Sieur Cazée from village assemblies.

seigneur are all or practically all property owners. . . . Most of the others do not own any land, or declared themselves too poor to take any part in the legal proceedings." Those twenty-five inhabitants were found to be cultivating the seigneur's land, rather than their own, and some were sharecroppers. The subdelegate ruled to disqualify them from voting in village assemblies because they were dependent upon and in debt to the seigneur.[48] In Missery, then, a minority was recognized as representing the "general will."

A majority vote usually did indicate the general will to the administration, but a majority could also form a cabal or act as a faction. To protect what they considered to be the general interest of the community, subdelegates sometimes intervened in village decisions to annul the work of such majority factions. In one such case, the intendant received a request from Villey-sur-Tille asking authorization to sue its seigneur. But only two-thirds of the inhabitants seemed to have been present at the meeting. The notary who had prepared the *délibération* assured the subdelegate that it was only the beggars (*mendiants*) who did not sign and were not present. The subdelegate ordered another meeting of the assembly, at which he discovered that "on the contrary, it was, in large part, the beggars who were there. . . . The inhabitants who have something to lose were not there and for the most part were not notified."[49] Here, too, the intendant was acting to protect "the will of the people from the clamour of a faction."[50] But here the faction represented a majority of the votes. Nevertheless, it was the general will, not the numerical majority, that was crucial, and only the intendant could distinguish from the multitude of voices those which represented the common interest and thus the general will.

48. AD, C-1651, 21 Oct. 1775, 22 Feb. 1776, 12 April 1778, 21 Aug. 1778: Procès-verbal, includes consultation with lawyer Ranfer and comments by Subdelegate Merle. The subdelegate's investigation revealed that the community apparently had not reported all of its properties during the verifications of Louis XIV because it did not trust the crown's intentions and feared that the verifications would be used to request taxes on communal properties.

49. AD, C-1308, Villey-sur-Tille; 13 Feb. 1780 and 12 Nov. 1782: Subdelegate to intendant.

50. Rousseau, *The Social Contract*, p. 147.

THE VILLAGE ASSEMBLY AS AN
INSTRUMENT OF COMPLIANCE

From the royal administration's point of view, one advantage of documented proof of full participation in the village assembly was that it could be used to bind recalcitrant minorities to decisions taken by the majority. After dealing with a case in which several inhabitants of St. Martin-de-la-Mer had refused to share "the costs of a legal action against their seigneur," the subdelegate commented on the advantages of using the minutes of a village assembly meeting called to verify the village's decision to go to court as a way of binding all inhabitants to that decision: "It happens every day that a resolution is not the fruit of the unanimous consent of those who make up the community; however, it binds everyone, and those who would have had the opposite opinion cannot go against the vote of the greatest number unless a surprise is discovered or a cabal has prevailed—otherwise the interests of the community would always be sacrificed to division that one should be careful to contain."[51] Administrators learned that the verification of the village's decision to go to court could later be used to prevent individuals from refusing to share the costs of a legal action on the ground that they were never consulted, or that the decision to sue was undertaken by "self-interested minorities."

Verification of the village's full participation in a decision to sue might also strengthen a community's position in court. It could prevent the community's adversaries from alleging that a claim represented only the will of a handful of *mutins* and not that of the majority. In Grenant, for example, the seigneur tried to persuade the parlement not to accept the village's case against him because five or six inhabitants were trying to sue him in the community's name. The subdelegate was called to oversee a meeting of the village assembly to verify that the claim indeed represented the general will. If it did, the community would have a stronger case.[52]

51. AD, C-1662, Saint Martin-de-la-Mer, 13 Aug. 1776: Subdelegate Merle to the intendant.
52. AD, C-659, 28 Sept. 1786: Letter from subdelegate to intendant.

In a similar situation, the lord of Talmay, hoping he could prevent his peasants from instituting a suit against him, wrote to the intendant in 1786 that a handful of *mutins* were urging that community to commence a foolish and poorly grounded legal action. The lord had already obtained a favorable decision in the seigneurial court, but the inhabitants were appealing to the Parlement of Paris. (Talmay was not within the legal jurisdiction of the Parlement of Dijon, but it was within the administrative jurisdiction of the Burgundian intendant.) The seigneur was confident that the community could be persuaded not to pursue this rash course "if the assembly were presided over by a commissioner who was able to override the few mutineers that govern the community." In a meeting of the village assembly, the subdelegate determined that the peasants who wanted to sue their seigneur (the majority) represented the general will. The subdelegate's testimony to this effect could be used to support the community's case in court.[53]

The Republicans

In an attempt to guarantee the smooth functioning of village assemblies, the crown issued numerous orders prohibiting individual troublemakers from participating in them. These difficult individuals were sometimes described as *républicains* or as possessing a spirit of republicanism. When in 1775 some inhabitants of Chaugey and Maison-Dieu were accused of abusing their communal rights, the subdelegate wrote that "the communities of Chaugey and Maison-Dieu are made up of republicans whom M. Amelot [the intendant] has had a difficult time in containing."[54] Having received numerous letters from the villagers of Grenant requesting permission to sue their seigneur, the subdelegate reported to the intendant that "all the items of the complaints brought against him [the lord] are so many imagined suppositions by a few seditious peasants in revolt against their lord, sentenced

53. AD, C-833, Talmay: Letter from intendant to subdelegate dated 28 Nov. 1786, Dijon.
54. AD, C-1601, Chaugey and Maison-Dieu, May 1775: The subdelegate reported that he had been ordered by the intendant to watch the community "in order to contain the republican spirit of the inhabitants."

by the local courts but whose republican spirit will submit neither to the lord's rights, nor to the rulings of his court, nor to the orders of M. the Intendant." Later that year, several inhabitants of Grenant refused to participate in the village lottery organized to draw the names of recruits for the king's militia. The subdelegate reported that the village had "fallen into the republican spirit that refuses to submit to the king's orders."[55]

If we understand what royal administrators meant by l'esprit républicain, we can better understand the kind of society the king's ministers were attempting to create. The writings of Turgot are particularly useful in this regard. Turgot claimed that republics were formed when the passions of individuals and parties were mistaken for those of the prince. Republicanism was more tyrannical than monarchy, because in a monarchy the powerful and the feeble could unite against a single tyrant or monarch. But in a republic, powerful individuals, with only the populace to combat, would unite to substitute their will for the general will. To Turgot, the source of tyranny was not the prince but uncontrolled intermediaries (persons or forces) between king and people. "Nothing," he wrote, "is so perilous as obedience paid to a party, which can always erect its passions into virtues." Because it embodied the general will and stood above the narrow interests of parties and factions, the monarchy was a guarantee against tyranny. In short, for Turgot the spirit of republicanism and the spirit of monarchy were opposites. Whereas republican government made a community vulnerable to abuses of power by the strong, a monarchy was the best defense against the tyranny of the powerful.[56] Moreover, the monarchy could quell or eradicate the factions, parties, and ideological divisions that arise in republics and threaten the unity of the state. The intendant's usage of the term "republicanism" at the local level was consistent with these dicta. This concern, to prevent particular interests from distorting expressions of the general interest, suggests why, during the last twenty years of the Old Regime, intendants adamantly refused all petitions from leading inhabitants to create Councils of Notables.

55. AD, C-659.
56. Anne-Robert-Jacques Turgot, Oeuvres de Turgot, ed. Dupont (Paris, 1811), 11:626–42.

Making Royal Supervision More Effective

If they were to make village assemblies a more efficient tool of administrative control, royal administrators also had to be able to punish village officers who were party to intrigues. For the intendant to supervise effectively, it was imperative that village officers not bend to pressure from powerful groups or individuals in the community.[57] In the 1760s, to make village *syndics* more responsive to the king and less responsive to village cliques, intendants began reviewing village accounts and rigorously prosecuting *syndics* for any abuse found during their tenure.

In 1767, suspecting that the *syndics* of Mont-St. Jean had been "too interested in the party of the strongest," the subdelegate requested a review of that community's fiscal records for the past twenty years. He recommended this measure because "this community has been governed for a long time by two or three of the richest inhabitants whose collusion was based not on the needs of public administration but instead on private interests. Fear or dependence made them masters of the vote; they had *syndics* named at their will." To demonstrate to the *syndics* of Mont-St. Jean the dangers of placing the interests of "the party of the strongest" above those of the community, the subdelegate threatened to hold *syndics* personally liable for all injustices in the distribution of that community's public charges committed during the previous twenty years. These *syndics* would not only be held financially responsible for all fiscal abuses during their respective terms of office but would also be "deprived of their rights as citizens." The subdelegate was persuaded that in the future, Mont-St. Jean's *syndics* would make greater efforts to "seek the means to bring relief to the miserable."[58]

Communal records after 1760 provide numerous examples of prosecutions of village *syndics* by intendants for irregularities in the management of their communities' financial obligations.

---

57. As noted earlier, one of the reasons for Colbert's mistrust of elected village officials was that they were too easily influenced by wealthy members of the community, too involved in networks of patronage and dependence to act for the good of all.

58. AD, C-1652, Mont-Saint Jean, June 1767: Letter from Subdelegate Merle to the intendant. Procès-verbal includes correspondence between the intendant and Subdelegate Merle.

Sieur Desgrey of Faye-Billot claimed that as *syndic* he was "ruined in his fortune and his estate . . . [and that] his furniture and goods [were] confiscated."[59] Because of this increased supervision by the intendant, the office of *syndic* may have become less attractive to the village's wealthy inhabitants.[60]

This increased surveillance of *syndics* might account to some extent for the growing pressures in favor of Councils of Notables. As supervision became more rigorous, wealthy individuals were finding the personal risks of service to be exceptionally high. In 1783 Bernard Carée, a leading inhabitant of Remilly-sur-Tille, refused to accept the position of village *échevin*, to which he had been elected. Carée presented the following explanation to the intendant:

The *échevin* of this village is charged with all the affairs of this community and must maintain the interests of the said community like his very own, given that he is obligated to render account of them without any indemnity. Consequently, because the *échevins* of this community are often interrupted in their work and initiative and spend a great number of days in supporting the interests of this community, during which time most inhabitants are at work and never have this responsibility, which is very costly and time-consuming for the person who has it, and because in this community there are only a dozen or so inhabitants who can and who are trusted to exercise this charge, in spite of the fact that this community is composed of sixty hearths, it is often the same ones who are obliged to exercise this charge, and because the suppliant, who performed the duties of *échevin* in the year 1772, was just forced to swear in before the local judge to perform the same function for the year 1784, without the community wishing to take any account of all the days that it is necessary to spend in order to support [communal] interests, which

59. AD, C-518, 1760. Desgrey attempted to sue the village to recover his losses. He claimed that most of the abuses for which he was prosecuted "fut commis pendant l'exercice de mes prédécesseurs." M. Desgrey had a four-page précis printed, in which he presented his case against the community: *Précis à Monseigneur l'Intendant de Bourgogne pour le Sieur Desgrey, Bachelier en Médecine, demeurant au Fays-Billot, province de Bourgogne, contre les habitans dudit lieu* (Paris, 1760). See also AD, C-578: the intendant approved Echirey's request to sue its tax assessor.

60. AD, C-1609, Montot, 1760. The administrative correspondence does not provide the best basis for generalizations about the declining attractiveness of village positions. It would be necessary to examine village assembly *délibérations* in conjunction with village tax records to determine whether these officials tended to be drawn more frequently from the wealthier peasantry after 1760. Unfortunately, few village archives are complete enough to allow the making of such an inquiry. One subdelegate wrote to the intendant, Amelot, in 1788 that "*échevins* are chosen only from the most distinguished inhabitants."

becomes too costly for the suppliant, who is appealing with trust to your authority.

My Lord, given that no one else must neglect his enterprise and lose his work to do good for the community, if it please you monseigneur, that when the suppliant renders his accounts before your subdelegate in the presence of the principal inhabitants, the community will be obligated to recognize the days that he spends, the price of which he will not be taxed, that by your decree, the suppliant hopes that the present document will be approved and then communicated to the said community, and then justice will be done.[61]

It seems reasonable to assume that wealthy inhabitants may have become more resentful about assuming (or at least more reluctant to assume) the post of village tax collector or *syndic.* That resentment may help explain why these inhabitants continued to push for the creation of Councils of Notables. They may have felt they had every right to hold a governing position in the village. Since they were doing all the work and bearing the most onerous responsibilities, why should they not set village policy? Several notables of the village of Fontaine-Française advanced another argument in favor of such councils. They claimed that in electing a *syndic,*

one usually chooses from among the notables—it is a necessary procedure because of the intelligence demanded for the administration of offices and the security necessary to maintain the communal patrimony. Therefore three-quarters of the time, one of the more substantial farmers is chosen *syndic.* But it is necessary that people of that condition pursue their farming, which is essential to society and to the good of the state. However, as *syndic,* the farmer must leave his precious occupation as often as the affairs of the community demand.[62]

---

61. AD, C-575, 27 Nov. 1783: Petition from Bernard Carée, inhabitant of Remilly-sur-Tille, to the intendant.

62. AD, C-1250, Fontaine-Française, 1774: Petition. Since the wealthy inhabitants would inevitably be held responsible for a community's failure to meet its financial obligations, an important incentive for these individuals to become a village *syndic* or tax collector was to prevent illiterate, insolvent inhabitants from occupying the post. But despite this incentive, many villagers complained that elected officials were too ignorant to perform their functions effectively. One subdelegate reported that it was rare for the village to elect "those among them who are capable of doing the job." The inhabitants, he remarked, elected as officials "only the most muddleheaded [*les gens les plus brouillons*] because they do not know how to dominate the others [*ne sçavent pas en imposer aux Autres*]."

As the solution to this problem, they suggested creation of a Council of Notables so that the work would be divided among a committee of substantial farmers.

Communal legal cases were one area in which the intendant's efforts to supervise village affairs and to arbitrate disputes were critical. The intendant wanted to prevent one faction in the village from initiating costly legal proceedings in the name of the community. Lawsuits against seigneurs, which were becoming increasingly common in the eighteenth century, were a primary concern,[63] for such suits could leave communities with massive debts. Villages instituted numerous suits against other villages, against townspeople, and against the lord's *fermier*. In 1782 the Estates of Burgundy reported that in the previous year, the intendant had approved the prosecution of four hundred community court cases involving claims totaling 400,000 livres. The court costs alone were 72,058 livres. The estates estimated that communities had, on average, lost nine out of ten cases.[64] In short, a large portion of the villages' collective income was being consumed by legal expenses.

As communal revenues grew during the eighteenth century, communities became more litigious than ever, and this resulted in a serious drain on their revenues. As early as 1683, the crown had decreed that "no person or persons can begin legal proceedings or make any deputation in the name of the community without first obtaining the consent of all inhabitants in a general assembly, confirmed and authorized by the intendant." Any individuals (*maires, échevins, syndics, jurats, consuls*) undertaking legal proceedings in the community's name but lacking proper authorization would be responsible in their "own and private names for the costs of the said legal proceedings without hope of appeal under any pretext at all and for the damages and interests of the said communities." Judges would be responsible for the community's costs for judgments rendered in cases that had been taken to court without the written consent of a majority in

---

63. See Pierre de Saint-Jacob, *Les paysans de la Bourgogne du nord au dernier siècle de l'Ancien Régime* (Dijon, 1960), p. 139.

64. AD, C-3519/44: *Mémoire* from the Estates of Burgundy, "Autorisation de plaider dans les affaires des communautés des habitans," pp. 6–7.

the village assembly. All court actions instituted by the village without the intendant's written permission would be terminated and the decisions annulled.

The edict of 1683 was not issued to prevent communities from exercising their right to go to court. Such legislation would have been arbitrary even by seventeenth-century standards, especially since communities had had this right since the Middle Ages. Rather, the legislation was aimed at preventing abuse by community officers. The monarchy's awareness of the problem is clearly stated in the preamble of the edict:

We are informed that, contrary to a disposition so advantageous to communities, *maires, échevins, syndics,* and the others who are charged with the administration of the affairs of the said communities, abusing their power, involve them every day, under different pretexts, without observing the formalities required by the said edicts, declarations, and *arrêts,* in legal proceedings that consume them in costs and that always go against the said communities because they are undertaken without legitimate basis.[65]

Far from always limiting communities' recourse to the courts of law, the monarchy was careful to guarantee access to them. In the eighteenth century, it issued numerous decrees confirming the intendant's right to approve any effort by a community to institute a court action.[66] In 1779 a subdelegate explained that the administration's vigilance was necessary only so that "factious, embittered, or stubborn people do not plead in the name of the community and against its will, and that is why a *délibération* containing the general will is required."[67] Before being granted approval of its request to go to court, a community had to obtain a written endorsement from a qualified lawyer stating that its claims were well founded. The subdelegate further explained that "in order that communities do not blindly involve themselves in expensive legal proceedings, . . . the wise practice was introduced of requiring a lawyer's opinion certifying that the inhabitants' claim was well founded [*bien fondé*]."[68]

65. AN, H-140; or BM, Fonds Saverot, vol. 47, no. 9.
66. The edict was reinforced by two *déclarations du roy* (2 Aug. 1687 and 29 Oct. 1703), and by an *arrêt du conseil* of 8 Aug. 1713 (AD, C-3331).
67. AD, C-1813, Massigny-les-Viteaux, 1779.
68. Ibid. The subdelegate was explaining why the intendant's authorization was necessary before the community could plead in court. He cited as well a

But once a community had received such certification, the intendant could do nothing beyond confirming that the *délibération* stating the community's intent to sue represented the general will of the community.

When the community of Saulx-le-Duc requested permission to sue its seigneur, the intendant wrote to the subdelegate: "Even though the right of the inhabitants appears well established by the consultation of M. ———, we believe that the community of Saulx-le-Duc should not be allowed to entangle itself in such considerable legal proceedings without first being assured of the will of the community. We propose, consequently, to order a general assembly." The intendant asked the subdelegate to conduct "in the accustomed manner an assembly of the said community which all inhabitants [meaning the heads of households] without legitimate excuse will be required to attend, to give their opinion, each separately, without confusion or uproar, [and] to declare which side they intend to take."[69] Such rigorous examinations had become standard procedure. Having each inhabitant explain the position he was taking was deemed the best way to verify that a claim represented the interests of the entire community. The Councils of Notables would have led to the closed, oligarchic government that royal administrators were trying to prevent by insisting that communal business be handled in open assemblies of the entire community. This concern emerges clearly from the intendant's objections to requests for the formation of Councils of Notables.

In 1774 the intendant received a petition from the wealthy inhabitants of Fontaine-Française requesting permission to create a Council of Notables composed of "twelve of the most enlightened among them." The community members reminded the intendant that "this practice [meeting in Councils of Notables] was followed earlier" at Fontaine-Française. Asserting that assemblies "are always tumultuous, often fruitless," they enu-

---

déclaration du roy of 29 Oct. 1703 and an *arrêt du conseil* of 8 Aug. 1713, both of which specified that the intendant's authorization was necessary before a community could initiate legal proceedings.

69. AD, C-1286, Saulx-le-Duc, 1777: Ordinance of the intendant, "Débat avec le seigneur engagiste pour la banalité du moulin de Tarsul."

merated their reasons for requesting the suppression of village assemblies in favor of a Council of Notables:

1. The community, with 260 households, is too large. There are many affairs that require frequent assemblies. The assemblies are so large that it is almost always impossible to come to an agreement on the contentions that concern the community and from which result cabals.

2. Assemblies are called on a moment's notice.

3. Rarely more than 30 inhabitants attend a single meeting. These 20 to 30 inhabitants pass a *délibération* for certification of which they pay 3 livres, and three days later they must convoke another assembly on the same subject resulting in another *délibération* no better than the first. Then a third, contrary *délibération* is passed two days later, making necessary a fourth *délibération* and added expenses. The secretary never forgets his employees and records a *délibération* even when only 15 or 20 inhabitants are present. These *délibérations* thus become extremely expensive.

4. We are obliged to assemble during the work week, and all the inhabitants, being at their work, are obliged to leave it and waste their time.

5. The *syndic* authorizes repairs or orders public works costing 800 livres, but according to the opinion of good workers it was work worth only 400 livres. The community is not informed of such abuses until after completion of the work.

6. The *syndic* and other village officials are almost always people who have no knowledge of business.[70]

But the intendant rejected the request, and his rejection reveals some of the theoretical presumptions that underlay the administration's preference for general assemblies over Councils of Notables. The intendant wrote that creation of a Council of Notables would "render these individuals absolute masters of the business. . . . This is so well known that previous intendants have rejected completely all requests of the same nature presented up to now." He preferred that communal business be settled in general assemblies, because at these meetings "one can watch a community more closely." For these reasons he decided that "it is better to continue to utilize general assemblies, and to take the

70. AD, C-1250, 17 April 1770. Includes notes of Subdelegate Charpy. The petition by the community's wealthy inhabitants was supported by the seigneur, M. de la Julien, in his letter to the intendant dated 17 April 1770, apparently written by the same individual who wrote the petition. The seigneur reiterated the reasons given by these inhabitants and, interestingly, used the same language.

necessary precautions so that everything proceeds in an orderly fashion."[71] In refusing a petition from the inhabitants of Lux to create a Council of Notables in 1771, the intendant explained that such a council "would lead to abuses, and it is more regular that business be taken directly to a general assembly that all inhabitants will be required to attend."[72] In another refusal eleven years later, the intendant noted that the wisdom of his predecessors had taught him that "we would see great abuse result if the business of the community were not treated with the knowledge of all the inhabitants."[73] In 1789 the intendant rejected the request of the village of Lamarche for establishment of a Council of Notables, citing his recent decisions as the basis for this one: "Every time that similar requests have been presented by a village community, they have been rejected, notably by Saucherance, the village neighboring Lamarche. This one should thus also be rejected, and all inhabitants should be enjoined to appear in the assemblies in the future as was recently decreed for the community of Faye-Billot."[74]

During the last twenty years of the Old Regime, the Burgundian intendant issued numerous ordinances for particular villages requiring inhabitants' full participation and setting fines for absences. These ordinances were issued in response to petitions for creation of Councils of Notables, following notification of abuse, or poor attendance. In one, the intendant specified the following formula for full participation: "We order all the inhabitants of the community who are not prevented by legitimate cause to attend the assemblies, which will be called by the *échevin*, to give their opinions, each separately, without confusion or tumult."[75]

71. Ibid., 23 Feb. 1774: Procès-verbal, includes request from Syndic Boudot, comments from the intendant, and letters from Subdelegate Perrenet dated 21 Oct. 1774 and 19 Oct. 1774.
72. AD, C-1259, Lux, 12 April 1771: Procès-verbal with notes from Subdelegate Charpy.
73. Ibid., Feb. 1782.
74. AD, C-786, 12 March 1789: Request from the community with intendant's comments recorded on margin of page. Another copy of the community's request with intendant's comments on back of page is dated March 1789. See also Subdelegate Suremain's report of January 1789.
75. Similar ordinances were issued for the villages of Fontaine-les-Sèches in 1761 (AD, C-1361); Lux in 1768 (AD, C-1259); Etalante in 1777, 1778 (AD, C-1088), and 1780 (AD, C-1123); Chenecaux in 1781 and 1785 (AD, C-1178); Genlis and Uchey in 1784 (AD, C-533); Chatillon in 1785 (AD, C-1123); Chivres in 1786 (AD, C-1468); Longchamp in 1787 (AD, C-773); and Echirey (AD, C-578).

In the late eighteenth century, wealthy inhabitants even began to claim that their interests were identical with those of the
community. At Gigny in 1781, a group of wealthy inhabitants
describing themselves as *propriétaires forains* (landowners who
lived on the outskirts of the village) and claiming the support of
their seigneur appealed to the seigneurial court to overturn a
decision of the village assembly, assented to by twenty-two of
the village's thirty-three inhabitants, to deny the sheep belonging to the *forains* access to the communal pasture. The *forains*,
who were the community's most highly taxed members, insisted that the assembly's sole motive for excluding their sheep
was its animosity toward them.[76] This animosity, as the landowners explained it, resulted from the ruling that they had obtained earlier requiring the community to divide two-thirds of
the timber annually cut from the communal woods according to
each individual's tax assessment.[77] Naturally, the highly taxed
landowners stood to benefit most from this ruling, which went
against the tradition of dividing all such timber equally among
all members of the community. The larger landowners, evidently hurt by the new decision, contended that their "sheep
were necessary because the soil in this region benefits most
from their manure" and maintained that they were calling upon
superior authority "out of a spirit of public interest." In contrast
to their own public spirit, "the multitude is all too often swayed
by partisan spirit to the extent that they [the multitude] are
ready to sacrifice their proper interests to satisfy the animosity
that moves them." Asking the court to repeal the assembly's *délibérations*, the larger landowners wrote that "the opinion of
the multitude—almost always blinded by partisan spirit—must
cede to individual votes when those votes are dictated by reflection and by motives of public utility; one must be, therefore,
even more receptive to the claims of the seigneur and land-

76. Those voting with the assembly's majority felt that there was not enough
pasture for both cattle and sheep. They wanted to eliminate the pasturing of
sheep on the commons since their cattle would have been difficult to feed otherwise. The wealthy inhabitants, by contrast, had private reserves of fodder for
their plow animals and cattle and wanted to use the communal pasture for their
large herds of sheep.
77. The issue of distributing communal wood will be discussed in detail in
Chapter 4.

owners, especially since they are the ones most interested in the progress of agriculture." In conclusion, the landowners compared their request, "founded on calculation and reflection," with that of the multitude, "blind and without reflection, victims of caprice and the spirit of partisanship."[78]

This case is exceptional in that there are few similar examples of even the better-off peasants claiming to be aligned in court cases with their lord. Nevertheless, it is evidence of a growing tendency for the well-to-do peasants to resent having to abide by decisions taken by the village assembly. Grievances such as those aired at Gigny often led leading inhabitants to petition the intendant for permission to create Councils of Notables. The Gigny case also indicates the emergence of a new conception of the general will and community participation. The earlier tradition of egalitarian participation in community affairs did not level social or economic distinctions between inhabitants. Rather, implicit in this tradition was the recognition of inequalities. The goal of community decision making had been to identify general interests in spite of differences in the inhabitants' wealth and education. What changed in the late eighteenth century was that the wealthy inhabitants, basing their argument on the concept of enlightened self-interest, began to insist that their own interests were those of the entire community. They argued that by promoting and increasing agricultural output, they advanced the long-term interests of the whole community. The logic that had formerly been the basis for defending egalitarian participation—that full participation was the best way to define the general will—had thus been declared invalid.

CURTAILING MINISTERIAL DESPOTISM

We have seen that wealthy peasants wanted to limit the role of village assemblies in favor of Councils of Notables so that they could consolidate their position as local political leaders. The councils would permit these wealthier inhabitants to differenti-

---

78 Précis pour lo soignour & les propriétaires-forains de Gigny, opposans a l'homologation de la délibération du 6 Août 1781 contre les habitans de la communauté du même lieu (Dijon, 1785), in BM, Fonds Saverot, vol. 67, no. 47.

ate their interests from those of the community. The well-to-do peasants were not the only group that wanted councils, however. After 1750, and especially after 1770, members of other elites also urged the creation of such councils. In general, the councils were seen as a way to limit the powers of the hated provincial intendancy and thereby to restore local independence. The local nobility, Jean Egret has speculated, regarded the councils as a means to regain its control over village affairs.[79] Those who opposed the crown saw village councils as a way to achieve the larger goal of curtailing absolutism. Seeking an alternative to arbitrary government, the crown's opponents, the "enlightened" political reformers mentioned earlier, spoke of creating institutions in which local notables would deliberate, determine, and express policy as representatives of the nation. But those opposing the monarchy had no institutional mechanisms through which to exert direct pressure on the crown. There was no legal means or forum for developing a joint program of action.

Nevertheless, as the fiscal crises escalated, the movement for economic and political change gained momentum, and in 1787 the king issued an edict that called for the restructuring of the entire royal administration. It was not the force of the opposition so much as the weakness of the crown, which was on the verge of bankruptcy, that led to the edict of 1787. The monarchy needed some way to negotiate with the nation's elites to obtain comprehensive tax reforms and expand the tax base, even if it meant offering political concessions. The edict of 1787 applied to the entire kingdom except the *pays d'états*, which included Burgundy.[80] It called for the creation of Councils of Notables in all villages. These councils were the bottom level in a hierarchy that included, in ascending order, village or municipal councils, *arrondissements*, departments, and provincial assemblies. Their members were elected in each village; membership was limited to substantial property owners. Each council was presided over

79. Jean Egret, *La prérévolution française* (Paris, 1962).
80. The *pays d'états* included the *généralités* of Languedoc (Montpellier and Montauban), Burgundy (Dijon), Flanders and Artois (Lille), Brittany (Rennes), Provence (Aix), Hainault and Cambrésis (Valenciennes). The smaller *pays d'états* of the Southwest were under the intendancy of Auch or Bordeaux. The *généralités* of Bourges and Montauban were also excluded.

by a lord or his agent (or in their absence an elected *syndic*). The councils were to choose two of their members to represent the village in the assembly of the *arrondissement*. The assembly of the *arrondissement*, in turn, elected representatives for the departmental assembly, which elected members for the provincial assembly. Most important, the creation of provincial assemblies implied the possible establishment of a truly representative national body. Egret suggests that the controller general, Brienne, believed that the provincial assemblies might eventually choose representatives to a national assembly (although this was not provided for in the edict of 1787).[81] In the *pays d'états*, the estates could choose representatives to a national assembly. This national assembly was to discuss with the king his yearly tax proposals. The hope was that it would ultimately be given powers to vote on taxes.

The hierarchy of assemblies created by the edict of 1787 would vote by head and not by order. The new bodies would divide among themselves the civil administrative functions (collectively referred to in the eighteenth century as the *police économique*) previously performed by the intendant, which included distribution of taxes, supervision of public works, maintenance of public buildings, organization of charity workshops, and control of poor relief. The intendant would retain only those powers necessary to guarantee civil obedience and to enforce the law.

In creating the assemblies, the crown sought to bypass the parlements and overcome their opposition to fiscal reform. The crown granted these assemblies the right to distribute taxes in the hope that their representatives would approve the fiscal reforms necessary to avoid the impending bankruptcy. The essential problem was to get tax-exempt groups to agree to surrender their exemptions.

The edict of 1787 marked a radical departure from the political and administrative traditions of royal absolutism. Contemporaries viewed it as a veritable revolution. (Tocqueville later wrote that the Revolution began with the administrative re-

81. Egret, *La prérévolution française,* 109–17.

forms of 1787.) Many applauded the program as a great victory for the cause of political liberty. For the nobility, the reforms promised renewed political power and control over village affairs. For the local community, the reforms meant a new degree of independence.[82]

Turgot, as controller general, had earlier considered a similar program for restructuring the kingdom's administration and had had his secretary write a long memorandum to the king. He thought the creation of a representative body could stem the tide of growing opposition to the crown. Turgot never presented his program to the king, however, because he feared that its implementation might transform the kingdom into a republic.[83] We know that Louis XVI only reluctantly supported the reforms of 1787. He wrote in the margin of Turgot's memorandum of 1775 (which the king read after Turgot was dismissed) that "the administration of intendants, except for a few abuses, is the best [feature of my kingdom]; not in that area is the state's chief difficulty to be found."[84]

By institutionalizing the powers of local notables, the edict of 1787 contradicted everything that administrative policy in Burgundy had been carefully calculated to achieve. The reforms were never implemented in Burgundy—that would have required suppression of the Burgundian estates and modification of the estates' tradition of representation by order so that their members would vote as equals. But we can assume that at a later date, similar reforms would have provided Burgundy with its own system of subordinate provincial assemblies. After 1787, however, the crown was too weak to control either the events or the people who would shape the future.

82. See M. P. Renouvin, Les assemblées provinciales de 1787 (Paris, 1921); C. Bloch, "Les assemblées municipales de 1787: Leur caractère économique, leur fonctionnement," in Etudes sur l'histoire économique de la France (1760–1789) (Paris, 1907); M. Lenonce de Lavergne, Les assemblées provinciales sous Louis XVI (Paris, 1864); Egret, La prérévolution française, pp. 109–22; Alexis de Tocqueville, L'Ancien Régime, 2 vols. (Paris, 1965), 1:239.

83. "Mémoire sur les municipalités," in Anne-Robert-Jacques Turgot, Oeuvres, 5 vols., ed. Gustave Schelle (Paris, 1913–1923), 4:568–628. Turgot never presented his reform program to Louis XV (p. 571). L'Abbé de Véri described Turgot's ambivalence toward the reform: "Turgot . . . ne voulait pas sacrifier la royauté à des idées trop républicaines" (p. 627).

84. Cited by Egret in La prérévolution française, p. 114.

THE VILLAGE AND THE
ENLIGHTENMENT

The Burgundian evidence suggests that in the matter of local political participation, the crown opted for a kingdom of established households rather than for a republic of property holders, which was the rival liberal goal. The crown's officials could exercise greater control over the peasantry by treating all households equally and binding each to the collective decisions of the assembly. Insisting upon general suffrage in full village assemblies, royal officials made it more difficult for wealthy inhabitants to dominate the village and ignore the rights of the poor. The wealthy could more easily hide their motives and intentions from the community in Councils of Notables, where they could collaborate with each other or with outsiders against the poor or in violation of common rights. If they were to control the appointment of such village officials as forest guards or shepherds, wealthy inhabitants could monopolize village properties. Royal administrators worried that the well-to-do, in pursuing their own short-term interests, might jeopardize the solvency of the village. This possibility is discussed more fully in Chapter 4, where we consider how communal rights figured in communal finances. The intendants' archives do not permit an assessment of how effective intendants really were in preventing chicanery, however, since such documents concern only abuses that were brought to their attention.

The royal administrators' insistence on full participation makes more sense when considered in conjunction with their efforts to increase collective fiscal and financial responsibility. Full participation was part of a package that included mechanisms for debt control and for linking the village to nationwide credit networks. The entire village voted; the entire village bore responsibility for communal debts. Creditors liked the arrangement because it was easier to get information about villages than about individual peasants, and because judges were more willing to believe that a commitment represented the general will of a community if the entire village had participated in the decision making. A decision that seemed to be the work of a cabal of wealthy inhabitants might not be recognized as the legal basis for a contract. Creditors increasingly appreciated full participation as a way of ensuring that the courts would recognize the validity of contracts to which villages were a party.

The emphasis that authorities placed on village assemblies increased the community's political effectiveness. We will see in Chapter 5 that the existence of a widely recognized forum for collective decision making meant that the village could defend its collective interests. This ability resulted in part from successful efforts to restrict the leadership of wealthy inhabitants in the village assemblies. Since authorities were not willing to deal with individuals, the rich peasants had to present themselves as agents of the community in order to be heard. This fact shaped internal political rhetoric; wealthy inhabitants had to describe even selfish goals to the assembly as serving the general welfare.

Royal officials considered it essential to establish bureaucratic hegemony over the more than one thousand villages in Burgundy. If creating a society that could be governed by administrative decree was the goal, ensuring that the rules were observed was much easier when the suffrage of all inhabitants could be scrutinized by the subdelegate in meetings of the entire village. The alternative, rich notables meeting in legally recognized bodies, was much more difficult to supervise. Full participation in open balloting under bureaucratic supervision was also a way to prevent the wealthy from controlling the assemblies. After so many efforts to curtail seigneurial administration, royal officials did not want powerful local men, whether lord or peasant, to stand between the monarchy and individual citizens.

Because they wanted to restrict the political role of wealthy inhabitants, royal officials did not want to endow the village with a government in which individuals delegated their sovereignty to village representatives. Bureaucrats had a vision of a state in which individuals would be equal before a distant and anonymous government that ruled for the good of all. Such a vision did not mean that bureaucrats were ready to abolish a society of orders, but they could and did recognize equality within the orders. A community of equal but atomized individuals could less easily resist the intendant's surveillance and domination. The policies designed to atomize the community were at once authoritarian and egalitarian but were nevertheless democratic: they extended suffrage to all male inhabitants. The threat to a state so conceived was posed by representative institutions rather than by equality.

The disputes between state and social groups over how villages should be governed enable us to assess the motives of Old Regime bureaucrats. They also help us to see that political change in eighteenth-century France cannot be explained in terms of a rising and irresistible democracy. The notion that there was a universal drive toward democracy obscures the fact that not one, but two, democratic traditions vied for dominance in eighteenth-century France. Each of these democratic traditions had different constituencies, and each promised France a different democratic future. One was supported by the administrative policies and traditions of the king's bureaucrats who, by insisting upon full participation in village assemblies, were enlarging the sphere of bureaucratic control. The other was supported by those ambitious elites, such as the well-off peasants and local seigneurs, who had found their opportunity to exercise political power limited by the growth of absolutism and administrative centralization.[85]

These conclusions about village government also lead to a generalization about the Enlightenment. The pressures exerted by wealthy peasants for creation of village councils might well appear to have been the work of the Enlightenment philosophes. Such an impression is misleading, however. The philosophes did not consult with the peasantry, nor did they know much about village practices. Few village leaders attended meetings of provincial literary societies or would have read works by those who favored curtailing absolutism. Nevertheless, the evidence from the village archives suggests a parallel movement of ideas among

85. Recognizing the dual nature of eighteenth-century democracy will help us to understand the contradictory nature of France's democratic traditions; it might help us to understand as well an important historical issue: the difference between the revolutions of 1789 and 1793. In his seminar on the historians of nineteenth-century France, given at the University of Michigan in 1981, François Furet emphasized the difference between the political legacies of the revolutions of 1789 and 1793. Guizot, Quinet, Tocqueville, Thiers, and Blanc, among others, posited that there were actually two French Revolutions. The revolution of 1789 could not have been the work of the same men, holding the same ideals, who created the revolution of 1793. To many nineteenth-century writers, the problem facing the 1789 revolutionaries was to create a society based on liberty; the problem in 1793 was to create a society based on equality.

people who did not read books. Just as the wealthy peasants clamored for village councils, the literary opponents of despotism sought a group of citizens who could replace the intendants as an intermediary between crown and nation. Perhaps, then, we should broaden the definition of the Enlightenment and speak of ideas shared in a common culture, the way Burckhardt spoke of the Renaissance.[86]

86. Carlo Ginzburg, in *The Cheese and the Worms: The Cosmos of a Sixteenth-Century Miller* (Baltimore, 1980), also speaks of circularity between the ideas of subordinate and ruling classes. Cultural diffusion and reciprocal influence between lower and dominant cultures can, perhaps, explain the striking consistency between the arguments of village notables in favor of councils and the programs proposed by the philosophes.

Four

The Politics of Agriculture

Readers of the king's edicts have generally found the royal intention to reform agricultural organization to be clearly stated. Beginning in the mid-eighteenth century, the elimination of common-use rights and properties was called for in the most explicit
terms. Historians have commonly assumed that the edicts accurately present the crown's intentions and have associated the
growth of state power with the promotion of agrarian individualism. But the programs for restructuring agriculture were never
implemented. In this chapter I suggest that the provincial intendants, rather than altering communal institutions, actually
helped communities to resist the reforms. Whereas crown and
intendant had earlier presented a united front in dealing with
communities, in the struggle over agrarian reform crown and
intendant seem to have separated and to have pursued divergent,
often antagonistic, courses.

RESTRUCTURING AGRICULTURE

According to royal policy statements of the late eighteenth century, agriculture in most of France was inefficient because it was
too tightly regulated by the community. Cultivation was governed by fixed routines and schedules set by the group. The
questions of what, when, and where to plant and to harvest were

decided collectively. In Burgundy, for example, the following procedure was routine. Arable land was divided into a few large open fields; peasants possessed strips in each field. (Separate, fenced-off parcels were not permitted.) The village assembly decided what would be planted in the open fields, which were divided into three *soles:* one-third was usually planted in wheat; one-third was planted in spring grain, either barley or oats; and one-third normally remained fallow. Thus, at least one-third of the tillable soil was fallow at all times. All village residents, including the seigneur, had the right to pasture their livestock on the fallow land or on wasteland. After the harvest, the cultivated area of the common fields was also made available to the village herd. The common fields thus consisted of wasteland and meadows, as well as the fallow and the harvested fields. According to the right of *vaine pâture,* all inhabitants, the seigneur included, could pasture livestock on the commons, the stubble of the open fields, or the fallow land. This right, along with the fragmentation of holdings, compelled individuals to sow and harvest at the same time as their neighbors, and to utilize the same crop rotation system. An additional disincentive to efficient agriculture was that the fragmentation of holdings and the scattering of plots and fields encouraged carelessness and dishonesty by neighbors. When one individual did not adequately drain his field, his neighbors' lands were often flooded; if someone carelessly turned a plow the wrong way, he might crush his neighbor's crop. The theft of a furrow or of a neighbor's crop was commonplace. The difficulty of policing fragmented holdings discouraged cultivators from investing their time or money in improvements.

Since artificial fertilizer did not exist, higher yields depended on manure, the supply of which depended on the quantity of livestock. However, an increase in livestock required an increase in the fallow land, which meant reducing the arable land. Thus, pasture could only be increased at the expense of arable land. Agronomists have referred to this dependence of livestock on fallow land as an "infernal circle." Whereas French peasants allowed one-third of their fields to lie fallow, the English developed an efficient way of increasing both arable land and livestock. On the fallow land rather than the tillable soil, they planted root crops, such as turnips, and grasses like sainfoin and clover, which enriched rather than exhausted the soil and could be used as feed. The introduction of these soil-restorative crops and the elimination of fallow land revolutionized English agriculture and society. A larger population could be supported because more livestock providing manure allowed more intensive cultivation of the arable land. More oats could be grown to support more horses, cows, and sheep, thus improving productivity.

The physiocrats, a group of eighteenth-century economists led by Quesnay, expressed the concerns about the technological conservatism of French agriculture in a theoretical formulation. They believed that only agriculture produced a surplus over the costs of production and that to guarantee the national welfare, France must have the largest possible agricultural surplus. To achieve this surplus, they postulated, high grain prices were desirable because a rise in agricultural income would mean an increase in net product, an expansion of the entire economy, and an increase in population. Rising agricultural incomes would also fuel growth in manufacturing because agrarian prosperity would create a market for urban goods.

To increase the capital invested in agriculture, the physiocrats considered it essential to emancipate the individual producer from traditions that dictated the communal regulation of agricultural routines. They called on the state to achieve this by redefining agrarian property rights. The reformers argued that individuals would be motivated to invest in improvements only if all legal obstacles to the full private ownership of land were removed. Only then would they be guaranteed the full benefits of their investments in enclosure, hedges, fences, and husbandry. Only then would they risk the considerable capital outlays necessary for the creation of artificial meadows. Basing their claims on the English example, the physiocrats asserted that since the right of common pasture made it a practical necessity to conform to the practices of one's neighbors, introducing new techniques required abolition of that right.

The preceding discussion of open-field agriculture, based on the royal edicts and the theory of the physiocrats, is simplified, but it is convenient for the purposes of this chapter. In actuality, there was great variety and flexibility in agricultural practices throughout France, but the argument of this chapter does not depend on recognition of that variation. The political and fiscal circumstances that prevented the implementation of the program for agricultural reform are our main concern here.

Ideas on how to escape the infernal circle—the dependence of livestock on fallow land—were part of a broader philosophy and program for economic growth, the goal of which was to increase long-term economic productivity for the benefit of the state. The physiocrats were convinced that France was underpopulated and that the soil, if properly cultivated, could support a much larger population. According to these economists, large populations were in themselves an important form of wealth. Since, according to the physiocrats, land was the basis of all wealth, the whole process of economic revitalization had to begin by bringing more money into agriculture. "Poor peasants mean a poor kingdom" was Quesnay's dictum. The first step was to free the grain trade from price controls.[1] The resulting higher grain prices would stimulate the entire economy in the long run. High grain prices would increase agricultural employment and wages and hence would also increase the demand for industrial products. This would result not in a shift of income between the industrial and agricultural sectors, but in an increase in the income of both. Rising profits would stimulate investment in new techniques that, by increasing agricultural productivity, would support the larger population, which would create more wealth.

But what about the interim, the period of adjustment to high prices for grain? What about the poor man who might lose his land because he could not afford the increased rent, or the worker who was unable to find the money to feed his family while waiting for wages to catch up with increased prices? Such problems were never discussed by the physiocrats, who eschewed sentimentality. Their concern was the building of a stronger, more populous state that could put more soldiers in the field and send more ships to sea. It was a political problem— France's defeat in the Seven Years' War—that elevated physiocratic ideas to prominence in many discussions.

---

1. See Steven L. Kaplan, *Bread, Politics, and Political Economy in the Reign of Louis XV* (The Hague, 1976).

In midcentury, the crown began to legislate the economic changes that the physiocrats had been proposing. It attempted on several occasions to remove price controls and export restrictions on grain, and to encourage and reward individual initiative. To these ends, the King's Council authorized the partitioning of common lands in 1770 and the enclosure of all lands in 1773. In addition, the right of common pasture was abolished with regard to enclosed lands so that individuals could withdraw their property from the villagewide system of crop rotation. Protected from the communal herd, owners might grow the root crops that had transformed English agriculture. The crown's program to reform and to restructure the agrarian economy is extensively covered in the literature on late-eighteenth-century France. The peasantry's opposition to those reforms has also received broad coverage in that literature. In most historical accounts, peasants are described as subsistence farmers who had little interest in producing for the market and opposed increases in grain prices. They desired, instead, protection from extreme price fluctuations. Because most peasants could not subsist on their crops alone—their holdings were often too small—they had to buy grain on the market and were interested in stable prices as consumers as much as (or more than) as producers. Lacking capital, they could neither afford nor benefit from enclosures. Moreover, the peasants feared that the loss of their collective rights would deprive them of a means of support, especially in times of need. Most peasants considered essential the right of common pasture, the use of the commons, equal shares of wood from the communal forest to use for fuel, and the right of gleaning stubble after the harvest.

Not so well known is that long before the monarchy issued orders abolishing collective practices, it was under pressure to do so from the Burgundian estates and Parlement. The reform legislation that was finally issued was the product of cooperation between the crown and those two provincial bodies, which are generally depicted as opponents of reform. Most historians are unaware that the reforms being sought by the King's Council were blocked by the royal bureaucracy. The intendant even upheld gleaning rights, which, in some regions, specified that farmers must use the sickle instead of the scythe. The sickle was less efficient; it left much more stubble in the fields, which became the property of the community. The sickle method also created more work for the field hands and reduced owners' profits.

There were essentially two reasons for the intendant's opposition to restricting these and other communal rights. The first was that loss of communal properties made it more difficult for communities to pay royal taxes. The reforms called for a break with the communities' tradition of common rights and required that common fields become the property of individuals; thus the community would lose them forever. But as was noted in Chapter 1, since Louis XIV's campaign to verify debts, such properties had become the basis of the communities' ability to borrow money. In the eighteenth century, leasing these properties became the usual way for communities to fund day-to-day expenses. The communities' financial solvency had come to depend on the preservation of communal rights; those rights provided communities with the means to cover their expenses. The intendant, whose foremost concern was that communities remain solvent so that they could pay royal taxes, was not willing to risk communal solvency for possible long-term gains in productivity. He might be blamed if tax yields fell short. The urgency of this fiscal preoccupation becomes clear when we consider that in the late 1770s and early 1780s, the crown was on the verge of bankruptcy. To support the costs of the American Revolution, the monarchy had incurred debts that were more than 50 percent of revenues in 1789. The problem of compensating the crown's financiers had become so serious that it jeopardized the monarchy's ability to borrow. The intendants feared that the loss of communal properties, by making it more difficult for communities to pay royal taxes, could aggravate a situation that was already critical.

The second reason was that the short-term dislocations caused by the new programs presented the intendant with urgent social problems. Although intendants may have personally supported the new ideas, economic progress was not their main administrative responsibility. The social problems, and in particular growing mendicity, were more important. They required the intendant's immediate attention, and they partly explain his opposition to the implementation of the new ideas. The fortunes of peasant families could change suddenly. One bad harvest, the billeting of troops, an epidemic, or the death of a cow or a few sheep could wipe out assets and impoverish a family. Communal rights and properties had traditionally functioned as a type of insurance for individual members of the community against sudden but temporary misfortune. The poorest inhabitants had been able to raise a cow, a pig, or a few sheep thanks to their communal pasture rights. A family in need could fall back on these resources and avoid destitution. In this sense, collective agricultural practices provided long-term security.

The physiocrats, however, did not believe that communal rights and properties should be social insurance against the mishaps and uncertainties that were the peasant's lot; advocates of physiocracy did not propose ways of coping with individual misfortune and poverty. They never considered what the possible alternatives would be once the community's resources could no longer provide welfare for individuals. Restricting communal rights forced many of the poor out of the village and onto the roads as itinerant workers or beggars. In a bad year, the number of roaming beggars sometimes exceeded the capacity of cities and charitable foundations to accommodate them. Historians today estimate that as much as 20 percent of the population of eighteenth-century France was indigent[2]—that is, over two million French were beggars or itinerant laborers. The authorities were unable to cope with the problems of controlling vagrancy, rehabilitating mendicants, or suppressing banditry. Roaming beggars threatened the security of the countryside and were a burden on the cities. For this reason, the intendant preferred that individuals remain in their communities of origin. If communal rights allowed a poor inhabitant to raise a cow or a pig or a few sheep on the communal pasture, then allowing him to retain those rights was preferable to forcing him out of the village and into dependence on charity or on the state. Therefore, preserving

2. See Olwen H. Hufton, *The Poor of Eighteenth-Century France, 1750–1789* (Oxford, 1974), p. 1; and Robert M. Schwartz, "Policing the Poor in Eighteenth-Century France: The Example of the Généralité of Caen," Ph.D. dissertation, University of Michigan, 1981.

collective rights was a way of maintaining the poor and keeping them in their villages. Also, so long as an inhabitant remained in the village he would pay some taxes. These taxes, no matter how minimal, would lighten the load on the others.[3]

COMMUNAL WOOD DISTRIBUTION

One issue on which the goals of the economic reformers collided with the older policies and procedures of the provincial intendant was communal wood distribution. According to provincial custom, the cooking and heating needs of each household were provided for by distributing communal wood equally to all tax-paying members of the community. In the 1730s, however, the Maîtrise des Eaux et Forêts began to encourage communities to divide timber cut from communal forests on the basis of a new standard: one-third divided equally among all inhabitants and two-thirds allocated to individuals in proportion to the royal taxes they paid. Previously, membership in the community had entitled an inhabitant to an equal share of the yearly timber allotment; now the important consideration was how much an individual contributed to community taxes. This change in the allocation of communal resources reflected the crown's broader

3. Many have interpreted the late-eighteenth-century attacks on gleaning rights as an effort to encourage the commercialization of agriculture by suppressing those communal aspects of agriculture that inhibited the incentives of large landholders. The curtailment of gleaning rights and other communal rights, however, cannot be understood without considering economic and demographic trends that the eighteenth-century French could not measure. Lacking reliable statistics, they were unaware of the long-term demographic problems that beset them. The disappearance of the plague after 1720, the extension of cottage industry, and administrative efforts to improve market communications all contributed to population growth. In the eighteenth century, population growth ceased to be limited by the pestilence and starvation that had periodically desolated entire localities and that had maintained a Malthusian balance between population and resources. The royal administration worked to mitigate the worst effects of local subsistence crises. With cessation of the crises, the poor were no longer threatened with imminent death. A distinct social class was emerging: the chronically poor, who were permanently undernourished but able to survive and to procreate. Community resources could no longer support these new demographic pressures. Contemporaries began to relate poverty to indolence, and indolence to communal rights. It was in this context that contemporaries began to question gleaning rights and other methods for dealing with poverty. Gleaning rights had always functioned as a type of insurance for community members against sudden but temporary misfortune; they were not intended to maintain permanent poverty.

program to increase long-term tax yields by giving more resources to wealthy peasants, who were likely to invest and
thereby to increase productivity. If individuals created more
wealth by increased investments, the tax base could be widened.
Over an extended period, this increased productivity would increase revenues and thus strengthen the state. Today we would
call such a theory supply-side economics. This approach marked
a striking departure from tradition in the eighteenth century. It
would eliminate the barriers to individuals' pursuit of economic
gain on the basis of self-interest and would elevate an individual's needs above those of the community.

This policy encountered community opposition. On this issue,
the intendants generally supported the communities. They feared
that the solidity of the existing tax base could be jeopardized for
the sake of long-term profits that might never materialize. If the
village poor lost their right to equal shares of timber, they would
have no legal way to get wood to heat their homes or cook their
meals. But the intendants opposed restricting that collective right
for yet another reason: the new wood policy decreased their authority over the village assembly. As we have seen in Chapter 3,
the intendant was committed to governance by majority rule in
the village assembly. The new policy, however, compromised the
assembly's authority. To change that policy, wealthy inhabitants
were henceforth supposed to appeal directly to the Maîtrise des
Eaux et Forêts, thus evading entirely the assembly's jurisdiction.
Such appeals were almost inevitable because a majority of inhabitants was not likely to support division of two-thirds of the wood
according to individual tax assessments. By allowing a vital community decision to be made outside the assembly's jurisdiction,
the new wood policy undermined the intendant's efforts to reinforce majority rule in the assemblies and threatened his principal
source of control over the peasantry—his supervision of the
village assembly. Intendants therefore resented the program and
generally were willing to help communities defy the authorities
who attempted to enforce the new system. The intendants' efforts were unsuccessful in the long run, however; other authorities had more direct jurisdiction over wood usage. Nevertheless,
an examination of the intendant's position with regard to the
wood distribution policy will reveal both how he acted to pre-

serve the peasantry's corporate traditions and how he worked against the reformers.

A royal edict of 1669 assigned the Maîtrise des Eaux et Forêts the final jurisdiction over all matters concerning the kingdom's woods.[4] It was not until the 1730s, however, that the maîtrise took an interest in how communities allotted their wood. In 1730 the King's Council ordered the Maîtrise des Eaux et Forêts to ensure that in the village of Braizey-sur-Plaine, "for all the years to come, wood must be distributed one-third by equal proportion and two-thirds by *le marc la livre* [according to the proportion of the community's taxes paid by a single inhabitant]."[5] The ordinance of 1730 seems to have applied to only one village; by the late eighteenth century, that policy had become the general rule throughout the province.

Even though the King's Council had assigned the Maîtrise des Eaux et Forêts final jurisdiction in matters that concerned forests, its authority soon came into conflict with that of the Parlement of Dijon. That parlement, on the basis of precedents going back to the sixteenth century, insisted that it had the right to oversee wood usage and refused to acknowledge that ministry's authority. The parlement was still ruling independently on distribution of wood from communal forests in the 1720s, and its decisions were often contrary to those of the maîtrise.[6] In the mid-eighteenth century, however, this situation began to change. When ruling on how communities should allocate their wood, the parlement generally upheld the royal legislation requiring the one-third, two-thirds distribution. There are indications that in the 1770s and 1780s, the parlement was going even further in the direction of individualism than the maîtrise by giving several communities permission to divide all their wood in proportion to the taxes paid by the inhabitants. In a letter to the intendant, the village of Aubaine cited a parlementary order giving that village permission to divide all their wood according to *le marc la livre*.[7] In 1777,

4. Ordonnance de la Maîtrise des Eaux et Forêts, April 1669. Text in Isambert, Jourdan, and Decrusy, *Recueil général des anciennes lois françaises depuis l'an 420 jusqu'à la Révolution de 1789*, 29 vols. (Paris, 1821–1833), 18:219–31.

5. *Règlement du conseil*, 29 Aug. 1730, art. 2; cited in an ordinance of M. Legrand, maître, Maîtrise des Eaux et Forêts, 12 Feb. 1773: AD, B²-256F.

6. See Chapter 2.

7. AD, C-901, Aubaine, July 1787: "Contestation avec le seigneur au sujet de l'affouage."

several inhabitants of Fontaine-Française insisted that there had been a similar parlementary ruling for their village.[8] In 1788, the inhabitants of Binges cited a parlementary decision of 1787 giving the *échevins* the right to divide the community's wood according to *le marc la livre*.[9] In this instance, then, the parlement went further in the direction of individualism than did the crown.

Both the parlement and the Maîtrise des Eaux et Forêts had more direct authority over wood distribution than did the intendant. Not only was a majority vote in the village assembly unnecessary to change wood allotments—the assembly did not have to be consulted at all. The request of a single wealthy inhabitant, with the approval of the seigneurial judge, was sufficient. As one subdelegate put it, for a community to change its distribution system, "all that is necessary is simply a request [to the maîtrise], and any inhabitant has the right to demand it, even though the common will might be opposed."[10] Thus, the assembly, and the intendant who supervised it, could offer no resistance to a decision to alter wood distribution. For example, in 1788, when the seigneurial judge of Blaisy-Bas approved a request from several of the inhabitants to change its distribution system, the village assembly met to discuss the change. Twenty-three families favored a return to equal distribution; only four families supported the new system. Nevertheless, the assembly's opposition to the new system was to no avail. There are many similar examples of village assemblies trying in vain to block or revoke the change to two-thirds distribution according to *le marc la livre*. Although the intendant had little direct jurisdiction over wood distribution, he did have an interest in helping these communities evade the new policy's requirements. We will see that the intendant's position did not change, but his methods for dealing with problems of wood distribution did.

The communities developed two arguments for reversing a decision by the maîtrise to require the one-third, two-thirds dis-

---

8. AD, C-1250, 18 Dec. 1777 to 9 Feb. 1778: Procès-verbal.
9. AD, C-472, Binges, June 1788: Procès-verbal, "Débats au sujet du partage de l'affouage."
10. AD, C-1803, Blaisy-Bas, March 1788: "Instances avec certains habitans, au sujet du mode de distribution de l'affouage." The village's troubles began in February 1770, when a group of inhabitants wrote to the intendant that the poor were not equally supporting the costs of maintaining the forests.

tribution. First, they argued that the annual payment of a customary fee to the seigneur, divided equally among the inhabitants
for the right to use the wood, exempted a community from compliance with the new allotment system. The sources do not reveal the basis or the origin of this argument, but they do reveal
that it was commonly resorted to by communities when the
majority of the inhabitants opposed the maîtrise's order. Second,
communities claimed exemption from the new system if what
remained after the wealthy inhabitants took their share was inadequate for the needs of the poor. The intendant supported both
arguments as possible grounds for exemption.

In 1773 the intendant was informed by a subdelegate that
some of the principal inhabitants of Avot "have imagined that it
was in their interest to have wood distributed according to the
tax rolls in the future." But the inhabitants, "assembled in very
great numbers, were almost unanimous in the opinion that they
should follow the usage of distributing their wood equally." The
community consulted a lawyer, "who claimed that the ordinance [issued by the Maîtrise des Eaux et Forêts requiring two-
thirds of the wood to be distributed according to *le marc la livre*]
is void of right because it was rendered on an anonymous and
basically unfair request that diverges from the established practice which excluded [from two-thirds distribution according to *le
marc la livre*] wood subject to a seigneurial fee paid by equal
portion." The intendant felt that Avot had sufficient grounds to
take its case to court.[11]

The following year, the intendant received a petition from a
majority of the inhabitants of Bissey-la-Côte opposing a judgment obtained by several inhabitants that required the community to distribute two-thirds of their wood according to *le marc
la livre*. The majority wanted to continue the equal distribution
of the wood and insisted that "if it was done otherwise in other
communities, that was because they had a lot of wood, but in
Bissey, which has only a dozen *arpent*s [one *arpent* equals approximately one acre] to divide among eighty-eight inhabitants,
if the distribution were done *au marc la livre*, the majority of
the inhabitants would hardly have one cart [*voiture*] each, which

11. AD, C-1223, Avot, 1773: Procès-verbal.

would cause pilfering either in the village commons or in the lord's woods." The intendant instructed the subdelegate that in communities where there was not much wood, he preferred equal distribution to avoid the inevitable theft by those unable to procure legally the firewood they felt was justly theirs.[12] We do not know the result of the subdelegate's efforts to continue equal distribution. But the administrative correspondence does indicate that in communities where a few wealthy families dominated the communal wood supplies, the intendant opposed abolishing equal distribution. With the price of wood escalating, the poor could not easily afford to buy on the free market the wood necessary to supplement their reduced supplies. The inhabitants of Fontaine-Française insisted that the poor, "deprived of wood that is due them, will now have to go foraging in the neighboring forests."[13] Reports of this nature were common. To contribute further to the indignation of the poor, implementation of the changed policy was often dictated by a handful of wealthy inhabitants. This was contrary to two fundamental premises of village management: government consistent with tradition, and majority rule.

In 1775 a subdelegate received a letter from the inhabitants of Chivre in which they "disclosed that every year it is usual to distribute equally wood from the twenty-five or twenty-six *arpents* of communal forest, but recently the principal inhabitants have seen fit to want the distribution on the basis of the *taille*, instead of by household, as it should be done. As a result these inhabitants have practically all the wood, and a poor inhabitant must scavenge for enough for his heating." The subdelegate thereupon sent the following note to the intendant:

Some of the inhabitants of Chivre, sir, have just sent me a request in which they disclose that traditionally they distributed communal wood by equal portions, but in recent years the principal inhabitants have judged it proper to distribute by *le marc la livre de la taille*. As a result, the portion received by the poorer inhabitants [the *manouvriers*] is not enough for their heating needs, and they ask that I remedy this abuse.

12. AD, C-1051, Bissey-la-Côte, 1774: "Débat avec plusieurs habitans au sujet de la distribution de l'affouage"; procès-verbal includes *délibérations* of the village assembly.

13. AD, C-1250, 1777: "Extrait des Registres des délibérations de la chambre commune de Fontaine-Française" and procès-verbal, Feb.

You know that the jurisprudence of the *arrêts* has held that the distribution of wood should be according to the circumstances, that is to say, that in the case where a community possesses its wood only because each inhabitant pays an equal portion of the fee for using the wood, then distribution is done by equal portion, but when a community possesses its wood without charge, then two-thirds must be distributed *au marc la livre de la taille* and the surplus, in equal portion. This is what I ask you to make the inhabitants of Chivre understand.[14]

The subdelegate's letter provides further proof that the intendant and his agents believed that if a community could prove it owned or used the wood because it paid a fee shared equally among the inhabitants, the community had reason to claim exemption from the two-thirds distribution. In another case, the village of Lux petitioned the intendant in 1779, stating that "the inhabitants of this community have followed the immemorial practice of sharing their wood by equal portion." They had just received a writ "requiring that in the future the wood be divided one-third by equal portion and the other two-thirds *au marc la livre de la taille royale.*" The inhabitants insisted that they had always paid their seigneur a yearly sum divided equally among all households for the right to use the wood, also divided equally. In a meeting of the village assembly, a majority decided to oppose the writ in court. The intendant endorsed the village custom as a valid basis for opposing implementation of the wood distribution policy recommended by the King's Council.[15]

That the intendant's efforts to aid communities in circumventing the maîtrise's policy failed is reflected in a decision handed down by the parlement in 1781. The community of Saulx-le-Duc, with the intendant's permission, had gone to court to seek the reversal of an order requiring unequal distribution that had been issued in 1777 by the Maîtrise des Eaux et Forêts. The inhabitants had made the familiar claim that, because they paid "equally a fee for the communal wood," they were entitled to divide it equally. This time, however, the claim was ineffective: the community lost. The parlement now went much further than it had previously and ruled that if the community had received an order from the maîtrise requiring that two-thirds of

14. AD, C-1468, Chivre, 1776: Procès-verbal.
15. AD, C-1259, Lux: Ordinance of the intendant.

their wood be distributed according to *le marc la livre*, it did not matter how they paid for their wood. An order from the maîtrise was final; the parlement ordered the inhabitants of Saulx-le-Duc to distribute their wood in accordance with it.[16] This parlementary decision seems to have influenced how the intendant handled subsequent requests to sue.

In July 1787, the inhabitants of Crépey asked the intendant for permission to sue Nicolas Degas, an inhabitant who had sought an order forcing the community to alter its allotment system. This community also asserted that its inhabitants had always paid the seigneurial dues equally. In 1788, the community hired two lawyers who planned to argue its claim on the grounds that wood distribution was regulated by custom and that Crépey had traditionally divided its wood equally. But the intendant refused to allow Crépey to go to court, explaining that "several times I have refused similar requests for authorization from inhabitants who would like to bring the same type of lawsuit."[17] Earlier he had refused to allow the inhabitants of Chanceaux to initiate a court case over the same issue; he reminded them that "the rule and the practice in the majority of communities is to distribute communal wood one-third by head between all the inhabitants and the remaining two-thirds by *le marc la livre de leur cottes de taille*."[18] The apparent reason for the change in the intendant's response was that since it was now clear that the parlement would rule against any community that attempted to maintain the traditional allotment system, there was no point in allowing such cases to go to court. He could not legally contradict this decision, since the parlement seemed to have upheld the royal policy in the matter. It was the intendant who was doubtful about the policy's validity. Moreover, since the King's Council had never contradicted the parlement's jurisprudence in this area, communities in effect had no legal recourse. When Thenissey asked the intendant for permission to appeal an order by the Maîtrise des Eaux et Forêts requiring the

16. AD, C-1286, Saulx-le-Duc, 21 July 1781 to Aug. 1781: Procès-verbal.

17. AD, C 901, Crépey, July 1787 to Jan. 1788: "Portion de bois de chauffage, les habitans contre Nicolas Degas." Procès-verbal includes comments from Sub-delegate Millot.

18. AD, C-1178, Chanceaux, 1783: Procès-verbal, includes a letter from Sub-delegate Gautherin dated Feb. 1786.

inhabitants to distribute their wood unequally, the subdelegate, citing the opinion of a lawyer who had expertise in the matter, responded that "one-third, two-thirds allotments were already practiced in the majority of communities."[19]

The intendant was still supportive of efforts to preserve equal distribution if they were dictated by a community's majority, and he was willing to support opposition as long as the village did not take its case to court. He did not want the community to waste resources on a court case it would surely lose. In Fontaine-les-Sèches in 1786, the intendant permitted a settlement that went against the ruling of the maîtrise. Fontaine-les-Sèches had not asked the intendant for permission to go to court, and the wealthy inhabitants of that village were willing to let the village assembly's decision stand. The intendant supported the community's opposition to the maîtrise's decision because neither side in the dispute had resorted to the courts.

Let us look more closely at what transpired at Fontaine-les-Sèches. In 1786, the *syndic* of that community wrote to the intendant requesting permission to maintain equal allotments. In support of his request, the *syndic* claimed that "it would be a means to make all inhabitants live in peace—alteration would result in much disorder." Two years earlier, the intendant had rejected a similar request from Fontaine-les-Sèches, saying that the community had no alternative but to divide two-thirds of its wood according to *le marc la livre*. The *syndic* explained that the community was ignoring that earlier order because the poor would be deprived of adequate wood supplies, and "as a result, neighbors will steal from neighbors and the poor will be driven to acts of brigandage in the woods." He continued that "if the equal sharing of wood were abolished, it would result in an infinite number of abuses. Soon, even the most highly taxed inhabitants would think that the tradition of dividing wood equally was a blessing." Moreover, the *syndic* concluded, "the charges relative to the wood are paid in equal portions, and this includes the salary of the communal forest warden." The subdelegate, who knew the situation firsthand, reported that the drawbacks to the two-thirds allotment were indeed substantial: "Those whom this arrangement

19. AD, C-1207, Thenissey, 1782.

[two-thirds allotment according to individual tax assessment] appears to benefit most would actually profit very little. It would be very difficult to prevent vandalism by the inhabitants. Besides, the division of communal wood by equal portion is rather generally observed [this may not have been true in other subdelegations] and even when it might seem abusive, it is perhaps less dangerous to tolerate than to abrogate it."

In April 1786 the intendant responded to the subdelegate's letter, pointing out that because "the inhabitants continue to insist that the wood be shared equally and not by the prescribed manner of these sentences, they do not need my authorization for that and no one will contradict their transaction."[20] This reply seems to indicate that so long as a court case was not contemplated, the intendant was willing to disregard violations.

When all else failed, one course still remained open to opponents of the new allotment system: settlement by *transaction*, that is, an out-of-court settlement in which a third party acted as intermediary. This is what happened in 1788 at Messigny. In 1787 the *échevin* there allowed the wood to be divided equally in defiance of an order by the *maîtrise*, issued the previous year, to divide two-thirds of the wood according to *le marc la livre*. The *échevin* was backed by a *délibération* of the village assembly, passed by eighty-one out of eighty-five households, in favor of equal distribution. Only five inhabitants, including the lord's *fermier* (who could not vote in the assembly), wanted the two-thirds, one-third allotment. Those five inhabitants took their case against the village to court. The court issued a subpoena forbidding the community to divide its wood again until a definitive sentence was handed down. At this point, the two parties, with the subdelegate acting as arbiter, reached a compromise solution. They agreed upon equal distribution for all those who paid taxes of more than twelve livres a year—this meant a majority of the inhabitants. The five inhabitants agreed to drop their case if the community would pay the court costs of their initial action. The subdelegate approved.[21] In both

20. AD, C-1361, Fontaine-les-Sèches, 14 April 1786: Procès-verbal, includes a letter from Subdelegate Cuneau de Mussy, 1 April 1786.
21. AD, C-552, Messigny, 1788 to 3 Jan. 1789: Procès-verbal, includes correspondence with Subdelegate Millot.

cases, Fontaine-les-Sèches and Messigny, we find that the intendant was willing to help communities evade the maîtrise's orders. In both cases the intendant upheld governance by majority rule and acted as the protector of the communities' corporate traditions. Thus, even though the intendant's actions seem inconsistent, there is consistency in his overall goal of preserving those traditions.

The conflicts between the intendant, the parlement, and the Maîtrise des Eaux et Forêts would at first seem to be just another instance of the tangled and overlapping jurisdictions characteristic of Old Regime institutions. But there was more to these disputes. A change in the wood distribution system implied a change in the concept of community. Implementation of the new policy violated the principle of governance by majority rule, and it challenged the protection traditionally afforded the poor members of the community. It also conflicted with traditions that Burgundian intendants were strongly committed to uphold. Even though the intendant's views did not prevail, his efforts to circumvent the new wood distribution policy suggest that he was more committed to the preservation of the community and its traditions than were the other officials who had jurisdiction over the peasantry. Evidently, the intendant believed that a strong and egalitarian community was the best solution to the most pressing social problems facing rural society.

The intendant refused to abolish collective rights, such as the equal distribution of wood, in part because he did not want responsibility for the poor inhabitants who would be forced out of the village. He also feared that the names of individuals who were forced to leave the village would disappear from the tax rolls, leaving a greater burden on those who remained. Moreover, he opposed the king's policy with regard to wood distribution because he wanted wealthy inhabitants to participate in village decision making as equals with the other inhabitants. In implementing its new policy, the crown allowed an important decision to be made without the village assembly's approval, hence without the intendant's intervention.

If the intendant's actions tell us anything about the Old Regime, it is that the higher ranks of government, whether intendant, parlement, or crown, regarded welfare as the responsibility of the community and not of the state. Neither central government officials nor local parlementaires wanted to collect national taxes that would be diverted to poor relief. They particularly shunned the creation of a national poor law system that the new agricultural reforms would make necessary. The French state's goals were simple and traditional: to avoid disorder by regulating the grain trade; to collect taxes levied on peasant's surplus production; to fight foreign wars and to compete internationally with other European states, no matter the cost.

THE PARTITION
OF COMMUNAL LANDS

In opposing the implementation of a program for the partition of common wastelands (lands set aside for pasture), the intendant championed policies that ran counter to the imperatives of the policymakers in the King's Council. The intendant's commitment to protecting communal rights in this matter even had him at loggerheads with the estates, with whom he rarely differed over matters concerning communal properties.

In a special report dated 1767, the Estates of Burgundy provided the king with a detailed program for improving agriculture. The run-down condition of common lands was one of the obstacles to agricultural improvement they cited. The estates reported that the lands, "called the commons, are a vast abandoned continent; no one gives them proper care or attention, they are continually fouled and devastated, and provide livestock with but very imperfect nourishment; because those abandoned lands are never allowed to mature, what they produce is of no value."[22]

In 1769 the estates reported more specifically on the sorry condition of the commons: "The common lands ceded to the inhabitants by the king and his ancestors, or by individual lords, having become arid by the lack of cultivation and by perpetual devastation, require your urgent attention, because these lands have the possibility of procuring for your peoples the most bene-

22. AD, C-3332, Estates of Burgundy, fols. 76–81v: Special report "présenté dans le but de développer l'agriculture," 1767.

ficial aid." The estates asserted that communal access to grazing areas had led to overgrazing, random breeding of animals, the spread of disease, and generally poor upkeep; collective ownership provided an incentive to overconsume and to underinvest in the commons. To prevent this, the estates called for the division of common lands into privately owned plots. "The partition of those goods has appeared to you, Sire, the only and unique means to procure from them [the commons] every advantage—already a great number of communities have asked, and obtained, permission to divide them among the inhabitants." To encourage communities to partition their commons, the estates asked the king to free lands, once they had been partitioned, from all royal taxes and from the tithe. The estates were convinced that partitioning common lands would provide an incentive for inhabitants to invest in land improvements. "Each inhabitant will hasten to increase [the lands'] value, to retain them and to turn them to the best account. These goods and lands, that are now lost to the State, would become a new resource for the poor inhabitants of the province."[23]

In 1773 the estates submitted another report on the matter. They envisioned that after being partitioned, the lands could be enclosed and that, in particular, this would result in the better conservation of meadows, thus increasing the province's livestock production.[24]

The king responded in 1774 by issuing an edict for Burgundy that permitted the partitioning of common lands. Such lands were to be divided equally among all inhabitants; "no inhabitant would be allowed more than one part." All portions would be hereditary in the direct line. If a direct heir was lacking, the portion would return to the community, which would then assign it to an inhabitant who, although possibly not possessing a portion because he did not live in the village at the time of the original allotment, was next in line as determined by length of village residence.

The edict assigned responsibility for partitioning to the village

23. Ibid., Cahier of 1769, art. 3.
24. Ibid., Cahier of 1773.

assembly.[25] A majority vote in the assembly, recorded by a notary, would begin the process. "The said *délibération* will contain the objections that can be made to the partition, be it by one or many inhabitants, and their cause: the same *délibération* must be signed by at least two-thirds of the inhabitants." The *délibération* would then be reviewed by the intendant, who would certify whether the proper formalities had been followed. He had no right to veto a community's decision. He could only sign the request and forward it to the Parlement of Dijon, which was required to register the village's decision without cost.[26]

The parlement did not register the edict until November 19, 1782.[27] Perhaps the parlement's reluctance was due to a desire to favor the interests of the well-off peasants, since common lands had always been more useful to those who owned the most livestock. The rich generally wanted to preserve the commons, which they monopolized. The poor generally supported partition into equal individual parcels. The controversy over partition continued even after the edict was registered, for substantial obstacles remained within the communities.

The difficulties of proving communal ownership often interfered with plans to partition. In Sombernon, according to a report compiled by the intendant's secretary, twenty-three inhabitants petitioned in June 1786 for permission to divide their communal lands in accordance with the edict of 1774. They insisted that partition would benefit the community because "the principal inhabitants [now] possess the greater part of the commons." The petitioners argued that "this privation [of the poor] is all the more prejudicial for the majority, because they have no pasture for their livestock." However, they were unable to provide information concerning "either the quantity, location, or quality of these usurpations," nor could they provide titles proving that what they called the communal lands actually belonged to the community. In the same year, the community's *syndic* wrote to the intendant that of Sombernon's 133

25. In England, by contrast, those owning a majority of the land could impose partition on the entire village.
26. AD, C-3523, no. 42, Jan 1774. Edict of *partage*, registered 19 Nov. 1782.
27. AD, B-12143, 19 Nov. 1782.

households, 64 were usurpers of communal properties.[28] Furthermore, most of these usurpations had occurred more than thirty
years earlier. Lacking titles, the community would find it difficult to recover the lands that had been usurped and that were
now under cultivation. Nor could the community hope to recover those usurped lands easily by instituting a lawsuit. According to provincial jurisprudence, in cases of alleged usurpation the burden of proof rested with the community and not
with the alleged usurpers. As we will see, Sombernon's problems
were not unique. Usurpations had become commonplace because the laws made it easier for the usurpers than for the communities to defend their claims.

A report on common lands issued by the estates in 1776
clearly describes the obstacles that communities faced when
attempting to partition those lands. In their report, the estates
called for the monarchy's intervention because usurpations
were so extensive as to menace the well-being of communities.
They reminded the monarch that common lands survived only
because of the crown's protection. "These lands, both necessary
and precious, would all have been dissipated if our kings had
not given and reiterated their orders to maintain and preserve
them. This was done by prohibiting the usurpations of commons and by forbidding communities to alienate those lands."
The estates insisted that "the alienation and usurpation of
common rights and properties is no longer to be feared. The
laws have provided for that. The laws make easy what they are
intended to prevent." The estates described the process of usurpation as follows.

One individual, by successive and barely noticeable advances, takes
possession of a part of the commons, and in his own good time joins
them to his family's land; another, more enterprising, clears it, and
puts himself in possession of it; if the usurper has influence and authority he silences the other inhabitants, and thus after thirty years
becomes the unquestioned owner; because most and even all communities, not having today any titles for their customs [usages] and com-

28. AD, C-1823, Sombernon, June 1786: Procès-verbal, "Partage des communaux demandé par les habitans."

mons, would attempt in vain to go against the usurper and ask him to relinquish a good that belongs to them; his thirty-year possession decides in his favor vis-à-vis the inhabitants who do not have the titles in their hands.

Communities were unlikely to continue to prosecute usurpers in court, because it was unlikely that they could win. "Discouraged by having to pay for court cases they continually lose, communities pay a sort of double *taille* in order to pursue usurpers. For this reason communities no longer try to curb usurpations; instead each inhabitant tries to make himself master of the commons and to appropriate them for himself; thus communities find themselves despoiled of the goods that are of the first necessity."

In an attempt to help communities recover usurped communal properties, the estates asked the king "to provide a law by which all communities would be ordered to assemble (during the three months after the registration and publication of this law) to name four principal inhabitants, or a greater number if they consider it necessary, to draw up a declaration of all communal woods, scrub, fields, swamps, heath, pasture, and all other properties belonging to each community." One can surmise that the principal inhabitants would be the group least likely to report fairly, since they were the most frequent usurpers of common lands. The estates believed such a law would "ensure the preservation and continuity of common lands, and rights, and other properties belonging to communities. It would enable communities to guarantee and to defend those properties from enterprises and usurpations; communities would then no longer be subject to continual lawsuits and to the loss of these most precious properties."[29] No such law was issued, however. In 1782, when the parlement finally registered the edict permitting the partitioning of communal lands, communities found, not surprisingly, that because they lacked information, they could not easily identify the lands they possessed in common.

29. AD, C-3332/182, Report of the estates, 1776, fols. 193–96: "Réclamation des mesures destinées à mettre fin aux usurpations commis sur les biens communs."

This lack, along with the opposition of wealthy inhabitants, de-layed the edict's implementation.

When Montmoyen tried to begin partitioning in 1787, it could not certify which lands belonged to the community. It met the same obstacle that had confronted Sombernon in 1786: although a majority of Montmoyen's inhabitants agreed to partition the common lands, the community could not produce titles to lands it claimed had been usurped. But most of the usurpations in Montmoyen, unlike those in Sombernon, were the work of a minority of wealthy inhabitants. The intendant took the side of those inhabitants of Montmoyen who wanted to partition the communal lands: "Neither the fact that those usurped lands were being put to fruitful use, nor the fact that they had long been in possession of the wealthy inhabitants who cultivated them, should prevent the community from advancing its desire to partition its commons." Furthermore, "poor inhabitants have a right to utilize [communal lands] as much as the well-off do; one cannot be stopped by the difficulties which continually pre-sent themselves in the execution of the edict of January 1774; it must be put into effect when a majority of inhabitants desire it." In his report to the intendant, the subdelegate said he thought that the legal obstacles preventing the partitions were substan-tial. In 1789 he wrote that "this partition has given way to an infinity of lawsuits because for over thirty years a number of individuals have possessed the lands and have already assarted and cultivated them."[30]

The logic of the intendant's position may at first seem confus-ing, but it is actually quite straightforward. His support of parti-tioning at Montmoyen was an exception that proves the rule. In general, intendants opposed partitioning for essentially two rea-sons. First, they believed that partitioned lands would inevitably fall into the hands of the wealthy. Second, they preferred that communities lease their commons so that they would be sure of a regular income from which to finance village expenditures. Intendants permitted partitioning to get back lands that had been usurped; that is, they supported partitioning when it was a

30. AD, C-1116, Montmoyen, 1787 to Aug. 1789: "Contestation au sujet du partage des communaux." Procès-verbal includes *délibérations* of the village assembly and correspondence between the intendant and the subdelegate.

means to turn usurpers into leasers. In examining the following cases, we will see how usurpations complicated matters for communities that wanted to partition, and for the intendant who wanted to prevent both usurpations and partitions. Partitions were generally prevented not by the intendant but by conflicts within communities.

The cases are complex when considered individually, but certain patterns clearly emerge. In Forléans in 1784, and in Remilly-sur-Tille in 1789, the partitioning of communal lands was blocked because the communities lacked titles.[31] Several inhabitants of Aisey-le-Duc decided to consider alternatives to partitioning communal lands and requested a meeting of the village assembly to identify them. First, the commons and the names of all presumed usurpers were to be listed. However, the community, because it lacked titles, had to accept an oral account of its properties. When recovery of the usurped lands was found to be impossible, the community insisted that a tax be levied on the usurpers in order to fund the village's general expenses. This was a compromise measure aimed at avoiding a lawsuit the community could not hope to win. A majority of inhabitants supported the measure because they knew that an oral account, given at a village assembly, would be of dubious value in court. The inhabitants proposed equal partition of the communal lands as a last resort, if the usurpers refused to pay the tax.[32]

There were thus three principal but related obstacles to the implementation of the crown's legislation regarding partition of communal lands: actual possession of the land by individuals, the absence of titles, and the almost universal opposition of the wealthy inhabitants to equal division of communal lands. It is

31. AD, C-1692, Forléans, 24 May 1784 to June 1786: Procès-verbal, includes *délibérations* of the village assembly (25 May 1784), during which a delegation was formed to attempt to "partager entre tous les feux ou ménages existant, la totalité, ou seulement partie des fonds communaux autres que les Bois." In February 1785 the inhabitants, at a meeting of the village assembly, agreed to hire a surveyor. It was at that point that the process got bogged down because of the difficulty of finding "the names, quality, and quantity of terrain usurped by whom and since when." See also AD, C-575, Remilly-sur-Tille, 1789.

32. AD, C-1026, Aisey-le-Duc: "Ordonnance de l'intendant qui authorise poursuites contre les usurpateurs des terrains communs." Similarly, in 1786 the intendant had ordered usurpers of communal lands in Puissey (AD, C-1526) to pay that community a tax in proportion to the value of the lands they had usurped. This order covered usurpations of the preceding forty years.

perhaps surprising to find that the wealthy inhabitants opposed partition, because they might be expected to be less supportive of common rights than were the poor. However, since they often monopolized the commons, they were among the staunchest defenders of this custom.

There was also a fourth obstacle. With partition came the problem of finding an alternative source of funds to replace those the community was accustomed to receiving from the lease of its communal properties. This financial problem was evident in 1782, when a majority of the inhabitants of Massigny-les-Semur agreed to partition their communal lands. With regard to that vote, the subdelegate explained: "If it cannot be said that it be the unanimous will, I am at least assured that it is shared by most, and that there are very few inhabitants who are against it." But the subdelegate opposed the proposed partition, because "basically I am persuaded that the well-employed revenue from those commons will be more useful to the inhabitants than what they get out of using those lands for pasture." The community had more to gain by leasing, the subdelegate reported, because leasing would provide a regular collective income, "and this means of underwriting their communal expenses will be less onerous than the taxes they will be forced to collect to replace [that income]." The intendant agreed with his subdelegate: "I am not disposed to approving partitions, especially if the usurpations that had already occurred are not recovered." As an alternative, he said, "it is necessary to place it all [the communal lands] in reserve; but for the good of the inhabitants, small portions can be leased at a modest price." In that way, many inhabitants could profit from the use of those lands, and at the same time the community could benefit from the continued revenues. If the community partitioned its lands, he continued, "in fifty years, the rich would have acquired all the commons, and the community would have nothing. Leasing seems preferable to me." Leasing was a way to prevent the properties from falling into the hands of the wealthy. In the long run, partitions would not improve the economic well-being of the poor, because the rich would inevitably acquire the lands outright.[33]

The intendant cited examples of partitions that eventually benefited the wealthy. Little trace remained of Marsannay-la-Côte's partition of its communal lands because "several of the inhabitants either had ceded or had sold their portions to the others."[34] When the community of Fontangy wanted to partition its commons, the intendant, Amelot, wrote to a subdelegate that he opposed the partition because "after a certain number of years, the commons would be inextricably mixed with the property of individuals. The principal purpose of the partitions then would not be attained. Moreover, the operation would have achieved the opposite of its stated goal, that of providing the poor with the resources for raising their livestock."[35] In the long run, partition would be harmful to the poor and would intensify the problem of poverty.

That the intendant also had financial reasons for opposing partitions is evident from his response to a petition from the inhabitants of Pagny-le-Château. At a meeting of the village assembly, the inhabitants decided to completely partition their commons. He wrote that the community would "suddenly lose 1,800 or 2,000 livres of revenues coming from the lease of the commons in question, and which are used for their needs which have greatly multiplied. How will it provide for its needs when it loses this resource?" Pagny-le-Château had already leased those lands for six years, and two years still remained in that lease. If the lease were terminated early, the community would immediately lose a source of income upon which it depended for payment of its yearly expenses.

The intendant asked the subdelegate, whom he described as an "enlightened man," for his opinion because "surely he will have the same thoughts as I do and he will provide some very good observations." Indeed, the subdelegate, Trullard, responded copiously and his response was recorded by the intendant's secretary. "M. Trullard definitely feels that the community is depriving itself, by this partition, of a resource that it had used to pay its debts, but he observes that even this consideration cannot stop the execution of the project authorized by the edict of

1774; thus, there is no other course to take than to approve the request." In his letter to the intendant, Trullard stated that "the edict solicited imprudently by the Estates for the partition of communal lands leaves the intendant only the futile right to approve [*viser*] the inhabitants' *délibération*. It does not leave him the power to prevent these dangerous partitions and their fatal consequences. The intendant could refuse to look at the request, but then he would have to account for that refusal to the *procureur général* of the parlement. It is necessary, then, to allow the inhabitants to do what they desire." In conclusion, the intendant wrote: "Unfortunately the edict of 1774 authorizes this kind of partition."[36]

The lands in question had always been in the community's possession and consequently could be safely leased. The intendant felt that Pagny-le-Château depended on income from the lands to finance its day-to-day expenditures as well as its rising debts. Replacing those funds with a village tax would place a substantial burden on this community.

The final case is that of Avelanges. In 1780 the poor laborers (*manouvriers*) of that community, who constituted its majority, refused to continue leasing their communal lands, preferring instead to divide them equally among all inhabitants. The subdelegate's report stated that "the principal inhabitants desire that the lease be renewed. The yield serves to pay the parish priest [*desservant*],[37] the schoolteacher, and the sacristan [*marguillier*]." The subdelegate and the intendant both rejected the proposed partition.[38] The intendant's decision was binding because this incident occurred two years before the Parlement registered the edict of 1774, which permitted partitions. The inhabitants could not appeal that decision for the same reason.

The cases we have studied suggest that the intendant's overriding concern in the problem of partition was that communities

36. AD, C-1764, Pagny-le-Château, March 1785: Procès-verbal, includes letter from Subdelegate Trullard, 2 April 1785. The inhabitants of Pagny-le-Château deliberated on the partitions in August 1784 and began partitioning in November 1784.

37. Vicar who served in the place of an absent curé. Whereas the curé was paid out of the *menu dîme*, the *desservant* received a salary paid out of the *fabrique* (funds belonging to the parish).

38. AD, C-1221, Avelanges, 19 Aug. 1780: Procès-verbal. Subdelegate Perrenet comments on the work of his predecessor, M. Charpy.

maintain possession of their communal properties and illustrate his commitment to protecting communal rights. He supported partitioning communal lands only as a means of recovering usurped land, as in Montmoyen. In situations where the community could lease the lands, the intendant supported that solution instead. As we have seen, the intendant was opposed to curtailment of communal rights, including the division of communal lands, because it intensified two problems. The first was the problem of poverty. Traditionally, communal properties and rights had served to protect the poor; implementation of the laws that permitted division of those properties would have dire consequences for them. The second problem was communal solvency and the collection of royal taxes. The intendant feared that partition of communal properties would contribute to communal insolvency and force communities to depend on loans, which could make the collection of royal taxes more difficult. The close relationship between fiscal solvency and the preservation of communal properties emerges clearly from the intendant's preference for the leasing of communal lands to the highest bidder, a practice referred to in the sources as *adjudication,* or auctioning.

THE LEASING OF COMMON LAND

As noted earlier, in the 1660s the monarchy began implementing a policy of forbidding communities to sell communal properties or to use those properties as surety for loans. To prevent sales of communal property, the intendants were assigned final jurisdiction over all matters concerning communal debts. These royal officials insisted that to pay debts or to finance current expenses, communities should lease communal lands instead. To ensure that traditional provincial institutions did not interfere with this plan, the crown issued an edict in 1669 that deprived provincial parlements of jurisdiction over cases concerning communal debts.[39]

39. Edict of 1669. See also Ordonnance of 1669, art. 7, title 25, which stipulated that "communaux qui ne sont pas utiles au pâturage" could be leased after a meeting of the assembly. Leasing made it possible for communities to use the revenues from collective properties, instead of the land itself, as collateral for

The Parlement of Dijon continued to dispute the exclusive jurisdiction of the king's officials over the leasing of communal lands well into the eighteenth century, largely because the leasing of communal woods, meadows, and wastelands to the highest bidder, usually for periods of six to nine years, became so widespread that the fees and the prestige connected with auctioning leases were of great value for those administering the auctions.[40] In an effort to recover its old right to authorize auctions, the Parlement of Dijon issued an *arrêt* in 1777 prohibiting the community of Saint-Usage from "proceeding with the said auction or any handing over of property elsewhere than before the judges of the place [seigneurial judges]." Since the parlement supervised seigneurial judges, it was trying indirectly to reestablish its own authority over the auctioning of leases. The parlementaires were hoping that in the event of a dispute, any transaction that had begun under the authority of the seigneurial judge would terminate before the parlement, not the intendant. But the parlement's efforts were short-lived. The following year, the king revoked the parlementary *arrêt* and ordered, once more, that leasing by auction take place under the authority of the intendant.[41] The king did not want his administrators to lose jurisdiction over an issue involving communal properties. Such a loss would have been a challenge to one of the intendant's principal functions—guaranteeing preservation of the communities' rights and properties.

During the eighteenth century royal officials, basing their authority on the edict of 1669, carefully supervised and encouraged the leasing of common lands while uniformly refusing requests to sell. When the community of Vic-les-Près, for example, asked for permission to sell some of its meadow to pay the costs of a court case it had lost, the intendant responded: "I never permit a com-

loans. The crown's commitment to leasing remained strong, and in the eighteenth century there was no reversal by royal policymakers. Crown and intendant continued to act as one in this regard until the Revolution.

40. Saint-Jacob mentioned a subdelegate from Auxonne who, in 1787, claimed that "almost all communities lease communal lands." See Pierre de Saint-Jacob, *Les paysans de la Bourgogne du nord au dernier siècle de l'Ancien Régime* (Dijon, 1960), p. 448.

41. AD, C-3523, 31 July 1778: Arrêt du Conseil d'Etat du Roi.

munity to pay the costs of a lawsuit by such means, which are against all principles and by which, if allowed, there would soon be no common lands."[42] When in 1770, the inhabitants of Blaisy-Bas wanted to sell communal lands in order to raise funds for improvement of their forests, the intendant similarly refused and insisted that the community lease the lands instead: "The price of the lease," he argued, "would be enough to pay the interest on the loan as well as other small communal expenses."[43] By contrast, the intendant welcomed requests for permission to lease communal lands, and to encourage that practice he was willing to do all that was necessary to protect the interests of both parties— the communities and the lessees of communal properties. To ensure the community's protection, a typical lease included the following stipulations:

The lessee will be held to use the said lands as a responsible head of household [en bon père de famille], and will be prohibited from changing the order of rotation. He must plow and fertilize the said lands, which he must maintain in good cultivation, to return them in the said state at the end of the present lease, the plow being used everywhere and subject to an inspection which will be at the expense of the lessee without appeal. The said lessee cannot recognize other jurisdictions than that of Monsieur the Intendant for any dispute that arises between him and the community about the lease.[44]

There were many instances in which intendants protected the interests of lessees. In 1774 the inhabitants of Losne, Chaugey, and Maison-Neuve refused to provide compensation to their lessees for losses suffered when the meadows they were leasing were entirely ruined by floods, thus damaging their harvest. The subdelegate reported to the intendant that "there was no negligence or delay on the part of these lessees." So quick and unforeseen were the floods that there was "not a single individual, even the most vigilant, who did not lose part or all of his meadows on account of this inundation." Accusing the community of "bad faith" for refusing to compensate the lessees, the subdele-

42. AD, C-969, Vic-les-Près, 1776: Ordinance of the intendant.
43. AD, C-1803, Blaisy-Bas, 1770: Ordinance of the intendant.
44. AD, C-1259, 1788: "Ordonnance de l'intendant, amodiation des communaux."

gate noted that the lease stipulated that, "in case of ordeals by floods or other unforeseen causes, the lessees will be compensated for all or part of their losses according to the estimate of experts who will be chosen amicably by both parties." "If these three communities," he added, "were allowed to act in such bad faith, they would embolden other communities to follow their example." The subdelegate recommended that the two parties share the expense of losses and that the community accept four hundred livres rent instead of the seven hundred livres due it. Moreover, the subdelegate concluded, "it is even a bad policy on the part of the inhabitants to mistreat those who would put value into their property. The inhabitants run the risk that their vexatious interference [tracasserie] will, in the years to come, cause the value of their lands to fall, and they will be refused by all individuals who would develop their land."[45] Rather than seeking to protect one party in preference to another, the intendant wanted to guarantee the integrity of the process so that the land's value would be maintained.

The intendant's promotion of the auctioning of leases did not deprive communities of direct control over their properties. Auctions were not imposed on unwilling communities by administrative fiat and were not a challenge to communal liberty. The numerous petitions found in the communal archives suggest that the initiative for auctions generally came from the community. Before approving a request for permission to auction the leases to communal lands, the intendant routinely requested that communities explain how they would employ the revenues thus gained and that they give an account of the community's assets and debts. Presiding at a meeting of the village assembly, the subdelegate attempted to verify that a majority supported the request for permission by requiring each inhabitant to testify to the existence of titles proving the community's possession of the lands in question, as well as to the extent, quality, and utility of those lands. The subdelegate then forwarded the minutes of the meeting with his comments to the intendant.

45. AD, C-1600, Jan. 1772: Procès-verbal, and letters to the intendant from Subdelegate Martène of Saint Jean-de-Losne, dated 22 Feb. 1767 and 1774.

The leasing of common lands was a particularly important way to protect them from usurpation by enterprising individuals within the community. The *échevins* of Chanceaux reported daily incursions into the common forests by inhabitants who assarted and converted them into private property. In this case, as in numerous similar cases, the intendant took action to protect the community by issuing an ordinance requiring the village to lease the assarted lands.[46] In 1778 the village of Lux complained to the intendant that "those portions of the commons which are of no utility are being usurped daily. The only means to conserve and to benefit from the lands is to put them on reserve and to lease them for the community's profit." The intendant wrote to his subdelegate that "the inhabitants of Lux have warned me of extensive usurpations of their commons, and in order to draw sufficient revenues for their local needs, they request that the commons be put on reserve, but before acting on the matter, I would like you to verify the approximate extent of the lands involved, whether the village is the proprietor, and whether one can put these lands aside without interfering with the right of passage belonging to neighboring communities."[47]

Such inquiries were routine and were used to help the intendant decide the value to assign communal lands so that communities would be assured the maximum return on their lands. For example, in 1788, when Longeault wanted to issue a twenty-nine-year lease, the intendant asked the subdelegate to verify that the community was getting the highest possible price.[48] The inquiries could also be used to guarantee that the lands actually belonged to the community and thus could be leased. Documentation of the majority's assent made it difficult for the community to renege on the agreement. Moreover, the subdelegate's attestation to that assent meant that the inhabitants could not later claim that they had been forced to lease the commons by a minority cabal.

46. AD, C-1178, Chanceaux, 1785: Procès-verbal. The intendant also ordered proceedings against the forest guards who did not report the usurpations.
47. AD, C-1259, 1778: "Poursuite contre les usurpateurs des terrains communaux."
48. AD, C-771, Longeault, 1788: Ordinance of the intendant.

By parceling the lands to be rented into large lots and requiring rental payments at the time of the auction, the intendants excluded the majority of villagers from the bidding and increased the likelihood that the lessees would be wealthy individuals. Had payments been required after the harvest, more individuals would have benefited, but the community as a group would have benefited less. The higher transaction and rent collection costs of leasing to a larger number of individuals (especially less solvent peasants) would have substantially reduced the profits to the village as a group.[49]

The crown's leasing policy may seem to have increased inequality within the village by increasing the political authority of the wealthy inhabitants. This was not necessarily so. Leasing communal property to the few wealthy villagers reduced the community's direct dependence on their capital to finance "extraordinary" or emergency expenses. When faced with such expenses, communities lacking the regular income provided by rentals depended exclusively on the imposition of special taxes, the largest proportion of which was paid by the well-to-do villagers.

An examination of the following cases suggests that leasing was often supported by the poorer peasantry but was resisted by the wealthy inhabitants, who were thereby prevented from usurping common lands. In 1768 a majority of the inhabitants of Chamblanc petitioned the intendant for permission to lease communal lands and to stop the usurpations that had become commonplace.[50] Similarly, in July 1782, the inhabitants of Labergement-Foigney petitioned the intendant for permission to lease the communal lands to prevent their being cultivated by the wealthy inhabitants. In his report to the intendant, the subdelegate said he supported this request because he believed that the continued usurpation of those lands would deprive the community of a necessary source of communal reve-

---

49. By contrast, Florence Gauthier views leasing as a threat to communal autonomy—a policy designed by the crown to deprive communities of their common rights. See her *La voie paysanne dans la Révolution française* (Paris, 1976).

50. AD, C-1748, Chamblanc, 1768.

nue.[51] In effect, by leasing the lands, the community was asking the wealthy inhabitants to pay for rights they were already enjoying without payment. The majority of the inhabitants of Perrière wanted to lease the commons simply because the revenue was needed to defray communal expenses. The wealthy villagers, led by a wealthy farmer, Jean Fleury, opposed the plan to lease and presented the intendant with a document in which they claimed that the commons were "indispensable for pasturing the common herd." The members of this group presented themselves as the majority, but the subdelegate discovered that they were really a minority of rich farmers and that their claims were false. The commons of the community of Perrière, he reported, were not indispensable except to the few who monopolized them.[52]

Conflict between rich and poor over leasing became evident in Barjon when, in 1781, the wealthy residents opposed partitions that were supported by a majority of inhabitants. But in this case, the intendant had originally proposed that the community lease its lands instead of partitioning them. The leading inhabitants had opposed this plan also. If they leased the lands from the community, the leading inhabitants would be paying to use what they were accustomed to using without charge. The subdelegate noted that "the *syndic* of this community reported to me that the commons were not leased because the four principal inhabitants, having shared them among themselves, enjoyed them without paying anything and did not want to desist from their use. The *syndic* admitted a strong desire to see your order implemented because he is among those who have no part in the commons."[53] As was so often true, the wealthy inhabitants, who possessed most of the livestock in the community, had monopolized the communal lands. Partition of the commons equally among the inhabitants would prevent them from doing so.

In the long run, the real threat to community well-being was

51. AD, C-769: Procès-verbal, 4 July 1782 (Paris) to 7 Aug. 1782 (Auxonne); includes comments from the subdelegate.

52. AD, C-1611, Perrière, April 1781.

53. AD, C-1225, 1781: Ordinance of the intendant.

not the leasing but the alienation of communal properties. French monarchs beginning with Louis XIV attempted to reverse the trend toward the loss of communal rights and properties. Royal administrators encouraged lease auctions as a way of providing communities with a regular income. In effect, communities could borrow money by offering the rights to the income from their land, rather than the land itself, as collateral for loans. Communities that borrowed did not risk losing their properties outright, as they would have otherwise. Leasing also protected a community's income against ecological uncertainties, since the community shared the risks with the wealthy inhabitants who leased the properties.

In sum, the crown's efforts to ensure the solvency of rural communities culminated in its attempts to encourage the leasing of communal properties. This policy did not deprive communities of their properties for the benefit of the wealthy inhabitants; rather, it ultimately increased the fiscal stability of communities. Leasing prevented the permanent loss of communal properties that would ordinarily be sold to meet exceptional expenses. Instead of selling communal lands, communities leased them to the highest bidder for a limited period. Thus, wealthy individuals could not actually acquire the lands; the communities' continued ownership was maintained. Moreover, leasing provided communities with a regular income. The long-term consequence of this policy was the protection of communal rights and properties.

Many historians of eighteenth-century France have asserted that communal properties were vestiges of a precapitalist culture that differed fundamentally from the newer culture of possessive individualism. According to this point of view, the intendants, as agents of the new capitalist culture, hastened the demise of communal properties by exposing them to the market. In this study I suggest instead that by treating collective properties as commodities to be traded at peak commercial value, intendants actually ensured the preservation of communal properties. Commercialization protected those properties from usurpation and dissolution. Thus, the differences between communal and capitalist property were reconciled. As communal rights became commercialized, they provided the capital that guaranteed the continued existence of communities.

ENCLOSURE

The dispute over enclosures involved another combination of forces and persons: the intendant and the estates were united against the unlikely alliance of the royal ministers and the Parlement of Dijon. Friction between the intendant and the crown peaked in this disagreement.

In their 1767 report on Burgundian agriculture, the Estates of Burgundy stated they hoped to persuade the king to issue regulations permitting the implementation of the physiocratic program for improving agriculture. They noted that many changes were necessary that would require the crown's assistance "to make it easier for landowners to find the means to best profit from their land by the most advantageous cultivation."

The estates lamented in the report that fragmentation of holdings prevented the efficient use of land and that scattered plots and fields were difficult to police; they presented a constant temptation to steal crops and even land. Elaborate precautions were therefore necessary to prevent infractions. In addition, poor draining or fencing by one neighbor or by the village reduced the productivity of adjacent properties. Thus fragmentation meant that the correspondence between a farmer's efforts and his rewards was not great. Fragmentation, the estates argued, invited slackness instead of diligence and discouraged enterprising individuals from making optimal investments of labor and capital.[54] A further obstacle to efficient farming was that farmers lost time going from one field to the next, and since parcels were rarely consolidated, specialization based on the quality of soil was unlikely.

But the principal obstacle to efficient agriculture was that land in the open fields was open to common grazing after the harvest and when the fields lay fallow. Most of the estates' report concentrated on explaining how communal grazing limited the production of livestock that was "necessary for the manure and plowing of the land." One problem was that "all owners

54. For a discussion of how "neighborhood effects" were disincentives to investment, see Donald McCloskey, "The Persistence of English Common Fields," in William N. Parker and Eric L. Jones, eds., *European Peasants and Their Markets* (Princeton, N.J., 1975), pp. 80–83.

were required to follow the same rotations": individuals could not withdraw their land from the mandatory fallow field. The right of common pasture guaranteed the persistence of the three-field crop rotation system, in which one field always remained fallow. Individual owners had no incentive to cultivate root crops, grasses, or other soil-restorative fodder crops on the third field because what "an individual would sow in the fallow area would necessarily be the prey of livestock, since the communal herd had the right to pasture there. It is the same with the meadows. The first cutting is usually leased, but after the harvest meadows are opened to the communal herd." Because the second cutting belonged to the community, individuals were discouraged from investing in artificial meadows. Another problem was that "no one can claim to be the absolute master of his land, nor is he, in effect, since he is not permitted to sow when he wants to nor how he wants to, because after the harvest, he has no more right to it than the poorest inhabitants of the parish, who do not possess one inch of land yet nourish their livestock at the expense of others."

"It is universally recognized," the estates continued, "that improvement and multiplication of livestock and the improvement in farming of arable land are mutually interdependent. They can prosper only one by the other." Insufficient livestock made intensive cultivation of the arable impossible. As the estates put it, "the earth can only give good and abundant products through animal power and manure. That power and manure must in turn come from the herds, which depend on the earth's abundance. Livestock is necessary to plow the fields, and to fertilize them. Abundant harvests are necessary to feed the livestock that make the earth fruitful." The province supported only half the livestock it needed because there was inadequate pasture in summer and a shortage of fodder in the winter. This was certainly not due to the quality of the soil, which "could be improved and could return to the owner the price of his care and industry." The true source of the difficulty was the organization of agriculture. The fragmentation of holdings and the right of common pasture "stifle the industry of the cultivator." In conclusion, the estates argued that escape from this cycle of dependence on fallow land could occur only if the right of common pasture were abolished so that individuals would be free to use the land as they saw fit. Improvement would not occur

so long as the parcels of family lands and fields remain divided and scattered here and there about the territory; as long as one is constrained to conform to the multitude regarding when and how to cultivate, to sow and to harvest; as long as it is not possible to use one's lands to cultivate that for which it is best suited; as long as the second cutting of the meadows is totally abandoned to the collectivity; as long as one cannot efficiently supplement natural meadows with artificial meadows.

As proof of their contentions, the estates cited the example of two *bailliages* in Burgundy, the Brionnais and the Charollais, where holdings had been consolidated and enclosed, "so that there is no distinction between pasture and arable land and where the master enjoys his properties as a true owner." These two *bailliages*, the estates reported, supported a far greater proportion of livestock than any other *bailliage*, and there livestock was "of far superior breed."

To begin the process of improvement, the estates asked the king to redefine property rights by issuing an edict permitting enclosure. To make enclosure attractive, it would be necessary first "to facilitate exchanges between owners." This meant allowing owners to unite their scattered possessions so that each individual could use his properties according to his needs. The estates suggested that the lands to be exchanged should be freed from all taxes and fees that were otherwise levied on land exchanges.[55]

The estates' principal concern was that the wastelands should be broken up and that the properties of individuals should be consolidated in parcels and then enclosed. The mere act of putting up hedges or fences did not guarantee improved farming, however. Improvement required abolition of the right of common pasture. Improvement also depended on eliminating the right of other communal herds to pass across village property to

55. AD, C-3332, Estates of Burgundy, fols. 76–81v: Special report "présenté dans le but de développer l'agriculture," 1767. The estates mentioned enclosures for the first time in the Cahier des remonstrances of 1764, art. 8 (AD, C-3332, fols. 43–44). The obligations of mortgages would be maintained, including all seigneurial and real-estate charges on the land that had existed before the exchanges.

get to water or meadow (*le droit de parcours*), as well as the right of individuals to pasture livestock on the commons. Only then would individuals enjoy full property ownership. So long as common grazing rights existed, the techniques essential to an increase in yields would not be introduced.

In 1769 the estates showed that they were reluctant to move too far or too fast. They again requested that the king issue an edict permitting owners to enclose but proposed limiting the portion enclosed to one-quarter of an owner's land. A larger proportion would be disruptive, even though in principle, unrestricted enclosure would be best for agriculture.[56] The estates were concerned with the social consequences of implementing enclosures too quickly. The king's adviser summarized the estates' reasons for wanting to move slowly:

[The estates] feared that too sudden and too general a change would bring about some inconveniences. The poor inhabitants of the countryside could not tranquilly observe an attempt to deprive them absolutely of what they regard as a right and as a resource. It can be predicted that if the permission to enclose is not restrained, they will strongly oppose enclosures, and especially at the beginning they will try to cross and degrade them. It thus appears more prudent to dismiss from their minds the idea of total loss, and prepare them by trials and bring them slowly to what those who reason and reflect desire.[57]

Before he issued an edict permitting enclosure in Burgundy, the king solicited the opinion of both the parlement and the intendant. The parlement shared the estates' opinion that such an edict would be "most useful to the Province" but disagreed with the estates on several critical points. Most important, the magistrates supported unlimited enclosures and stated three objections to the estates' proposal that enclosures be limited to one-quarter of the village's properties. First, "the restriction would be onerous for owners of small holdings, whose possessions are not extensive enough so that the cost of fences or hedges would be greater than the benefits they could draw by

---

56. AD, C-3332, fols. 43–44v (Cahier of 1764, art. 8). See also AN, H-173/9 and H-173/26; and AN, H-173/10: "Précis du Mémoire des Etats de Bourgogne sur les avantages de clôture."

57. AN, H-173/12, fols. 6–7.

enclosing their properties." Second, the parlement assumed that the wealthy inhabitants would simply defy the edict and enclose more than a quarter of their lands. The village would be unable to prevent their doing so, because "they [the wealthy inhabitants] would maintain their projects by rendering themselves, by their influence, masters of the deliberations of the village communities." Third, limiting enclosures to one-quarter of village property would only "engage communities in continual disputes," and it was unrealistic; it could not be enforced. The court described what would happen:

If owners were permitted to enclose random portions of their lands, they would use this power with respect to their most valuable properties and would only leave the most arid lands for pasture of livestock by right of *vaine pâture*. Because permission for unlimited enclosure was accorded to Lorraine and Champagne, we cannot see any reason to limit it in Burgundy; even the estates have thought along the same lines as the parlement in this respect, presenting in the memoir with their request that villages be constrained to enclose one-quarter of their holdings in order not to frighten those who, lacking knowledge and reflection, would still hold to the old prejudice; but the ideas of unenlightened individuals must not be considered when it is a question of public interest.[58]

Another major disagreement between the estates and the parlement concerned abolition of rights. The estates wanted to abolish the right of common pasture, which included the right of *parcours* (passage), as a precondition to enclosure of one-quarter of the land. The parlement, however, did not wish to go that far.

With respect to the right of *parcours*, the parlement thinks there is no reason to abolish it since when it is decided that the enclosed holdings will not be subject either to the right of *vaine pâture* or to the right of *parcours*, it will be of little importance that those [holdings] which are open to *vaine pâturage* of the livestock of one community be so equally for the livestock of its neighbors.

The parlement observes in this regard that according to the municipal statute of the province, communities can have the right of *parcours*

58. AN, H-173/24, 1770: "Mémoire concernant le projet d'édit." See also AN, H-173/27: "Mémoire concernant la clôture des héritages et le droit de parcours"; AN, H-173/20, 1770: "Clôture d'héritages"; and AN, H-173/29.

in three ways: when they have a title, when they pay a tax to the seigneur, and when the right is reciprocal. To abolish this right in the first two cases would uselessly deprive communities and seigneurs of a right that belongs to them.[59]

Abolishing the right of *parcours* was not necessary, the parlement argued, since all an individual needed to do to eliminate it was to enclose his fields. The law had given the claims of an encloser priority over those of the community. To curtail the right of *parcours* or the right of *vaine pâture* directly, however, was an encroachment on a community property right. To deny communities a right of property, such as the pasture right, for an uncertain reason would only lead them to refuse the payment of seigneurial dues on the grounds that those dues were payment for the pasture right. They could not assert similar claims if the pasture right were curtailed on account of enclosure because enclosure was the assertion of a superior right of property. In other words, enclosures would eliminate the right of *parcours*.

The parlement did agree with the estates on the need to eliminate the legal fees for consolidating parcels. "The parlement insists, moreover, on the necessity of facilitating exchanges by the suppression of all fees to which they [owners] are subject. In so doing, owners would be motivated to bring together in a single holding the parcels they possess in different places, without which the permission to enclose would be of no utility."[60]

The intendant also submitted a report on enclosure, which reveals his position as being much closer to that of the estates. He agreed with them on the need to abolish the common pasture right as a precondition for enclosure.

M. the intendant observes, in this case, that if the right of passage provides for landless inhabitants the means to feed a few head of livestock, which, in turn, helps in their subsistence, this slight advantage is balanced by many inconveniences in that the owner, deprived of the freedom to enclose his possessions, neglects to improve them, limits himself to following the old routine, and fears making expenditures in

59. AN, H-173/24: "Mémoire concernant le projet d'édit"; includes "Le mémoire et le projet d'édit envoyés par le Parlement de Dijon" and the intendant's response, with observation from M. Bertin, adviser to the king on agriculture.

60. Ibid. Nevertheless, parlements and estates differed on the question of mortgages.

fences or ditches that customs like the right of common pasture render useless. The owner knows that the success of his project would be rendered very uncertain by the persistence of pasture rights. On the other hand, the owner would reacquire, by the abolition of the right of passage, the natural right to enclose his lands and to use them in the most advantageous way; then industry and emulation would be reborn among the cultivators who, being convinced by experience that the improvement and multiplication of livestock is an essential part of agriculture, would venture taking risks, would improve natural meadows and make artificial ones.

Individuals, the intendant believed, would not risk investing in hedges, fences, or ditches unless they were assured in advance that the right of common pasture would be abolished. He disagreed with the parlement's contention that abolishing the common pasture right on enclosed properties would motivate owners to enclose. That the right of common pasture had to be abolished as a precondition to all other improvements, the intendant argued, was

founded on the experience of several cantons of Burgundy where passage does not occur, such as the Morvan, which produces the most grain, and the *bailliages* of Montcenis, Bourbon-Lancey, Charolles, and Semur-en-Auxois, which are the only cantons where steers are fattened and where there is a slightly profitable commerce.

M. the intendant adds that there is another obstacle to the progress of agriculture in Burgundy, to wit, the division into several parcels, scattered here and there, of the holdings belonging to the same owner in the area of a single parish. This division, he said, is a source of lawsuits between owners of neighboring parcels because of the difficulty of distinguishing boundary markers, and he thinks that this division will render the permission to enclose less useful, given that the owners will be stopped, either by the considerable expense that the enclosure of many separated parcels brings about, or by the necessity for those whose lands are surrounded to allow passage across their properties. He thinks that the most dependable means of remedying this inconvenience would be to facilitate exchanges of lands situated within the boundaries of the same parish, by according the exchange contracts the exemption requested by the estates, which could, furthermore, arrange the surrender of the rights in question, if only his majesty can suspend or reduce them to this condition.[61]

61. Ibid. See also AN, H-173/15, pp. 7–9.

Like the estates, the intendant opposed rapid change. Unrestricted enclosures might outrage the poor. "It should be feared that a change, too abrupt and too general, would bring about some disadvantages for the poor inhabitants of the countryside, who would not peacefully watch themselves be deprived of what they consider as a right. It would thus be more prudent to dismiss from their minds the idea of total deprivation and to lead them slowly and by degrees to that which appears to be the will of most of those who reason and reflect."[62] Besides, if agricultural progress occurred less rapidly more peasants would benefit.

The intendant and the estates must have collaborated on the topic of enclosures, because in their correspondence with Paris both used the same phrases. Although estates and intendant disagreed on the question of partitioning the commons, the estates were generally acquiescent if not cooperative with the intendant on all issues of communal rights. For example, in the reports they made to the king every three years, the estates argued in favor of increasing the intendant's supervision of village finances. Especially after 1770, when communal lawsuits were growing in scope and frequency, the estates also argued that the intendant's power to authorize and review communal lawsuits was essential. The estates' concern with fiscality (that is, that the province pay the taxes it was annually assessed) might explain their willingness to cooperate with the intendant on such matters. Also, large sums of capital were required to pay the king's debts and substantial loans were floated through the estates. In this regard, the estates were the link between the province and the financial groups discussed in Chapter 1. The estates included a permanent body, the Elus, that worked closely with the *contrôleur général*. Both the estates and the intendant shared a concern with provincial finance: both wanted the financial resources of the province to remain available to the king. This concern about provincial finance probably made the estates much more conservative than the parlement on issues of communal rights. In the seventeenth century and earlier, the estates, not the parlement, were viewed as the defender of provincial

---

62. AN, H-173/24. For more on the intendant's position, see AN, H-173/12: Letter of Intendant Amelot on enclosure, 27 March 1769.

liberties. By the eighteenth century, however, the opposite seems to have been true. Many of the positions the estates took on communal rights and on the intendant's role may seem paradoxical until we recognize that above all, the estates represented financial interests. They did not want to arouse unrest in the countryside that might thwart the annual tax collection process, or to risk disrupting a system that had been the basis of tax collection and credit for more than a century.[63]

Finally, in August 1770, the king issued an edict permitting unlimited enclosures in Burgundy. The edict followed closely the suggestions of the parlement, which promptly registered it on March 20, 1771. Although the edict did not abolish the right of passage, as the estates had hoped, it did give enclosers an exemption from taxes, if only for six years. The exchange of land parcels of less than ten *arpents* was exempted from the *centième denier* and from other royal and seigneurial taxes, with the exception of the registration tax, but exchanged land remained subject to seigneurial and real estate taxes and to the tithe. The estates, however, had to indemnify the farmer general who collected the king's taxes for any loss in income that resulted from exchanges.[64] This clause opened up a new area of contention.

In 1776 the estates asked the king to extend the exemptions. They insisted that "the motives that have determined this law remain in all their strength" and argued that not extending the exemptions would inhibit the progress of enclosure, which had already encountered many obstacles. "The absence of walls, the difficulty of making arrangements with others, were among the causes that obstructed exchanges. But circumstances vary, and time brings together even the most opposite of interests. The exchanges that your subjects have not yet been able to complete can be done at a more favorable moment."[65] But that moment never came. The monarchy's refusal to extend perpetual indem-

63. These are only speculations because little is known about provincial finance and credit. No study has yet been made of the financial functions of the estates.

64. AN, H-173/23: "Edit du Roi concernant les clôtures en Bourgogne," Aug. 1770. By omitting the question of mortgages, the king had, in effect, supported the parlement's position, that is, permitting creditors to maintain their mortgages on lands to be regrouped.

65. AD, C-3332, art. 2, fol. 183.

nities to would-be enclosers is probably not a sufficient explanation for the absence of an enclosure movement in Burgundy, however.[66]

CONCLUSION: WHY FRENCH AGRICULTURE STAGNATED

The Burgundian enclosure edict seems to have left many problems unresolved. The greatest obstacle to enclosure was the complexity of negotiating exchanges between individuals. Individuals had many good reasons for holding out. They might have wanted to build up a consolidated holding slowly, not wanting to risk that the new parcel might be worse than the old. Smallholders might have held out as a means of bargaining for a larger share of the reallotments. A way was needed to prevent individuals from blocking an enclosure by holding out for the best possible return, such as the English parliamentary enclosure bills, which extinguished all communal rights at the same time. The vote for enclosure in England was registered in proportion to the size of holdings. Once agreement of the parties who owned four-fifths of the land had been obtained, all village landholders were compelled to enclose simultaneously.[67] To arrive at a general agreement by a single decision required such stringently undemocratic measures. By contrast, the French edict made it necessary for each individual to negotiate with his neighbor—an extremely awkward and seemingly endless process. The transformation of agrarian organization and the large-scale improvements French reformers were seeking would have required a method for reaching a general agreement.

Another weakness of the Burgundian enclosure edict was that it left unsolved the problem of how the costs of enclosures would be shared. Because there were no clauses pertaining to the

66. There were two instances of enclosure: (1) the inhabitants of Fée informed the intendant of a program to enclose their properties in accordance with the edict of 1770 (AD, C-1691, 20 Nov. 1779); (2) the intendant informed the inhabitants of Marmagne that he could not oppose two individuals who wanted to enclose their properties (AD, C-1370).

67. For a discussion of the English enclosures, see J. A. Yelling, *Common Field and Enclosure in England, 1450–1850* (London, 1977).

costs of building fences between adjacent plots, a party could refuse to share the cost of constructing a fence in anticipation that his neighbor would absorb the entire cost. Thus, the costs of enclosure were not divided equally among the village inhabitants but rather were borne by the individual who initiated the enclosure. An additional disincentive was that the village was not prohibited from exercising its traditional right of common pasture. What was to prevent a village from grazing its herd on an individual's enclosed fields planted in clover? For an individual to sue his village in court would be an expensive and slow process, the outcome of which would not be known for years.

Not surprisingly, neither individuals nor communities responded to the opportunities made available by the edict of 1770; the Burgundian peasantry showed few signs of interest in enclosure before 1789. An agricultural revolution that never occurred left few documents. Since no legislation ever made enclosures mandatory, peasants did not meet in village assemblies to discuss why they did not want to enclose their lands. To understand why an enclosure movement did not occur in Burgundy, it is useful to analyze the movement that did occur in England.

English historians now tell us that the enclosure movement of the late eighteenth century was the culmination of a long process of land reallotments, reclamations, and fencing in of separate parcels. This piecemeal process resulted in the enclosure of more English land than did the parliamentary enclosure bills of the late eighteenth and early nineteenth centuries.[68] The amalgamation of small farms into larger consolidated units caused the dispossession of unsuccessful peasant smallholders and tenants.[69]

High grain prices provided owners with an additional incentive to enclose. Even though the English countryside was gradually enclosed, the records suggest that consolidation and enclosure were most frequent during periods when grain prices were

68. J. R. Wordie, "The Chronology of English Enclosure, 1500–1914," *Economic History Review*, 2d ser., 36 (Nov. 1983): 483-505; Eric Kerridge, *Agrarian Problems in the Sixteenth Century and After* (London, 1969); John Harold Clapham, *An Economic History of Modern Britain* (Cambridge, 1949), 1:19.

69. E. L. Jones, ed., *Agriculture and Economic Growth in England, 1650–1815* (London, 1967).

at their peak.[70] When grain prices were high, landlords could earn higher profits by consolidating holdings and enclosing the land because famers were then willing to pay twice as much for enclosed farms.[71] Beginning in 1725, prices for Burgundian grain also escalated steadily; they peaked in 1770–1771 and remained high through 1789.[72] Why were rising grain prices not an incentive for landlords in France to enclose?[73] The fiscal politics that reinforced communal property rights account for the absence of enclosures in Burgundy.

Viewed in historical perspective, the most serious challenge to open-field agriculture in Burgundy seems to have been the steady expropriation of communal properties, which began with the Wars of Religion and ended in the 1660s. To preserve what remained, the crown prohibited communities from alienating communal properties. The administration's protection ended a century of devastation and explains why communities did not suffer further reduction of communal properties during the economic crisis that spanned the years 1685–1715. By protecting open-field agriculture from the loss of one of its most essential elements—communal pasture—the monarchy also guaranteed the survival of those smallholders who depended on communal pasture to support a minimum number of livestock. To protect smallholders further, the crown prohibited the confiscation of peasant livestock for payment of debts. Thus, smallholders were

70. P. Deane, *The First Industrial Revolution* (Cambridge, 1965), pp. 40–45. On English grain prices, see A. H. John, "The Course of Agricultural Change, 1660–1760," in L. S. Pressnell, ed., *Studies in the Industrial Revolution* (London, 1960).

71. J. D. Chambers and G. E. Mingay, *The Agricultural Revolution, 1750–1880* (London, 1966), pp. 39–52.

72. F. Braudel and C. E. Labrousse, eds., *Histoire économique et sociale de la France* (Paris, 1970), 2:386–87. On grain prices in Burgundy, see Saint-Jacob, *Les paysans*, pp. 239, 461; C. E. Labrousse, *Esquisse du mouvement des prix et des revenus en France au XVIIIe siècle*, 2 vols. (Paris, 1933).

73. There is considerable evidence that because there was more common land in Burgundy, it was considerably easier to usurp and to assart communal land there than in other provinces. The availability of unassarted lands may have hindered the progress of enclosure by diverting attention, at least temporarily, from its advantages. Enterprising individuals may have channeled their energies instead to usurping and assarting uncultivated communal lands. But even if this were the case, it could be no more than a partial explanation for the slow progress of enclosure in Burgundy.

cushioned from the economic downswings that resulted in massive expropriation in England.

The smallholder had little to gain from enclosures. Not only would he have had trouble meeting the legal and fencing costs of enclosures, but he would have been unable to invest in improving his holdings or buying livestock. A majority of the Burgundian peasants were probably smallholders.[74] Thus in the long run, the crown's policies were at least partly responsible for the survival of a substantial group within the peasantry that was committed to the continuation of open fields, mandatory fallow land, and communal pastures.

The well-to-do peasants also had much to gain from the preservation of communal properties and rights because the crown's policies provided that group with economic opportunities within the open-field system. The king's communal wood distribution policy, his refusal to create harsh legislation to punish usurpers of common lands, and his policy with regard to the leasing of common lands all provided ways for wealthy peasants to profit from the preservation of communal properties and to neglect enclosure. Most important, by increasing their herds, wealthy peasants were able to benefit most from communal rights and properties. As we have seen, the wealthy inhabitants resisted the partitioning of the commons.

The monarchy's policy therefore reinforced the commitment of both rich and poor peasants to the open-field system. That communitywide consensus existed in favor of abolishing the right of *vaine pâture* or the three-field rotation system was unlikely because most members of the community identified their interests with preservation of the open fields. It was the

74. Unfortunately, the documents consulted for this study did not provide reliable information on the social structure of the village. They do reveal, however, that the intendants were generally of the opinion that large holdings were not as common in Burgundy as in the provinces that provided grain to Paris. A sample of tax rolls from twenty villages revealed that about 30 percent of the inhabitants paid an average of 30 livres per year. This suggests that these peasants had holdings that enabled them to be self-sufficient. The same sample indicated that a very small percentage of peasants paid more than 70 livres; a handful of peasants paid between 100 and 150 livres. Even these holdings were insubstantial in comparison with the largest holdings in England. The average size of holdings was considerably larger in England than in Burgundy, and large holdings constituted a far greater percentage of total acreage.

demands of the seigneurie, not the open-field system, that peasants, rich and poor alike, saw as obstructing attainment of their economic goals. After 1770, the community concentrated its energies not on enclosures and improvements but on limiting seigneurial rights and evading payment of seigneurial dues.

An agricultural revolution could not be legislated into existence. In the final analysis, an enclosure movement never occurred in France because the economic incentives for enclosure were inhibited by royal policies that, on the one hand, cushioned the smallholder from the devastating effects of downswings in the economy and, on the other, extended economic opportunities within the open-field system to well-off peasants.

Finally, the reorganization of Burgundian agriculture was blocked by the actions of Burgundy's intendants. In the seventeenth century, intendants protected communal rights and properties from seigneurs and townsmen; in the eighteenth century, they protected those same rights and properties from "enlightened" reformers within the King's Council. The intendants responded unfavorably to royal policies that gave wealthy inhabitants a portion of wood in proportion to their individual tax assessments. Intendants often prevented the partitioning of common lands, again contravening the policies of the King's Council. When the monarchy launched a nationwide campaign in the 1780s to curtail gleaning rights, the Burgundian intendant, Dupleix, attempted to protect those rights by writing to the controller general, Calonne, "that [gleaning rights] gave relief to the poor inhabitants."[75] Thus, intendants contributed to preservation of the traditional peasant community and its open-field system of agriculture.

75. AD, C-14, 19 Aug. 1780: Correspondence between Intendant Dupleix and Controller General Calonne.

Five

Challenging the Seigneurie: Community and Contention on the Eve of the Revolution

In Burgundy, community contention was aided, not inhibited, by the growth of state power. By strengthening the community, and by providing the peasantry with the means to interact effectively with the authorities, the state had made collective action possible. However, the efforts to strengthen the community backfired, for in the end, the crown also became a target.

We have seen in Chapter 2 that state officials allied themselves with the community to undermine village dependence on local landlords. The king's officials then reinforced the communal decision-making structure by establishing a permanent set of rules and procedures for the village assembly and by insisting on full participation (Chapter 3); they also staunchly defended the preservation of communal properties and collective agricultural practices (Chapter 4). The village of the late eighteenth century could better defend its interests to the outside as a result of these efforts by state makers. Communal properties were pro-

An earlier version of this chapter, with the same title, appeared in the *Journal of Modern History* 57 (Dec. 1985):652–81. It was awarded the Chester Higby Prize for best article in modern European history for the years 1985–86.

tected in rural jurisprudence and the village was given greater freedom from seigneurial control. In this chapter, we will see that the state not only made the communal village stronger but also encouraged the peasants to challenge the payment of seigneurial dues.

COURT CASES AS EVIDENCE
OF CHANGING RELATIONS
BETWEEN LORDS AND PEASANTS

In July 1789, peasants in several parts of France attempted to defend their own cause by attacking the châteaux of their lords. The peasantry wanted to force a renunciation of manorial dues, even if that required burning the documents that authorized their payment. In areas where the peasants did not attack, they resisted by refusing to pay. These outbreaks may have surprised contemporaries, but hostility to manorial dues was not new. The July revolts had been prefigured by several decades of difficulty during which peasant communities initiated numerous court cases in an attempt to reduce the burden of feudal dues. In Burgundy, a great deal of documentation concerning these disputes survives in both the judicial and administrative archives of the Old Regime. Yet, those historians seeking to understand the outbreaks of 1789 have spent little time studying records of that litigation. This lack of interest in such a rich archival source can be explained very simply. The consensus among historians has been that the resistance of the peasantry was a reaction to the increased demands of the seigneurie for payment of lapsed feudal dues during a period of economic recession. Most historians have seen no need to examine documents concerning the court cases, since the explanation for their proliferation has been thought to be well established.

Had the court cases received greater attention, it would have become clear that the origins of the peasantry's discontent were much more complicated. The revolts were not necessarily precipitated by new or unprecedented exactions or innovative ways of enforcing traditional obligations; under attack were seigneurial rights and privileges that had gone largely unquestioned for centuries. The analysis of the litigation presented here suggests that a

different hypothesis is necessary to explain the growing antiseigneurialism. An examination of administrative channels through
which the court cases had to pass reveals much about the institutional changes that had destabilized society. Those cases had important ideological consequences and played a part in preparing for
the night of August 4, 1789, when the Constituent Assembly
abolished feudal dues, for the assembly drew ideas from the court
cases and personnel from groups that were active in them.

In this chapter it will be suggested that as early as the middle
of the eighteenth century, peasant communities had already begun to contest seigneurial authority in court, using terms similar to those that would later be used by the Constituent Assembly. In those cases, peasants were not only questioning specific
feudal dues; they were challenging for the first time the principles of lordship. It is this widening of the attack that needs to be
explained.

Peasant communities in Burgundy had a long tradition of being able to sue their seigneurs; records of communities using the
king's courts for that purpose go back to the fourteenth century.
Although suits between lord and peasant were not a novelty, it
appeared to eighteenth-century observers that the amount of litigation was increasing and, more important, that the issues were
now broader and the rhetoric more aggressive. It seemed that
there was not a single seigneurial right, no matter how ancient,
that could not be subject to scrutiny and to reevaluation.

Legal proceedings were a relatively sophisticated form of collective resistance compared with the popular rebellions of the
seventeenth century. In the process of challenging seigneurial
authority in court, peasant communities acquired a legal education. The lawyers who defended peasant communities also developed new ways of viewing seigneurial rights and acquired the
vocabulary necessary to discuss more effectively the grievances
of their persistent clients in the countryside. In this sense, communities participated in the creation of the terminology that
was used during the Revolution to dismantle feudal rights over
the land. Many of the ideas we generally associate with the
events of 1789 are clearly stated in the records of those court
cases. Moreover, many lawyers who would later appear in the
revolutionary assemblies, and whose participation and expertise

were necessary when questions concerning feudal rights were raised, had acquired that expertise when serving as consultants in disputes between lord and peasant. Nevertheless, their efforts in the years before 1789 to restrain or to redefine feudal rights were to little avail. Although access to the courts provided both the peasantry and the lawyers with a more effective means to express discontent, the peasants lost case after case. Taking the disputes to court may have only heightened tensions and increased communities' opposition to their lords. The Revolution achieved through violence what a generation of litigation had failed to accomplish peacefully.

In the face of repeated failure, how did communities find the means and the encouragement to bring costly suits challenging time-honored seigneurial rights? In this chapter I suggest that state administrators, by taking over many of the governmental functions previously performed by seigneurial officials, deprived the seigneurs of a significant justification for the continued collection of feudal dues. Those royal officials offered the peasants protection as an alternative to the traditional local governing authority of the seigneurs. As feudal dues became residual, they became increasingly detestable. Royal administrators encouraged communities to question their obligations to their feudal lords. By promising their support, the king's officials inspired communities with the confidence to take their complaints to court.

The principal goal of this chapter is to explain why, in the litigation of the late eighteenth century, peasants were no longer simply questioning specific feudal dues but were also beginning to question the general principles of seigneurial authority. First, I will define several of the feudal rights that were most commonly disputed in court and whose assertion led to attacks on lordship. Then I shall explore the question of why antiseigneurialism increased and why it was expressed in court. The explanation begins with an attempt to answer the most obvious question: How did communities find the financial means to sue their lords? A subsequent discussion focuses on the increasing role of the legal profession and the changing strategies used by lawyers to dispute seigneurial rights. I shall conclude that the growth of the centralizing state explains the changing attitudes of the village toward the seigneurie.

RESISTANCE MOUNTS:
THE DISPUTES

In 1766 the inhabitants of Epoisse were asked to contribute 1,600 livres to repair the walls of the lord's château. The community had always been responsible for the upkeep of the walls, so it is not surprising that the community complied with the lord's request. In 1785 the walls again needed repairs estimated at 2,000 livres. This time, however, the community of Epoisse refused to pay and even went so far as to insist on examining the titles that justified the lord's request. The community's stated reason for refusing was that "the castle of this place can no longer be considered a fortified castle; the bridge, and that which fortified it, having been destroyed for a long time."[1] The castle at Epoisse had not been fortified for almost a century when the community had consented to repair it in 1766. The refusal, nineteen years later, to honor an arrangement that had never been questioned was evidence of the changing relations between lord and peasants in late eighteenth-century Burgundy.

The village Epoisse was but one of many in Burgundy whose inhabitants, in the eighteenth century, refused payment demanded under the seigneurial prerogative known as *guet et garde*. It had been customary for seigneurs to have their châteaux repaired at the expense of their *guettables*. Behind the walls of the châteaux, peasants had found facilities, such as ovens and mills, necessary for self-sufficiency and for survival in times of danger. In the seventeenth century, some members of most communities could remember occasions when the shelter of the lord's château had protected their livestock, their families, and their grain from marauding armies. Those facilities were needed less frequently for that purpose in the eighteenth century, since Franche-Comté, which had been annexed in 1678, provided a buffer between Burgundy and the battlefields in Germany. Once the dangers posed by unsupervised mercenary armies had been eliminated, seigneurs began to transform the old fortresses into country residences. Instead of maintaining facilities necessary to secure a village under siege, they built other kinds of accommodations

1. Archives Départementales, Côte-d'Or, Dijon B²-583, 12 April 1785; "Délibération des habitants d'Epoisse concernant le mur du château."

designed for the recreation and amusement of family and guests. The walls no longer provided protection, but privacy.

By the early eighteenth century, disputes were erupting over who, the lords or the peasants, should pay for these innovations to the châteaux. The intendants often had to intervene. The archives of the intendant record eighteen such interventions between 1716 and 1738. Of the 160 villages involved in those eighteen disputes, all conceded and finally agreed to an out-of-court settlement with the seigneur. The intendant helped some of these communities arrive at more favorable agreements, but in all the cases the communities finally did pay.[2] By midcentury, however, peasants were not only asking for the intendant to intervene in disputes over *guet et garde* but were going to court, sometimes as far as the parlement, when all else failed. Typical was the dispute in 1753 between the inhabitants of Echarnment and Grandmont and their seigneur, M. de Ganay. Those two villages had refused to pay for repairs of the château walls. "The château," the communities' lawyers insisted, "has neither towers nor other fortifications; it has been transformed into a modern building, it can neither house the entire village nor does it have the necessary ovens, mills, and, since it lacks a drawbridge, what good is the moat?" In short, the château was now no more than a personal residence; it could no longer serve as a shelter. The case went to court and the community lost. Among the lord's defenses was the question: If the communities' case was just, why had the grievances been raised so suddenly? Twice since the château had been transformed they had paid the same charges. This, the lord's lawyers argued, constituted proof that the community had already recognized the legitimacy of those rights.[3] Such reasoning led peasants to question whether custom alone justified the continuation of *guet et garde*. That is what happened at Baugy in 1755, when the inhabitants rejected the lord's request for funds to repair his château. They insisted that structural changes had

2. AD, C-2940, 1716; C-2944, 1719; C-2945, 1720; C-2946, 1721; C-2949, 1724; C-2950, 1724; C-2951, 1725; C-2953, 1727; C-2957, 1731; C-2958, 1732; C-2962, 1736; C-2964, 1738. Judgments of Intendant de la Briffe.

3. AD, E-877. Papers of M. de Ganay, seigneur of Lusigny, Echarnment, and Grandmont, 1753. Includes correspondence with Messrs. Disson and Guyot, lawyers for the village, and decision of the parlement in favor of M. de Ganay.

rendered it unsuitable for defense and argued that these changed circumstances warranted a reconsideration of the lord's collection of *guet et garde*.[4] In 1762 the inhabitants of Menessaire and Bèze informed their lord, Leopold d'Aussy, that they would not pay *guet et garde* as usual until their lawyers had examined the lord's titles to that right.[5] In 1770 the inhabitants of Nolay informed their lord, the duke d'Aumont, that they would no longer pay the twenty sols they were assessed annually for *guet et garde*. They, too, wanted to review the lord's titles. Their lawyers recommended that they fight the duke in court, and the intendant gave his approval.[6]

By 1775 the disputes had escalated. Now requests for payment of *guet et garde* were leading many communities to reject all seigneurial dues. In 1775 such a dispute arose between the inhabitants of Missery and their seigneur, M. de Flammerans. The inhabitants questioned whether they should continue to maintain the château, since the lord had transformed it. "It is no longer fortified," they disclosed, and "it has become a pleasant country residence." Flammerans completely ignored these arguments and asserted that in 1716, and again in 1766, the inhabitants had complied with an identical request. Therefore, he insisted, the community had no grounds to withhold payment. The inhabitants reacted to this stubborn refusal to even consider their objections by calling for a review of all seigneurial dues. Their lawyers attacked Flammerans's right to collect a number of dues that were listed in the *terrier*. However, in September 1783, the parlement ruled against them.[7] In the 1780s, communities no sooner received a request for *guet et garde* than they were on their way to consult a lawyer. The days when peasants would honor a feudal obligation just because they had done so in

4. AD, C-2967: Judgments of Intendant Joly de Fleury ordering "la visite des travaux à la charge des retrayants du château de Baugy," 17 Feb. 1756.

5. AD, C-1651, Menessaire, "Débats avec le seigneur pour la curée des fosses et la réparation de menus emparements du château," 1762.

6. AD, C-940, "Intervention de la commune dans un procès contre le duc d'Aumont, à fin d'obtenir la suppression d'une redevance de 20 sols pour exemption de guet et garde," 1770.

7. AD, C-1651: Procès-verbal, 26 Aug. 1775, 17 Feb. 1777, and 27 March 1779, terminating with the decision of the parlement against the community on 8 Sept. 1783.

the past were over.[8] The attacks on *guet et garde* were not unique. Other seigneurial rights, such as *triage, indire,* and the *four banal,* were also being challenged.

Marc Bloch commented that *triage* was the most common source of conflict between lords and peasants in the last part of the eighteenth century.[9] In Burgundy, *triage* was but one of several seigneurial rights that were regularly disputed. *Triage* had received royal recognition in an ordinance of 1669, which affirmed the lord's right to reserve one-third of the communal woods for his personal use.[10] A lord could claim *triage* in the absence of titles proving his ownership of the woods simply by arguing that the woods were originally ceded gratuitously. The burden of proof was placed on the community, and few of them had titles documenting how communal woods were acquired.

More often than not in the seventeenth and early eighteenth centuries, claims to *triage* were settled by an out-of-court agreement. Marguerite Blocaille has studied claims to *triage* made between 1669 and 1789 in the heavily wooded subdelegation of Arc-sur-Tille. Between 1669 and 1719, only three of twenty-six such claims resulted in lawsuits. Of eight claims asserted between 1719 and 1750, three resulted in lawsuits. But between 1750 and 1789, nine of fourteen claims ended in the courts and another was on its way to court when the Revolution broke out.[11] Blocaille's conclusion was that at the end of the eighteenth century, in this subdelegation, communities were much

8. For example, the inhabitants of Chauvirey, Diancy, and Jonchery, the communities that were traditionally responsible for the upkeep of the château at Vianges, refused in 1781 to contribute to the maintenance of the bridges and moat. Diancy and Jonchery were condemned by the local seigneurial court but persisted in their refusal. They argued that "even if the occasion should arise, the château would not be able to shelter the inhabitants since its fortifications had been destroyed" (AD, C-655, 28 Nov. 1781). In 1782 the inhabitants of Busserotte refused to continue yearly payments for maintenance of the château belonging to the seigneur of Grancey. The lord's agent asked the intendant to order the inhabitants to pay. Instead, on 29 March 1785, the intendant permitted Busserotte to sue (AD, C-1234, procès-verbal, 1782, Aug. 1784, and Feb. 1785, terminating on 29 March 1785 with the intendant's authorization to sue).

9. Marc Bloch, *Les caractères originaux de l'histoire rurale française,* 2:193.

10. Ordinance of Aug. 1669, title 25, arts. 4, 5. Text in Isambert, Jourdan, and Decrusy, *Recueil général des anciennes lois françaises depuis l'an 420 jusqu'à la Révolution de 1789,* 29 vols. (Paris, 1821–1833), 18:219–311.

11. Marguerite Blocaille, "Forêts, seigneurs, et communautés au dernier siècle de l'Ancien Régime," Thèse, Diplôme des Etudes Supérieures, Université de Dijon, 1973.

more likely to dispute *triage* in court. Higher costs for wood might explain the growing number of claims to *triage*, but they do not explain the larger percentage of such claims that were ending up in the courts. There is no reason to assume that this trend was peculiar to Arc-sur-Tille.

The *droit d'indire* permitted the lord to double seigneurial dues for one year for any of the following reasons: an overseas voyage by the lord, his being dubbed or receiving a new title, the marriage of the lord's eldest daughter, or to provide ransom if the lord were kidnapped or captured. In the eighteenth century, a marriage was the most frequent pretext. The intensity with which communities resented *indire* was noted by contemporaries, and the more prudent seigneurs exercised great caution when claiming this right, to avoid ending up in court. In 1779, for example, the lord of Ecotigny claimed only 600 livres by virtue of *indire* when he was entitled to more. He wanted to avoid trouble, ill will, and a possible lawsuit.[12] In contrast, when the count of Saulx-Tavanes was made a duke in 1786, he promptly doubled the seigneurial dues payable by all those within his jurisdiction, as well as those of the *forains*, who lived on the outskirts of his village and were not subject to his jurisdiction. Six of his nine communities united with their traditional rivals, the *forains*, in opposition to his request.[13] Opposition to *indire* usually did not succeed, however. Communities continued to dispute the right, but in vain; for example, the community of Beaumont-sur-Vingeanne was defeated in 1788.[14]

The right of *four banal* required the peasants to bake their

12. AD, C-922: Report of the subdelegate, March 1779: "Il a reclamé de ses vassaux un droit d'indire qu'il a bien voulu restraindre à 600 livres."

13. AD, C-1260, Lux, 1786: Petition to the intendant for permission to begin legal proceedings.

14. Examples of disputes over *triage* and *indire* follow. Gissy-sur-Ouche, 1763: members of the community went to court to dispute the claim of *triage* asserted by the seigneur (the comtesse de Rochechouart); the community lost (AD, C-658). Mirabeau, 1764: the town claimed it could not afford the *indire* imposed by the seigneur, M. de Bauffremont (AD, C-793). Villiers-la-Faye, 9 Sept. 1766: Prince de Bauffremont claimed *indire* because of the marriage of his daughter (AD, C-1551). Auxey, July 1769: the community repudiated the lord's claim of *indire*. The lord's lawyers commented: "Les moyens des habitants sont invincibles" (AD, H-903). Villey-sur-Tille, February 1782: the village had to take a loan to pay the dues demanded by virtue of *indire* (AD, C-1308). Beaumont-sur-Vigeanne, 1787: the Marquis de Tavanes claimed the right of *indire* on the occasion of his promotion to "chevalier des ordres du roi" (AD, C-1226).

bread in the lord's oven and prohibited them from maintaining ovens of their own. Undisputed assertion of this right had been common throughout France during the Middle Ages, when it provided an economical way for large numbers of people to bake their bread in common; in the eighteenth century, many could afford ovens of their own and resented paying the lord's baker. By the late eighteenth century, seigneurs in most of the kingdom, with the exception of Burgundy, were no longer claiming this right.

A SEIGNEURIAL REACTION IN BURGUNDY?

Many historians of Burgundy, and of France in general, have characterized the eighteenth century as a series of "seigneurial reactions" that began in the 1730s and 1740s. In essence, they argue that seigneurs were seeking to consolidate their rights over the peasantry and to achieve more efficient estate management by hiring specialized lawyers, called *feudistes*, to rediscover seigneurial dues that had either been allowed to lapse or were not strictly enforced. The result was a period of increasingly difficult relations between lords and peasants. The communal archives, however, suggest that by the 1770s it was no longer clear who was on the offensive, the community or the seigneurie. The seigneur's eagerness to reimpose long-forgotten dues was matched by the peasantry's willingness to challenge all seigneurial rights and privileges.

Were seigneurial dues more hateful in the late eighteenth century than they had been in the past? Pierre de Saint-Jacob, the foremost historian of rural Burgundy, suggests that an economic crisis and mounting misery made seigneurial dues seem unendurable, especially because seigneurs were reasserting a claim to dues that had long since lapsed. Nevertheless, times were probably harder for Burgundian peasants, and seigneurs were even more aggressive in reinforcing their authority over them, in both the sixteenth and seventeenth centuries. And if times were so bad, how did communities find the means to sue? Moreover, a great deal of organization is required to bring grievances to court. Financial resources, support from legal and political authorities, and some hope of winning were all necessary. These Saint-Jacob does not consider, however. Most important, the court cases after 1750 were not just disputes over the collection of seigneurial dues, and contemporaries did not conceive of them as such. Well-informed observers expressed concern that much more was at stake. Peasants, they felt, were challenging the nature of the bonds that had governed men and women for over a thousand years. But they were not only questioning the legal basis of the lord's authority (his *terrier*); they were also disputing the moral and historical justification of that authority. In feudal law, the right to collect seigneurial dues was supported by elaborate moral and historical arguments, and in the court cases of the seventeenth and early eighteenth centuries those justifications were not at issue. The disputes focused on the legality of specific dues, methods of collection, and assessment. Does the lord's previous *terrier* document the rights he claims in the new *terrier*? Can the lord document his assertion that the inhabitants owe a yearly fee for the privilege of watering the village herd in the moat of the château? Can they fish in his streams or market their wine without a license? Has the village acquired, by the payment of seigneurial dues, the right to pasture the herd in the village's meadow or woodlands, or did that privilege originate as a grant from the seigneur? Do the titles verify the lord's insistence on the tongue of each head of cattle slaughtered in the village? Or must he provide an agent to supervise the slaughter before he can expect the tongue? The cases after 1770 generally went beyond such specific issues. The strategy had shifted: the historical justifications of seigneurial authority were now being questioned along with the exactions they supported. It is this change in strategy that I want to explain.

Since the Middle Ages, lords had periodically rewritten their *terriers*, that is, renewed their titles. There was nothing new in that. But if these efforts were not novel in the eighteenth century, the failure of lords and peasants to agree amicably on the rewritten *terriers* was, and it was alarming to contemporaries. The rewriting of *terriers*, an activity described in the documents as *reconnaissance*, became the topic of heated debates that were often ended by the intervention of the courts. In such disputes, the lord's lawyers usually claimed that what should have been no more than a routine recognition of the lord's traditional rights had become an opportunity for inhabitants to challenge the basis of traditions previously unquestioned.

In 1777 two lawyers from the town of Auxois commented that "we do not understand in the slightest what [spirit of] giddiness has taken hold of the people of the countryside recently. Nor do we have an inkling by what motive they have persuaded themselves that they can avoid with impunity paying various *droits* they owe their seigneur. But this sort of contagion is becoming so widespread that even vassals who do not, without forewarning, go so far as a decided refusal, require at least that their seigneurs produce the titles that justify the payments they collect."[15] A lawyer representing the seigneur of Cormaranche expressed the same concern: "The imprudence and rashness with which village communities constantly undertake dreadful lawsuits, without right, without motives, and without interest, and the inconveniences that result, have not escaped the attention of the law. It [the law] has sought to provide a remedy, but experience only reinforces the knowledge that the usual remedies are powerless."[16] When the community of Saint-Julien refused to acknowledge its seigneurial titles in 1788, a president of the Parlement of Dijon, Jean Pérard, commented: "The allegations that the communities have just used to support their case provide convincing proof that there are no rights, however legitimate, that cannot be questioned today."[17] Peasants were even going so far as to discontinue payment of certain seigneurial dues on the grounds that the rights to them had been acquired by violence during darker and more barbaric times.

The inhabitants of Sergey claimed that in the sixteenth century, the community had been improperly forced to pay for the use of certain properties that had always belonged to them. The community lost in the *bailliage* court, and the case was on its

---

15. AD, H-581, 1777.

16. "Mémoire pour dame Louise le Bret de Corcelles contre les habitans et communauté de Cormaranche," 1782. BM, Fonds Saverot, vol. 16, no. 5, title 65.

17. In the eighteenth century, the parlement had nine presidents at all times but only one *premier président*. BM, Fonds Saverot, vol. 37, no. 27: "Mémoire responsif par messire Jean Pérard, chevalier, président au Parlement de Bourgogne contre les habitans et communauté de Saint-Julien," 1788.

way to the parlement when Pierre de la Forest, the lord of Sergey and count of Rumilly, published a *factum* in which his lawyers asserted that "the *bailliage* of Gex viewed this attempt [by the community] as a chimera, born of this spirit of independence that is so easy these days to inspire in the country dwellers." La Forest's lawyers explained that "for many centuries there has not passed one year without the inhabitants rendering a new homage to the property of their seigneurs, since each year they have paid him exactly in his capacity as owner of the woods. How, then, after a possession so ancient, so peaceful, so continuous, and so consistent with the most respectable and most authentic titles, could the inhabitants of Sergey seriously question their seigneurs regarding a property that they have, until today, so dutifully and solemnly recognized?" It seemed to these lawyers that the community was guilty of misapprehension, or was suffering from some kind of delusion. The lawyers said that they would "discuss, in order, the allegations, the frivolous reasons that serve as the basis of this claim. Assuredly, much skill would be needed to persuade us that a community, having paid different sorts of dues for many centuries in order to enjoy rights of usage in the woods of any seigneurie, is not the user, but the owner, of these same woods."

But the villagers were convinced that the lord had usurped the woods from the community during times of disorder. The fact that they paid for the right to use the woods did not establish the seigneur's innocence. Custom was not enough; they required that the lord show the original titles to prove his ownership. The community's lawyers stated the villagers' request as follows: "According to this community, all the titles that have just been analyzed should be ignored; moreover, the immemorial possession that accompanies them should be disregarded because, they say, other titles exist, much older than these *terriers* and transactions, and in the matter of seigneurial rights, one should always resort to the oldest title."[18]

Even the wealthiest seigneur in all Burgundy, the duke of Saulx-Tavanes, was having trouble asserting his seigneurial

18. BM, Fonds Saverot, vol. 37, no. 5. "Mémoire pour M. Pierre de la Forest, comte de Rumilly, etc. contre les habitans de la communauté de Sergy appelans de la sentence rendue au bailliage de Gex," 18 Aug. 1783.

rights. In 1785 the inhabitants of one of the duke's villages refused outright to acknowledge a renewal of his *terrier*. Evidently
their refusal pertained to three-quarters of the articles contained
in the new *terrier*. The duke decided to present his case publicly;
his lawyers argued the points at length in a *factum*.

Nothing was more frivolous than the pretexts alleged by the inhabitants of Lux to color their refusal of the recognition requested of them.
They were perfectly well aware of these *droits*, listed in the draft of
which they were given a copy, since the exercise of the *droits* has never
been interrupted. Most are purely customary *droits*, basic to seigneurial
justice and administration, and common to seigneurial justice throughout the province. Lastly, seigneurial justice, essential to the character of
the territorial seigneur, could not be considered by the inhabitants as an
exorbitant *droit*. However, they stubbornly refused any kind of recognition. They say that they need a copy of all the titles, as if reason
and customary practice could have authorized such a procedure. They
asked to see the seigneurial archives, with travel expenses paid. Their
procureurs-syndics did not want to enter the drawing room of the
château of Lux, where the titles necessary for the writing of the new
terrier were spread out, in spite of the fact that the salon of the château
was a perfectly free place, the château being occupied at the time only
by the commissioners in charge of the renewal. They [also] refused to
see the titles at the office of the clerk of Lux, under the pretext that the
clerk sold wine, although the deposit of the documents would have
been done in a safe room, quiet and far from noise.

Because the duke of Saulx-Tavanes has found it necessary to sue the
inhabitants in the *bailliage* court, he has to prove all of his *droits*, without exception, since the inhabitants declared that they did not wish to
recognize any. If they [the inhabitants] had had the prudence to indicate
those they wanted to contest, the seigneur's request would have been
limited to those particular rights, which would have considerably diminished the costs of the lawsuit and investigation. It is instead necessary to
draw up all the *droits*, to indicate the titles that verified them, to give
copies to the litigants, as was requested by the inhabitants themselves,
to make, in a word, an enormous suit from a discussion that could have
been reduced to a few main points, if the inhabitants had had the prudence to restrain their refusal to the *droits* they wanted to contest.

At last, after a multitude of delays, the inhabitants of Lux furnished
their defense, which attacked close to two-thirds of the *droits* that
they were asked to recognize, and which constituted thirty-one separate articles.[19]

19. AD, C-1260: "Mémoire pour Charles-François Casimir, duc de Saulx-
Tavanes, . . . contre les syndics et habitans de la communauté de Lux, appelans
de la sentence rendue au bailliage de Dijon, le 27 Août 1785."

Litigation of this nature was so common that a village dossier that does not include mention of a lawsuit is exceptional. Communities were contracting debts, postponing necessary repairs and construction, and even delaying the payment of royal taxes to pay the costs incurred in court cases. Those authorities who supervised communal finances were seeking ways to curtail this drain on communal resources. The Estates of Burgundy, which were charged with provincial tax collection, were foremost among the provincial authorities who wanted to restrain peasant litigiousness. In the 1780s the estates composed a *mémoire* to the king defending the intendant's right to review and to approve, on the basis of his own authority, all communal requests to sue. The Parlement of Dijon claimed that it alone could decide whether a case was well founded. The intendant, the parlement asserted, was not authorized to interpret the laws. The estates argued that this right was part of the intendant's authority as the tutor of communities, and that the parlement could hardly be expected to limit the lawsuits by villages since those lawsuits enriched the parlementaires. In defending their position, the estates reported that communities initiated about four hundred court cases a year, at an annual cost of about 400,000 livres. This meant an average of one lawsuit per community every five years. The estates reported that in a good year, the communities lost 90 percent of the suits. Their titles were often in disarray or missing, their counselors poorly prepared. "Their lawsuits are only good for the money they pay out"; moreover, "the results of these judicial costs must be the desiccation of the countryside, misery, poverty, and incapacity to pay royal taxes. All plans for improvement, for reform, can be nothing but illusory speculations so long as this epidemic wind corrupts production at its roots and makes all the wealth of the earth disappear in one moment." The estates concluded that the intendant's right to review and to approve communities' requests to sue had to be preserved. "This wound can only be healed by reinforcing the powers of the posted commissioners."[20]

The estates were not alone in this desire to eliminate un-

---

20. AD, C-5085: Undated *mémoire* by the Estates of Burgundy. Its context indicates its approximate date.

sound court cases. The subdelegate of Saulieu offered a bold solution: creation of a bureau of four or five lawyers charged exclusively with approving all community requests to sue. The bureau would have the power to veto any requests it considered poorly founded; no suit could be filed without its consent. This "precaution," the subdelegate claimed, "would make many abuses cease."[21] The subdelegate suggested a council of nonpartisan lawyers who would provide communities free legal aid. The intendant did not like the idea. First, the council would be very costly, and the intendant was already faced with financial problems; he regularly petitioned both the king and the estates for more funds. Second, the council would be opposed by the parlement on the grounds that it infringed on the parlement's exclusive authority to interpret the law. Third, the council of lawyers would inevitably become embroiled in the court cases it supervised. Finally, who would supervise the council to ensure that it remained free from abuse, did not accept bribes, and was not otherwise manipulated?

Court cases in which lord was pitted against peasant constituted a large proportion of the increase in communal lawsuits. And these were the cases that most concerned the authorities. Even if those suits were not the majority, they were the most expensive. If seigneurs were dissatisfied with the decisions of the lower courts, they had the privilege of appealing to the parlement. The stakes were high in cases involving lord and peasant.

It is not possible to calculate what percentage of Burgundian communities initiated these expensive lawsuits against their lords. However, to obtain some indication of the number of such cases, we might consider what was happening in Langres, the *généralité* north of Burgundy. In his study, Jean-Jacques Clère found that in 1789, three-quarters of the communities of Langres had previously instituted or were presently involved in lawsuits against the seigneur.[22] The concerns expressed in these lawsuits

---

21. AD, C-1662, 13 Aug. 1776: Subdelegate Merle to intendant.
22. Jean-Jacques Clère, "Les paysans de la Haute-Marne et la Révolution française (1780–1825): Recherches sur la communauté villageoise," Thèse, Droit, Université de Dijon, 1980, p. 256. "If you take into account affairs of *triages*, of *cantonnements*, of claims, of property emanating from the seigneurs, in short, usurpations of commons, claimed or real, more than three-quarters of the communities were led to sue their seigneurs during the last fifty years of the Ancien Régime."

illuminate the actions of Burgundian communities during the Revolution. In Langres, just as in Burgundy, there were antistatist, antifiscal, and even anticlerical outbreaks during the Revolution, but the most distinctive feature of rural unrest in both regions was its antiseigneurialism.

For communities to initiate lawsuits against their seigneurs—suits that would be very expensive and very long, and that would envenom their relations with the seigneur for many years—three conditions had to exist. The first was shared and increasing animosity toward the seigneur. Few historians would disagree that it existed. Such animosity, many historians have argued, was an outcome of the economic struggle with the seigneurie, and of an economic situation after 1770 that was devastating to many small and medium-sized producers. The second condition was that communities had to have considerable financial resources, especially if their case went to the parlement. There are, however, many indications that communities were wealthier in the eighteenth century than they had been previously. Because communal properties—forests in particular—had increased in value, communities could finance court cases on a scale that had never been possible. The third condition, hope, is the most difficult to pinpoint, and of the three conditions it has been discussed the least. It was certainly as important as animosity or means. Hope of liberation from feudal dues had two key sources: the expanding legal profession and the growing royal bureaucracy. Both of these groups, by recognizing and supporting communal rights, raised the peasantry's expectations. Animosity, resources, and hope—had one of these ingredients been lacking, the events leading up to the great struggle of 1789 might not have occurred.

THE MISERY THESIS

Animosity toward the seigneurie has received much attention in works on the peasantry and the French Revolution. In fact, historians have concentrated on the economic grievances that led to the peasantry's revolt against the seigneurs, almost to the exclusion of all other considerations. In his comprehensive study of the eighteenth-century Burgundian peasantry, Saint-Jacob presents

the most commonly held explanation of peasant unrest after
1770: The peasantry's growing hostility to the seigneurie was an
outcome of the community's competition with the seigneurie for
declining profits in agriculture.[23] Saint-Jacob argued that a land
shortage, caused by new practices of land management, hampered
peasants' efforts to produce for themselves.[24] Although they had
previously leased small parcels to numerous small producers,
seigneurs now preferred to lease large consolidated plots to the
fermiers, who had larger sums of cash in hand and were more
likely to be solvent than were smallholders. *Fermiers* signed six-
or nine-year leases that specified a fixed rent. Lords would sometimes lease to a single large tenant, called the *fermier* or the
fermier général, but this practice was not common in Burgundy.
Such an arrangement assured the lord a regular return and made
the tenant responsible for the many details of farming, such as
providing the livestock, plows, and tools; collecting the rents and
dues of subleasers; bargaining with the grain and wood merchants; making the repairs; and paying the royal taxes. Saint-
Jacob called these new leasing practices "physiocratic." (Perhaps
this is not the best term, for seigneurs were not concerned with
improving agriculture in order to increase agricultural yields, as
the term "physiocracy" would imply; rather, they were motivated by a desire to rationalize seigneurial revenues.) The leasing
practices created among the poor "a hunger for land . . . after so
much dearth, now the worst of all, a dearth of land." This scarcity, Saint-Jacob asserted, was "the big event of the new times."[25]
Because of the new practices, seigneurial lands were closed to
small and medium-sized producers. This group, traditionally dependent on the leasing of seigneurial lands, was thus ruined.[26]
Unable to find small parcels to lease, small producers were transformed into an agricultural proletariat at a time when wages were
not keeping up with the general increase in prices.[27] Large num-

23. Pierre de Saint-Jacob, *Les paysans de la Bourgogne du nord au dernier
siècle de l'Ancien Régime* (Dijon, 1960).
24. Many peasants cultivated lands they did not own. Large tenants often
owned no land of their own. Smallholders frequently rounded out their farms by
cultivating adjoining land under lease.
25. Saint-Jacob, *Les paysans*, p. 432.
26. Ibid. The *manouvrier* could not find "le lopin de terre qui lui permettrait
de compléter son salaire de tâcheron" (p. 432).
27. Ibid., p. 458.

bers of them were thrown into the labor market, causing wages
to decline. Worse than declining wages, Saint-Jacob insisted, was
the loss of self-respect experienced by independent peasants who
were accustomed to producing either for the market or for their
own consumption and were now reduced to the status of day
laborers.[28]

The common lands were also diminishing. Peasants, who had
despaired of finding private land at a reasonable price, "tried to
encroach upon public property."[29] But it was the wealthy inhabitants who did most of the usurping. One contemporary observed
that "the richest and strongest seized everything that they
wanted."[30] In 1776 Intendant Amelot issued a report that contained a similar observation: "The principal inhabitants have, in
a certain way, divided up the commons among themselves."
This had devastating consequences for the poor. The intendant
added that "the poor *manouvriers*, who earlier raised their families with the aid of a few cows, were deprived of this resource
and exposed to death from hunger because they did not dare
complain and did not have the means of making themselves
heard."[31] The problem, he would learn, was that the communities could not defend themselves against usurpation because
they rarely possessed titles. Dependent on oral reports and on
the memory of individuals, communities could not hope to sub-
stantiate their claims in court.

Saint-Jacob pointed out that there was yet another cause of
the land shortage: the leasing of communal properties. This
practice, which became increasingly widespread during the
eighteenth century and which was supported by the royal administration, further reduced the lands available to the poor.
The leasing of communal lands had become an important
source of income for communities. With communal lands diminishing, the poor could not raise livestock and were deprived

28. "A proletariat was growing in the village. They lacked money, livestock,
and land on which they could make a living. Their purchasing power had decreased by 80 percent in half a century. They went after their enemies." Ibid., p.
444.
   29. AD, C-1092: Letter from Chanoine Petit, June 1768; cited by Saint-Jacob,
Les paysans, p. 447.
   30. AD, C-1043, 1776; cited by Saint-Jacob, *Les paysans*, p. 447.
   31. Saint-Jacob, *Les paysans*, p. 469.

of their principal source of capital. Lack of capital made it even harder for them to rent the lands that were still available.

As if the land shortage were not enough, another factor contributed to mounting peasant misery. After 1775, grain prices declined dramatically while the price of leases continued to increase. Landowners and tenants had signed leases with the expectation that grain prices would rise, continuing a long-term trend that was assumed to be permanent.[32] Grain prices never again recovered the same rate of increase after 1775, however. Declining grain prices should have lowered the living expenses of the poor, but Saint-Jacob claimed that this did not happen. The land shortage, along with population growth (the population is estimated to have increased 10 percent since 1715), had thrown more workers into the job market. Because of the abundance of unemployed workers, salaries were low and rose less rapidly than prices. The depression "did not lower the price of wheat nor did it change the grain market sufficiently to obtain for the poor any meaningful relief. On the contrary, the economic depression rendered *fermiers* even more nervous and demanding, they undoubtedly skimped more than ever on wages, and *manouvriers* were even less certain of finding work."[33] Even if reduced grain prices did lower living expenses for the poor, Saint-Jacob insisted that an improved standard of living, including lower food costs, could never compensate peasants for the loss of self-respect that resulted from their loss of independence.

Saint-Jacob claimed that "the great economic and social fact of the century was the power of the *fermier*, a general land speculation, a domination of the traditional means of modest agricultural cultivation by money."[34] During the fifty years before the Revolution, speculation had transformed rural society. The money of the "new men" had begun to disturb the ancient market of land and of grain, while dearth had eliminated the smallholders. "This was a cruelly resented social failure and a source of bitter animosity among a class as careful and proud of its freedom as it was hostile to a newborn capitalism."[35] The

32. Ibid., p. 484.
33. Ibid., p. 437.
34. Ibid., p. 569.
35. Ibid., p. 572.

"newborn" capitalism was advancing at the expense of common pasture, woodlands, and grazing rights—all of which had traditionally protected the peasantry from the full force of fluctuations in the grain market. Worse still for the smallholders, the new leasing practices meant consolidation of the dispersed plots that had formerly been leased to them. Saint-Jacob summarized the situation faced by the growing rural proletariat on the eve of the Revolution. Its standard of living, its source of capital, and its supply of livestock had decreased. Unable to find lands to rent, peasants were condemned to toil on the land of their richer neighbors. As this dispossessed peasantry grew, so too did anti-seigneurial sentiment.

In the new land management policies the community found its explanation for peasant debts and for the increasing pauperism. It was the seigneur, along with wealthy *fermiers*, who had introduced and promoted the new policies; they were the principal beneficiaries of the new economic regime. Since the seigneurie was leading the attack on communal practices, it was responsible for the land shortage as well. The peasants resented the penetration of urban financial interests into the countryside and held the seigneur responsible for introducing those interests in the person of the *fermier*.

In short, there is no equivocation in Saint-Jacob's explanation of what led the peasantry to revolution. As living standards in the village declined, the sense of insecurity became generalized. The culprit was undeniably the seigneur. Misery finally led the peasantry to rebellion.[36]

My purpose here is not to dispute Saint-Jacob's economic analysis, nor his conclusion that the deteriorating economic situation created pressures and tensions that intensified antagonisms between lord and peasant, especially since the seigneurs

---

36. "The mediocrity that instilled itself in the village led to rebellion. The spirit of resistance became general. Everywhere seigneurial rights were discussed. *Reconnaissances* of previous *terriers* no longer sufficed. Inhabitants wanted to see the original titles. The entire seigneurial system was suspect. Contemporaries were struck by the new spirit of independence. Resistance was being organized. In their briefs, lawyers were using audacious expressions that further discredited the seigneurial regime; the ecclesiastical seigneurs were particularly singled out. Thus everywhere the winds of revolt blew." Ibid., pp. 463–65. Saint-Jacob's assumption that the overwhelming misery led to revolt needs to be tested, however.

seemed to be profiting from the peasants' misery. But why in Burgundy was that hostility expressed collectively rather than individually? As E. P. Thompson has pointed out, the peasants in England had much to complain about in the eighteenth century, but their grievances led to individual rather than collective resistance. English peasants resorted to vandalism and acts of personal violence against their lords.[37] Saint-Jacob did not consider it necessary to explain the collective strength of French communities. Like most historians writing about the French peasantry, he took for granted that group's most striking characteristic—its collective organization in response to oppression. The English peasantry did not react to oppression collectively because, unlike their French counterparts, they had neither a village assembly to represent them, nor collective rights and properties to unite them. In the remainder of this chapter I will explain how French communities found the resources and the hope that enabled them collectively to oppose the seigneur.

BEYOND THE MISERY THESIS:
INCREASING COMMUNAL REVENUES

Communal wealth was one of the conditions that made possible concerted opposition to the seigneur. Ironically, communities on the whole were becoming wealthier at a time when personal poverty was increasing. This communal prosperity began when over a century of constant invasion and pillaging ended. Mercenaries had lived off the land since the 1560s, but beginning in the seventeenth century, the crown took measures to isolate soldiers from the civilian population. The regiments were supervised by the intendants, and the military commanders were made to answer personally for abuses committed by their troops. The records left by Burgundy's first intendants suggest that efforts were indeed made to carry out the king's instructions. Although the new arrangements gave civilian authorities unprecedented rights of supervision over the military, the immediate result was to give the military greater incentives to police itself.

In order to protect the peasants, the intendants were in-

37. E. P. Thompson, *Whigs and Hunters* (New York, 1975).

structed to report misdemeanors committed by the troops directly to the king and simultaneously to the military authorities. In addition, the intendants were authorized to bring suits against the delinquent soldiers and to see that the courts followed through, even if that required going to the highest level of jurisdiction. Soldiers were directed to inform civilian authorities of their movements, follow prescribed routes, and maintain discipline in transit, all in accordance with the intendant's orders. The intendants received additional powers of supervision over activities that affected the military, such as the furnishing of horses and supplies by inhabitants, the provisioning of barracks, the lodging of the troops, and the raising of the village militia. The king authorized the intendant to verify that civilian proprietors near military encampments were reimbursed for property damage caused by troop movements. Despite all these measures, the wars of Louis XIV had to stop before the countryside really began to recover from the devastation caused by military maneuvers.

Control of the troops, as much as or more than any other factor, made possible the economic recovery and relative prosperity of communities in eighteenth-century Burgundy. Prosperity permitted the population to increase, and grain prices went up since yields remained unchanged. This price increase brought good fortune to some individuals but adversity to many.[38] For communities in general, however, peace increased communal wealth. In wartime, many communities had had to sell communal resources to recover the costs of damages caused by campaigning troops.

The increased value of communal properties, particularly forests, was the key to the new communal wealth. The demand for wood had greatly increased.[39] Naval construction, metallurgy, increased housing construction, and more elaborate home fur-

38. Pierre Quarré and Jean Richard, "Campagnes et villes de Bourgogne sous l'Ancien Régime," in Jean Richard, ed., Histoire de la Bourgogne (Toulouse, 1978), p. 261. "In its totality the province had in 1786–1788 approximately 1,100,000 inhabitants, which represented an increase of about 10 percent since the beginning of the century. The hardships of the twenty years previous to 1784 did not compromise demographic progress. The essential point was overcoming the misery of the end of the seventeenth century and of 1709."

39. Parts of Burgundy were specially designated to provide timber for the government's shipbuilding operations at Toulon.

nishings for a larger and wealthier population put pressures on dwindling wood reserves. Since wood was France's principal fuel, historians can today speak of an energy crisis occurring in the late eighteenth century. This crisis resulted in an estimated 91 percent increase in the national price of wood between 1726 and 1787.[40] As holders of substantial portions of the kingdom's woods, rural communities were among the first to benefit. At least 50 percent of the communities in Burgundy had wood surpluses and could profit from the inflation in wood prices.

The evidence with regard to wood prices in eighteenth-century Burgundy is fragmentary but the trends are clear. There are indications that wood prices may have actually exceeded the estimated national increase of 91 percent. In 1666 Intendant Bouchu estimated that the timber from one *arpent* of woods in the village of Gissey was worth between 8 livres and 25 livres. In 1746 the same timber sold for 55 livres. In 1785 wood from 25 *arpents* was auctioned in Gissey for 1,850 livres, or 74 livres per *arpent*.[41] In Dijon, a *moule* of wood worth 4 livres 10 sols in 1716 was worth 13 livres in 1787.[42] The largest increases occurred after 1770, the period when communities were most litigious. Saint-Jacob found that timber from the Comte de Beaumont's woods, worth 73 livres in 1776, was worth 110 livres in 1786 and 160 livres in 1788.[43] Because communities could acquire large sums by selling communal wood, there was considerable incentive to defend the woods against such threats as seigneurial *triage*. Thus, woods became an important subject of court cases as well as an important source of funds to support court costs. As we will see in this chapter, the higher commercial value of wood was not the sole reason for the frequency and the intensity of the disputes.

Communities could also reap important new profits by leas-

40. C. E. Labrousse, *Esquisse du mouvement des prix et des revenus en France au XVIIIe siècle* (Paris, 1933), p. 346, and F. Braudel and C. E. Labrousse, eds., *Histoire économique et sociale de la France* (Paris, 1970), 2:331.

41. B. de Varine, *Villages de la vallée de l'Ouche aux 17e et 18e siècles: La seigneurie de Marigny-sur-Ouche* (Roanne, 1979), p. 80. Gissey is in the valley of the Ouche, which during the eighteenth century supplied much of Dijon's wood.

42. M. Devèze, *Histoire des forêts* (Paris, 1965), chap. 5; and Devèze, "Les forêts françaises à la veille de la Révolution," *Revue d'histoire moderne et contemporaine* 13 (1966):241–72.

43. Saint-Jacob, *Les paysans*, p. 488.

ing their collectively owned meadow and pasture lands. That practice had become widespread. The result—fewer opportunities to raise livestock—meant that some individuals within the community might have been poorer, but again, communities were becoming wealthier.

The community was not the sole manager of communal properties; its two protectors, the Maîtrise des Eaux et Forêts and the intendant, both oversaw their management. The public forests supervised by the maîtrise included the forests owned by the king and those owned by the communities. The maîtrise's principal concern was the rational harvesting of timber to provision the navy with mature lumber necessary for shipbuilding. These supplies were crucial to national security as well as to France's colonial competition with England. However, the maîtrise had little control over forests owned by individuals. Its jurisdiction, like that of most branches of the royal bureaucracy, was limited to properties that the king could define as public goods. The maîtrise refused to allow communities to sell their woodlands to individuals because forests owned by individuals were not clearly within its jurisdiction. Therefore, the maîtrise was continually engaged in conflict with communities that wanted to sell their collectively owned forests to pay village debts. The maîtrise also restricted the premature sale of firewood to ensure that wood supplies would not be depleted by communities anxious to defray current expenses. These sales could be sources of quick, short-term profits for communities, but they limited the availability of the older, more substantial lumber required by the navy. Individual owners, however, could not be dissuaded from attempting to benefit from the escalating profits to be gained from the sale of firewood. The rising value of firewood not only made more difficult the maîtrise's struggle to maintain communal possession of forests but invited usurpation and abuse of those forests. By the late eighteenth century, communities were becoming less able to prevent lords or wealthy peasants from usurping communal forests.

The opposition of the maîtrise to the alienation of communal forests and the premature sale of firewood deprived the community of control over its single most important source of revenue. Communities complained that communal liberty was being trampled on by an increasingly despotic administration—a complaint not without justification.[44] Ironically, this lack of liberty—the inability to sell communal properties—contributed to the communities' survival. The forests provided communities with a regular source of income; without them communities found it difficult to raise money for village expenditures. The knowledge that communal forests would remain intact encouraged wood merchants to offer communities remuneration for the right to harvest timber from the communal woods. This practice permitted large wood merchants to monopolize wood supplies, thus driving small dealers out of the market. Communities' contacts with large suppliers often helped them gain access to credit. This was a much more satisfactory method of meeting current expenses than the alienation of forests. It meant that communities did not lose possession of their communal properties, and when they did harvest the wood, they received the maximum value.

The intendant, like the maîtrise, did not allow communities to alienate communal properties. But they forbade the practice for different reasons. As we saw in Chapter 4, the intendant was concerned not with the navy but with ensuring that the payment of municipal charges did not interfere with the collection of royal taxes. To ensure that communities did not sell communal properties, the intendant supervised how communities used collective pasture, wastelands, and meadows. Communities in need of funds were encouraged to lease rather than to sell communal properties; if that was not sufficient, they could borrow money by using the anticipated rental income as collateral for loans. As a result, the communal patrimony was preserved and the village had access to credit. In addition, to prevent closed auctions in which communal property was leased to preferred customers at special prices, the intendant made sure that auctions were widely publicized and supervised by subdelegates.

Both the maîtrise and the intendant had a veto power over the use of communal funds. Communities that wanted to contract public works had to get the intendant's authorization. Builders' estimates had to be submitted to the intendant for approval and,

44. On those complaints, see Andrée Corvol, "Forêts et communautés en Basse-Bourgogne au XVIIIe siècle," *Revue historique* 256 (1976):15–36.

most important, communities could not pay directly for public works. The bills for any construction or repairs involving the village and the payments from the sale or lease of communal property were delivered to either the maîtrise or the intendant. The bills were paid only when the authorities were satisfied with the completed project. Builders who wanted to do business with communities had to prove that their price was right and that the quality would meet certain standards. If the intendant felt that the project was frivolous or that the price was excessive, he could exercise his veto. At the least, several years were usually required for a transaction to be arranged.[45] Communities complained, often bitterly, that the delays restricted communal independence.

Court expenses were one communal expenditure for which the intendant could not refuse authorization. The community's right to sue in the King's Court had a long history. During the early Middle Ages, access to the King's Court endowed communities with an increasingly well-defined legal identity. By the eighteenth century, the village's right to use the royal courts as a corporate body was firmly established. As communal properties became more valuable, communities exercised that right more frequently. If a community wanted to sue, all that was necessary was the opinion of two lawyers that the suit was well founded. An intendant could not deny authorization once their favorable opinion had been documented. The lawyers, in effect, could write their own paychecks, drawn on communal coffers. Both the intendant and the Estates of Burgundy resented the power the legal community had over the use of communal funds; both tried repeatedly to curtail that power, but in vain.

The question facing communities was how to employ their increased revenues. Distribution among the inhabitants—the most obvious answer—was not even a possibility, for the intendant routinely rejected such requests. His position was clear: collective revenues, like those properties from which they were derived, could be used only collectively. Requests for permission to use communal funds to pay royal taxes were also rejected.

45. For a fuller discussion of how royal bureaucrats supervised the management of communal properties and how those properties were affected by fiscal practices, see Chapter 4.

The latter policy was not so rigidly enforced. For example, in 1773 the inhabitants of Authume leased their commons for 400 livres in order to make payments still owed on the *taille*. In 1779 Châtelet asked for permission to pay the *taille* out of communal revenues. The intendant denied the request, claiming that it benefited the wealthy inhabitants more than the poor. Finally, the intendant did permit that community to pay the *capitation* out of communal revenues.[46]

Another possible use for collective revenues was agricultural improvements, such as drainage or villagewide enclosure.[47] These possibilities were never discussed, however. The funds obtained from wood sales that were not employed for construction or repairs were almost inevitably used to initiate court cases. Once a community had sold timber from the communal forests, it was not long before the lord would be called to court to defend his prerogatives. As one subdelegate put it, "The inhabitants of Thorey have forests, consequently they have lawsuits."[48] Communities were either going to court to protect their woods from their lords or selling timber to sue the lord. Many communities revived disputes that had been in litigation for years. The argument in a specific case often included references to a string of earlier disputes. Once grievances had gone to court, they became part of the community's patrimony. Just as two peasants sometimes inherited the vendettas between their fathers, communities frequently inherited their fathers' disputes with the seigneur.

The connection between the increase in communal revenues and the frequency of litigation was obvious to contemporaries. In 1776 a subdelegate remarked bluntly, "It is certain that the

46. In Authume, the intendant opposed the leasing of the commons to make up back payments on the *taille* because it benefited the rich more than the poor (AD, C-1743, intendant to community, reprimanding the community). In 1774 Châtelet paid 1,152 livres of the *taille* from communal revenues. In 1779 the intendant refused to allow Châtelet to pay its taxes out of communal revenues: "This would have many disadvantages and would result in much abuse in communities." In the end, he allowed Châtelet to pay its 1779 *capitation* out of the communal coffer (AD, C-1751, intendant to the community of Châtelet). In 1750 Flagey sold timber from the communal woods to pay taxes (AD, C-758, *délibération* of the village assembly).

47. Enclosure would have made little sense unless an entire area were regrouped.

48. AD, C-683, April 1788: Subdelegate to intendant.

communities which do not have communal revenues, or where the inhabitants are not well off, sue much less than those who have cash in hand and whose inhabitants are rich." To control the tendency of communities to institute court cases, he suggested preventing communities from using the funds obtained from the sale of wood or from the leasing of communal properties to pay court costs. He wrote to the intendant, "It is thus with the greatest circumspection that one should permit a community to pay the costs of a lawsuit out of communal revenues; if one obliged the inhabitants to pay by imposition, they would not so easily decide to sue again." The problem was that because court cases were financed out of communal funds, individuals felt "that it costs them nothing." Thus, "communities eagerly engage in court cases that are rather poorly founded."[49] In 1780, with the intendant's permission, the village of Montot sued its curé over the amount of the *menu dîme* ("dîme des menus grains"). The subdelegate complained that the *maison commune*, which was also the home of the school rector, needed repairs but that the inhabitants of Montot thought only of lawsuits. He concluded: "If the costs of the lawsuit are paid out of the money from the sale of wood, the inhabitants will not be corrected in their desire to go to court."[50]

THE LEGAL PROFESSION AND
THE DEVELOPMENT OF
A REVOLUTIONARY DISCOURSE

The growth of the legal profession also contributed to a heightening of tensions between lord and peasant. The number of legally trained professionals increased much faster in the eighteenth century than did the population as a whole.[51] This increase in the number of law graduates had the effect of encouraging both more intervention and more litigation. To earn a living, legal practitioners developed a wide range of new cases that they could present on behalf of communities. With

49. AD, C-1609, Jan. 1776: Procès-verbal, includes a letter to the intendant from the curé.
50. Ibid., 1780: Subdelegate to intendant.
51. Richard L. Kagan, "Law Students and Careers in Eighteenth-Century France," *Past and Present* 68 (Aug. 1975):38–72.

changes in legal theory, new precedents were being established that were often based on new theories and that increased the areas of possible intervention.

Legal officials (such as *greffiers* and notaries), with whom peasants had regular contact, were better educated than their predecessors and therefore generally possessed some background in law. Many notaries were in fact lawyers. Enterprising notaries made it their business to keep up with developments in the *bailliage* courts and in the parlement—hence their reputation among seigneurial officials as troublemakers. In writing up the minutes of a village assembly, a notary might include a suggestion that the inhabitants seek legal advice and question the traditional seigneurial exactions. When the inhabitants of Buffon formally denounced certain seigneurial rights, the lord quickly responded that the notary who had drawn up the denunciation must have instigated their act. Considering the agitation by the notary, he said, the community's sudden refusal to acknowledge long-standing seigneurial rights should not be surprising. He noted sarcastically, "This seems to have come out of the air, that is, if one puts aside the role of the notary." The notary, he claimed, "was able to make the poor, illiterate peasants believe whatever he wanted them to."[52] Seigneurs and their attorneys often singled out notaries for abuse in this way.

Keeping up with developments in the field of law allowed a local notary to make himself more valuable to communities and to justify an increase in his own fees. Pride, however, also moved local notaries to keep abreast of what was happening in the courts in the provincial capital, particularly in parlement. Having a knowledge of Dijon's legal events and personalities was a way to cut a good figure in local society. To understand this we need to look at the importance of the law courts in the provincial capital of Dijon.

One thousand families (5,000 individuals, or 20 percent of Dijon's population) owned offices in eighteenth-century Dijon. Court cases were an item of concern and conversation among families that had some contact with the law. Their interest in legal

52. "Factum pour les habitans de Buffon, défendeurs contre Messire Guillaume Languet-Robelin, seigneur de Rochefort." BM, Fonds Saverot, vol. 13, no. 21, n.d. (probably after 1704).

issues was intensified by the fact that the parlement was becoming the center of provincial consciousness. It had replaced the estates as the protector of and spokesman for provincial liberties.[53] As members of the most prestigious provincial institution, parlementaires were some of the most influential members of the town, and they belonged to the wealthiest families in the province.[54] The eighteenth-century residences built by the wealthy members of parlement were among the most prominent architectural additions to the city; they expressed in stone the legal profession's dramatic expansion, just as the cathedrals built in the twelfth century dramatized the church's growing wealth and authority.

Considering Dijon's position as an administrative and judicial capital, one can appreciate the stir that could be caused by a court case such as the one in 1785 between the duke of Saulx-Tavanes and the village of Lux.[55] Five years earlier, the king had made the count of Saulx-Tavanes a duke, in recognition of one of "the greatest houses in the realm," and had incorporated his seven villages in Burgundy into a duchy. No sooner had the duke's properties acquired special judicial status as a ducal *bailliage* than the village of Lux refused to acknowledge or to sign the lord's recently revised *terrier*. Their refusal was doubly annoying to the duke because as recently as 1781, he had retained a group of lawyers to renew his titles at a cost of three thousand to four thousand livres a year.[56] The duke's lawyers did not in-

53. On account of their fiscal responsibilities, the estates often cooperated with the intendant, thus compromising their traditional role as guardians of provincial liberty. On that role, see H. Drouot, *Mayenne et la Bourgogne.* 2 vols. (Paris, 1937), 1:94–102.

54. In 1770–1771 the parlement had 76 members and 5 honorary members. Most members were nobles and all were wealthy, for they owned both rural and urban property. In a study of 120 magistrates, Colombet found that the majority (92 percent) were either of noble birth or recently ennobled. However, 50 percent had inherited their seats in parlement from their fathers. In the second half of the eighteenth century, the parlementaires expanded and embellished their homes in Dijon. Colombet found that they also increased their rural holdings at the expense of both the nobility of the sword and the bourgeoisie. They had acquired many châteaux, parks, and large landed estates; in fact, ownership of land in the countryside became their principal form of wealth. See A. Colombet, *Les parlementaires bourguignons à la fin du XVIIIe siècle* (Dijon, 1937).

55. AD, C-1260: "Mémoire pour . . . duc de Saulx-Tavanes . . . contre . . . la communauté de Lux."

56. See Robert Forster, *The House of Saulx-Tavanes: Versailles and Burgundy, 1700–1830* (Baltimore, 1971), p. 94. Forster treats "the 'seigneurial reaction' practiced by the Duc de Saulx-Tavanes," pp. 92–108.

timidate the community and force it to quickly accept the *terrier*, as the duke had hoped, but rather seem to have had the opposite effect. When they offered the community several hours to review the new titles, the community demanded several months. The villagers found the majority (thirty-one) of the articles unacceptable. Could provincial society fail to notice that, shortly after he was made a duke, the wealthiest seigneur in the province was unable to bring his peasants to recognize his most fundamental seigneurial rights? What kind of example would this set for the subjects of less distinguished seigneurs? Similar rumbles of opposition were being heard in other villages.

Lawyers took both sides in these disputes. The same lawyer who helped a peasant community resist its seigneur might turn around and rewrite a *terrier* that enabled a lord to assert a claim to neglected seigneurial dues and to his ownership of previously communal properties.

Will an examination of their social origins help illuminate what motivated the lawyers? In the eighteenth century, most of the new lawyers had roots in urban areas. Only 2 percent of Dijon's law students came from peasant families, and sons of seigneurs seldom chose a career in law. Thus, the countryside was not well represented in the legal profession. The fathers of 50 percent of Dijon's law students were members of the legal profession, however.[57] Lawyers, regardless of their background, stood to gain from the escalating fees charged in suits between lords and peasants. Their willingness to work for either side needs no other explanation.

Nevertheless, other explanations have been offered. A number of writers have stressed that lawyers were often destitute and resented a system that allowed few opportunities for professional success. Bouchard, a Burgundian historian writing about Burgundy, described the lawyers who worked for peasants as professionally frustrated, living a hand-to-mouth existence (like many of their clients), and willing to take up any cause. The Robespierres of late-eighteenth-century France were recruited from this group. Distinct from the high nobility of the robe, confined to subordinate work, and despised by the parlemen-

57. Kagan, "Law Students."

taires, some of them seem to have hated privilege and the parlementary nobility as much as the peasants did. Thus the parlementary nobility and the expanding ranks of bourgeois lawyers had no community of interests. Bouchard insisted that the barrier to social mobility and the contempt of the high nobility of the robe for these lawyers weakened the solidarity of the legal profession. "The bar is now a closed career in which one feels stifled. Those who practice law no longer have anything in common with the magistrates before whom they appear, nor do they share in fortune, for theirs is modest; nor origin, for they know themselves to be sons of the people before a hereditary nobility; nor ambitions, for they know they will never be seated on fleurs-de-lys."[58]

In pointing out the differences between non-noble legal practitioners and the magisterial elite of the parlement, Bouchard may have overemphasized the divisions within the profession as a whole. Unity of the common practitioners may have existed despite that group's alienation from the high robe. Bouchard also ignored the fact that the same lawyers often worked alternately for both seigneurs and peasants, as did Ranfer. In discussing the frustrations of poverty and the absence of opportunities for professional advancement, Bouchard ignored the frustration that comes from persistently being unable to win cases for clients. Moreover, there is no evidence that lawyers ever went hungry.

Do the lawsuits instituted at the end of the eighteenth century suggest that lawyers were becoming revolutionary activists? Or, as Bouchard and, more recently, Maurice Gresset have argued, do they reflect the resentment of a disgruntled, frustrated group of individuals blocked in its efforts to enter the magistracy?[59] Bouchard asserted that lawyers' development of new ideas that would abet peasants in evading feudal dues was proof that the common practitioners had joined the peasants to form a class front against the seigneurs. The creation of legal theory by practitioners to serve the interests of clients was not

58. M. Bouchard, *De l'humanisme à l'Encylopédie: L'esprit public en Bourgogne sous l'Ancien Régime* (Paris, 1930), pp. 554–55; see also p. 855.

59. Maurice Gresset, *Gens de justice à Besançon: De la conquête par Louis XIV à la Révolution française, 1674–1789* (Paris, 1978). Gresset argues that resentment led the middle ranks of the legal profession to embrace radical ideas in 1789.

unique to the late eighteenth century. Jonathan Dewald noted
that the lawyers of the sixteenth-century Parlement of Rouen
were also creating legal theory. It was not class interest but
professionalism that motivated those lawyers. Dewald claimed
that in developing these ideas, lawyers were not revolutionary
ideologues but professionals doing what legal practitioners had
always done on behalf of all of their clients—even in private law,
where political considerations were minimal. Lawyers were also
seeking to encourage magistrates to make their decisions more
theoretically explicit. The parlement tried to keep secret the
theoretical premises of its decision making and presented its
decisions in nontheoretical terms so that they would be more
difficult to attack. Dewald reported that magistrates were "not
in the habit of giving reasons for [their] decisions."[60] In short, by
developing theory, lawyers were not attempting to foment political revolution but to overcome the judicial secrecy of the
magistrates and to win points for their clients. By its very nature, litigation frequently created new viewpoints that could be
used by future litigants.

The records of the court cases, however, suggest that the
changes in legal theory during the late eighteenth century were
reflected in the positions taken by the Constituent Assembly
during the Revolution. The peasants' lawsuits established a set
of categories into which the new grievances could be fitted and a
vocabulary with which they could be described.

One of the first seigneurial rights to be attacked by lawyers
employing the radically new kind of argumentation was the *four
banal.* In 1765 a lawyer working for the community of Tilchâtel
(in Champagne) explained: "All the authors concede that most
banalités derive from the violence of seigneurs. It is these rights,
which are not stipulated in the fiefs, that have always been
odious and that justice has attempted to restrain as much as
possible according to the maxim *odia sunt restringenda* [evil
things are to be restrained]."[61] Even though lawyers were questioning all seigneurial rights and privileges not stipulated in the
original fief, privilege still had its powerful defenders, such as

60. Jonathan Dewald, *The Formation of a Provincial Nobility* (Princeton,
N.J., 1980), pp. 32–33, 67.
61. AD, C-1976, Tilchâtel, 1765: Procès-verbal.

the seigneurial judge of Talmay who, in 1781, ordered forty-six inhabitants to demolish their private ovens and set stiff penalties for future infractions. This incensed and unified the community, which took its objection to the local *bailliage* court. When that court ruled in the lord's favor, the community, convinced that the lord had originally acquired this right by resorting to violence, and committed to redressing injustices of the past, hired two lawyers. They found the community's case to be sound because

1. The right of *banalité* is not a seigneurial right; it is not attached to the fief or to [its] justice, but it is an extraordinary right that can only subsist by virtue of an explicit convention. . . . It is a personal servitude, which, according to customary law, must be established by title.

2. Each individual who makes up a community cannot be forced by his community to obey an act that imposes a charge on him *ut singule* [as an individual].

The intendant reviewed the case, but before approving the community's petition to sue, he ordered the subdelegate to convoke a meeting of the village assembly to determine whether a majority favored bringing suit. In that meeting, 129 of 157 inhabitants voted to sue. The intendant then authorized the suit, commenting that "one could not desire a more numerous or unanimous deliberation." It is interesting to note that although only 46 inhabitants had ovens, 129 inhabitants favored instituting suit.[62]

The argument used against seigneurial *banalité* had implications for the *droit d'indire* as well. There was good reason to believe that it did not derive from the original fief either. In the most recent compilation of Burgundian customs (1740–1742), precedents for *indire* had been cited dating back to 1333.[63] As a

---

62. AD, C-833, Talmay, 1782, Jan. 1783–1786: Procès-verbal, includes *délibération* of the community, sentence of the *bailliage* court, and correspondence between the intendant and the subdelegate.

63. M. Bouhier, *Les coûtumiers du duché de Bourgogne avec les anciens coûtumes et observations de M. Bouhier, président à mortier*, 2 vols. (Dijon, 1742, 1746), 2:287–89, 319–20; Taisand, *Coûtumes générales du pays et duché de Bourgogne* (Dijon, 1698). Taisand and Bouhier, chroniclers of Burgundian customs, had different explanations of *indire*, but both supported seigneurial rights. Taisand argued that *indire* was an attribute of seigneurial justice; Bouhier viewed *indire* as originating in the charters of enfranchisement. In Taisand's interpretation, it was a personal obligation of all those subject to high justice. A seigneur could request *indire* from all who, "being his men were subject to his justice." Thus vassal, *mainmortable censitaire*, and *homme coûtumier* must all

right possessed by lords of high justice, however, it was not
generally recognized or regulated until the late seventeenth century. The speculation of jurists was that the right had originated
in the charters of enfranchisement. Serfs were not subject to
indire, but the Burgundian charters referred to the enfranchised
peasants as vassals, and it is possible that lords began to collect
indire from the community on the grounds that as their vassals,
these newly enfranchised serfs should bear the obligations of
liberty. But peasants now claimed that, as a responsibility associated with liberty, *indire* should not be forced: it should flow
from generosity alone. Its mandatory collection was extortion. A
group of lawyers arguing for their client, the village of Arc-sur-
Tille, advanced the position that *indire* was "at its origin purely
voluntary, offered in certain cases by vassals to their lords."
Moreover, they argued that the practice did not derive from the
charters of enfranchisement and that not all peasants had been
mainmortables.[64] Evidently, lords and peasants now disagreed on
a very fundamental quesion—the meaning of the word "vassal."

In 1785 a curé in the village of Thorey-sous-Charny wrote to
the intendant to protest the claim of the local seigneur, the
Comtesse de Brionne, for *indire.* Actually, it was a request for a
double *indire:* one for her daughter's marriage and one for her
dead husband's promotion to a chivalric order in 1758. The curé
appealed to the intendant to help the community resist the
lord's efforts "to extort such an unjust tribute." He described
indire as an "onerous and baroque imposition" and suggested
that "it would be interesting, perhaps, to investigate the origin
of the *droit d'indire* and to go back to the heart of the Republic
of Rome to discover it. It would be surprising, perhaps, to find a
simple tribute of gratitude from the clients of the Republic

---

pay as subjects of high justice. Bouhier pointed out, however, that "there is not
the least mention of *indire* in our oldest custom; it would seem that in the
Custom of 1459, *indire* was introduced in the interest of lords of high justice."
To explain this absence from the earlier compilation of customs, Bouhier asserted that *indire* was not an original seigneurial right but the result of a later
contract between lords and peasants. Assuming that all Burgundian peasants had
once been *mainmortables,* Bouhier argued that all were subject to *indire.* In
application, there was little difference between the theories of the two authors.
The parlement could cite both to defend seigneurial rights against peasant rights.

64. AD, E-1743 and C-459: "Débat avec le seigneur pour le droit d'indire."

transformed into a very onerous duty for the French peasant."[65]
The argumentation is somewhat fanciful, but the point is that
indire was resented on the grounds that, although it had originated as a courtesy, it had become arbitrary and the amounts
exorbitant.

The inhabitants of Buffon used a similar argument in a case
concerning *guet et garde*. They asserted that "the right of personal *guet et garde* is one that was introduced by the necessity
of wars, and by the need that seigneurs had for the villagers to
defend and to guard their châteaux, and the need that villagers
had to find in the châteaux of their seigneurs a sure haven for
their effects and for their persons." The seigneurs' use of force
had transformed what had begun as a voluntary and reciprocal
agreement into an onerous and mandatory imposition. The community's lawyers asserted that "because its original motivation
was only a sort of tacit agreement between seigneurs and
villagers, founded on the reciprocal need they had of each other
in case of imminent peril, it follows that everything that tends
to charge or inconvenience the latter [villagers], without bringing them any utility, is regarded as having been usurped by violence and in consequence odious."[66] Just as in the arguments
against the *four banal* and *indire*, the peasants were arguing that
this seigneurial right had originated in times of disorder and
when weak kings permitted lords to resort to violence.

Lawyers working for communities also began insisting that
seigneurial rights had to be uniform throughout the province.
Rights that were not uniform were *préscriptibles*. Despite their
antiquity, they could be curtailed simply because they were inconsistent with provincewide custom. This was exactly what
the lawyers of Lux were claiming in that community's dispute
with the duke of Saulx-Tavanes: "The seigneurial rights that
exceed [custom] in one territory that which custom authorizes
in the others must be restrained." In effect, lawyers were arguing
that, regardless of a previous contract, peasants were not bound
to honor rights exceeding or contradicting principles established
for the province as a whole. In his defense, the duke's lawyers

65. AD, C-1709: Letter from the curé dated 25 Nov. 1785, pp. 1–2.
66. BM, Fonds Saverot, vol. 13, no. 21.

insisted that "because these rights are based on an individual contract, it is fair to abide by the titles that establish them."[67] The community's position was novel, but premature; it did not influence the outcome of the case. Although communities were losing most of the cases, the important point is that having gotten seigneurial lawyers to address their claims, the peasants and their lawyers were able to define the terms of the dialogue, and they extended the range of discourse to include concepts whose implications would be detrimental to seigneurial rights.

More important than the attack on any single seigneurial right was the fact that the lord's *terrier*, the juridical basis of his traditional right to collect seigneurial dues, was being challenged. Lawyers working for peasant communities insisted that provincial and national laws should take precedence over the lord's *terrier* in court. Just as the National Convention would later claim that it could override particular and historic privileges in making laws for all of France, lawyers after the 1770s claimed that the particular rights of seigneurs stated in their *terriers* could be contradicted by laws that applied to the entire province. Although lords were still able to defend most of their rights and privileges, they had to agree to a discussion of terms and concepts developed by the opposition. Thus, the status of seigneurial titles had shifted dramatically—their validity could now be challenged. The new legal battles were important because what had been based on custom and tradition now became a problem to be discussed.

In the legal briefs one cannot easily distinguish the lawyers' attitudes from those of their peasant clients. Lawyers and peasants had different reasons for challenging seigneurial authority, however. Lawyers could increase their fees; peasants could hope to reduce their feudal dues. Invoking the idea of a class alliance to account for their collaboration is gratuitous; advancing the notion that hostility to privilege motivated the lawyers is likewise gratuitous. Lawyers were being paid to do a job and utilized whatever legal arguments were at hand.

The assault on seigneurial rights had only just begun when

---

67. AD, C-1260: "Mémoire pour Charles-François Casimir, duc de Saulx-Tavanes, . . . le 27 Août 1785."

the Constituent Assembly attacked the entire seigneurial system in 1789. The Revolution accomplished in months what lawyers might have taken decades to achieve in the courts. But the language used by the Constituent Assembly to dissolve the feudal system in 1789 was already being used with increasing regularity in court cases that pitted lord against peasant during the last half of the eighteenth century. The lawsuits of the 1770s and 1780s introduced the language used on the night of August 4, 1789.[68]

A DISRUPTIVE FORCE: THE GROWTH OF THE ROYAL BUREAUCRACY

The spirit of communal independence and the readiness of communities to take the seigneur to court coincided with the intendant's more active intervention in village affairs. The institution of a court action was one area in which the intendant's supervision and consent were critical. The intendant's endorsement of a community's case frequently provided the final incentive for a community to stand firm against its seigneur. For example, in 1771 the intendant, mistrustful of the seigneur's efforts to rewrite the *terrier*, instructed the inhabitants of Thorey-sous-Charny to insist on examining the lord's titles. Intendant Amelot wrote to the subdelegate that a thorough investigation of the titles should be undertaken, "all the more rightly since it was already discovered that M. de Gamay intends to create certain *droits* which have never existed."[69] In 1782, when giving permis-

68. The changing language and strategy used in the late-eighteenth-century court cases between lord and peasant is still largely an unexplored area, research in which promises substantial rewards for those seeking to understand the Revolution. The problem is not the dearth but the abundance of sources. Access to the material is barred by its sheer volume and lack of organization. Because it has yet to find an archivist, the history of these cases has not found a historian. The *facta* collected in the Fonds Saverot and Fonds Carnot in Dijon's public library are the most important and best-cataloged source, but they are not complete enough to allow anything more than a preliminary treatment of the subject. Those collections rarely contain *facta* from both sides in a dispute. Nor do they present the decision of the judge. But they do suggest tendencies and raise questions. Thorough research of this unexplored area depends on the still uninventoried archives of the parlement.

69. AD, C-1709, Thorey-sous-Charny, 1771: "Débats avec M. de Canay, coseigneur de Thorey, au sujet de la reconnaissance de ses droits." Includes correspondence of subdelegate with the intendant.

sion to the inhabitants of Talmay to dispute the lord's *four banal*, the intendant suggested that since the community was going to court, they question as well "whether they must suffer
the servitude of the right of passage that M. de Talmay claims to
have in the meadow of the said place."[70] After losing their case
in the local *bailliage* court, the inhabitants of Saulx-le-Duc were
reluctant to continue their suit disputing the lord's *terrier*. The
community's lawyer, M. Pataille, wrote to the intendant asking
him to persuade the community to carry its case to the next
level of jurisdiction.[71] Obviously, Pataille had some reason to
believe that the intendant would support the community's case
and could influence its decision.

The intendant's intervention on the side of peasant rights was
equally direct in 1774, when M. de Flammerans, the seigneur of
Missery, asked the inhabitants to sign a new *terrier*. Because the
lord had refused to consider reducing an annual fee for *guet et
garde*, the community hesitated and demanded more time so
that a lawyer could review the titles. First, the community
needed the intendant's permission to impose a *taille négotialle*
to finance the preliminary review. The intendant's approval
angered Flammerans. The subdelegate reported: "There was no
recourse other than a tax. The inhabitants asked for it, [and] to
refuse them the tax would have been to take away their means
of self-defense; that is what determined the ordinance of September 30, 1774; and that was what angered M. de Flammerans
because it put weapons into the hands of his inhabitants against
him."

The review suggested that the legal basis of some of the articles in the new *terrier* was not verifiable from the lord's titles.
The lord was unwilling to negotiate, however; he argued that his
lawyers were experts who could not be mistaken. The community was left with no recourse but to seek satisfaction in court.
It presented to the intendant a *délibération* in which fifty of
fifty-eight inhabitants asked for permission to collect a tax to
pay a lawyer to research the lord's titles. In endorsing this second request, the intendant further angered Flammerans, who

70. AD, C-833, Talmay, 1782: Procès-verbal; comments from the intendant,
p. 5.
71. AD, C-1223, Saulx-le-Duc, 1782: Pataille to intendant.

then accused him of intriguing with the inhabitants of Missery. The lord decided to make a personal visit to Missery to persuade the inhabitants to abandon their suit. The subdelegate observed that apparently "M. de Flammerans, seeing that he had not been able to abuse the good faith of M. Amelot [the intendant], schemed in his parish. Besides, he was not afraid of showing himself to be soliciting for the opponents, though from decency he should not have appeared to take any side in this affair or to involve himself in it." Flammerans successfully intimidated forty-three inhabitants, who petitioned to have the case withdrawn. The intendant rejected that petition because he was certain the seigneur had pressured those forty-three inhabitants to sign. Since he was certain that the community's grievances were well founded, he ordered the inhabitants who did not sign to continue the suit and instructed them that communal funds could still be used to finance the case. The intendant commented: "The more one examines this affair, the more one sees reign the pettiness and spirit of intrigue that the seigneur of Missery has not feared exhibiting from the outset of this dispute and that was all the more ridiculous since he [the lord] was shown a *délibération* of fifty inhabitants who wished to sue against eight who did not."[72]

Intendants often intervened to help communities resist requests for *guet et garde*. In 1766 the inhabitants of Chazelle were asked by their seigneur, M. Voisenet, to repair the doors of the château. The seigneur even agreed to contribute half of the expenses if the village agreed to rebuild the door totally in iron. He further promised to discharge them from all repairs for one hundred years. Despite these inducements, Intendant Amelot ordered the community to delay until an expert could report on the state of the doors and advise the best way to repair them.[73] In 1774 the subdelegate commented that the request by the seigneur of Missery for *guet et garde* should be treated with caution since the seigneur had transformed the structure into a "château agréable"

---

72. AD, C-1651, Missery, 1774: Debates with the seigneur over the "reconnaissance générale des droits seigneuriaux."

73. AD, C-1649, Chazelle, 1766: Procès-verbal containing "Débats avec le seigneur et les habitants de Chazelle-l'Echo, au sujet des réparations de la porte et des menus emparements du château."

at the inhabitants' expense. "The changes to the château," the subdelegate argued, "had altered the nature of the place, and since it could no longer offer shelter to the inhabitants, they should be liberated from all maintenance expenses." He said he thought the community could find legal grounds for refusing payment. Nevertheless, the village inhabitants feared the seigneur might increase the amount of his request and were about to consent. The intendant objected. He insisted that as protection for the community, at least an eighteen-year limit be placed upon the seigneur's right to ask again for payment. To further protect the inhabitants, the intendant ordered a survey of the present state of the moat, as well as an additional report once the work was completed. After the affair was terminated, the subdelegate made clear that he strongly objected to the seigneur's request: "The continuation of *guet et garde* is of dubious utility. Public tranquility does not require the maintenance of those old fortresses, most of which today have become no more than country residences; their present appointments in no way correspond to their original functions."[74] In 1781 the community of Chauvirey reported that it would pay the charges requested for *guet et garde* "to avoid legal costs that could be considerable." Intendant Feydeau remarked to the inhabitants of Diancy and Jonchery, who, unlike those of Chauvirey, had refused to pay, that they had taken a much wiser course in seeking legal consultation. He added that "it seems the inhabitants of Chauvirey would acquit themselves without reflection. It is the wisdom of the tutors of communities to stop them." The intendant insisted that acquiescence to the lord now would only invite new charges later, so he ordered the community of Chauvirey to obtain the advice of two lawyers.[75] In 1782 the seigneurial agent at the château of Vianges requested contributions from the fourteen villages that once had depended on the château for protection in times of danger. The intendant was incensed. He wrote to the subdelegate:

I notice that he [the seigneurial agent] has actively but uselessly prosecuted these communities. It would have been easy to avoid those prosecu-

74. AD, C-1651, Missery: Subdelegate to intendant, 24 Feb. 1777.
75. AD, C-655: Judgment of the intendant, 1781. "Obligation des habitants de Jonchery et de Chauvirey, de contribuer aux menus emparements du château de Vianges."

tions if only I had been consulted directly. I am persuaded that Madame la marquise de Vianges would disapprove if only she were informed. Please inform her agent that I am very ill-disposed toward his conduct and that I recommend that he does not put any further money into pursuing his object. The expenses will only fatigue the communities without procuring for him the funds he desires. After all, he can only receive payment if I authorize the community to raise the funds. Thus, you should try to make him understand that the interests of his constituents require that he address me, and not the inhabitants.[76]

The intendant wanted to protect communities from unreasonable imposts, but he also wanted to prevent future lawsuits that would drain communal resources. Consenting to an illegal *reconnaissance* or an unsound claim to *triage* would only lead to future conflicts. Thus, the intendant encouraged communities to be sure that seigneurial claims were well established in the hope that such issues might be resolved once and for all. It was to this end, and not to foment trouble between lord and peasant, that intendants recommended that communities ask a lawyer to examine and to verify the lord's titles before agreeing to a claim to *triage* or *reconnaissance*. For example, in 1781 the intendant recommended that to prevent future strife, the community of Villers-la-Faye carefully investigate the lord's titles before consenting to his claim to one-third of the communal woods under the right of *triage*. The intendant wrote: "It is much better that the inhabitants require from now on the verification of the seigneur's titles than to cede to him what he requests today." It would be much better to be sure now than to be sorry later. He added, "I painfully observe communities sustaining lawsuits, but I must not allow them to give up their properties without just cause."[77]

The preceding examples would seem to indicate that the intendants were unsympathetic to feudal exactions such as seigneurial *banalités*. Although they strongly believed in protecting private property, the intendants would probably have distinguished between feudal property and purely economic property such as rent. Such distinctions were already being made by the

76. AD, C-1646, Bar-le-Regulier: Intendant to subdelegate, March 1782. "Imposition pour la réparation des ponts et fossés du château de Vianges."

77. AD, C-1551, Villers-la-Faye, July 1781: "Contestation avec le seigneur au sujet du droit de triage."

Parlement of Paris, but there was a tendency for the Parlement of Dijon to refuse to cite the precedents of the Parisian parlement. Leaders of the Burgundian parlement, such as its last *premier président*, Bouhier, opposed following the lead of Paris and insisted that all rulings of courts in Burgundy be consistent with Burgundian customs. Despite such strong opposition from the parlementary magistrates, lawyers in Dijon cited decisions handed down by the Parlement of Paris on behalf of their clients. From the evidence it is not clear whether the intendants consistently supported one side or the other in these broader disputes over the autonomy of Burgundian jurisprudence. Such tactics as citing the precedents of the Parisian parlement had at least their tacit approval, for the intendants authorized many cases that were built upon arguments originating in the Parisian court. This is not to say that the intendants believed the Parlement of Paris should dictate the laws of the nation. It does suggest that, in decisions concerning the seigneurs' right to collect dues in general, the intendants favored the most liberal jurisprudence.[78]

The growth of the intendant's power had a far-reaching influence on relationships between lord and peasant. We have just seen the effect on such relationships of the intendant's direct and immediate support of communal rights. More significant is that the king's servants were increasing their power at the expense of seigneurial authority. By the second half of the eighteenth century, whenever matters concerning village finances were at issue, the community could bypass its lord and correspond directly with the king's bureaucratic representative in the province. This trend paved the way for the collapse of the seigneur's leadership of the village. In the late eighteenth century, the lord and his agents had little contact with the daily routines of village government. The village *syndic* was now directly responsible to the intendant and not to the seigneurial judge. The bureaucracy never became so strong and efficient that it could eliminate entirely the seigneur's local role, but it was strong enough to give the peasants an alternative to his authority in the

78. See AD, C-833, 1782: Procès-verbal, p. 2. Also AD, C-747, Cheuge, March 1789: "Débat avec le fermier du seigneur pour la banalité du four," with decision of the intendant.

village. As a result of being able to choose between two alternatives, the community became more assertive.

In the early seventeenth century, Burgundian seigneurs still protected their peasants against marauding armies, brigands, and even royal taxes. The seigneurs provided, as well, a wide range of administrative and judicial services, and in the Estates of Burgundy, they represented the villages before the king. In the eighteenth century, seigneurs performed few such services. Moreover, many of the seigneur's administrative functions were now performed by the intendant. And, in a complete reversal of roles, the intendant was beginning to protect inhabitants from seigneurial exactions. In many areas, the intendant's protection was more extensive than the seigneurs' had ever been. The intendant attempted to find ways to indemnify communities that were victims of natural disasters.[79] By improving market communications, the intendant sought to guarantee food supplies in time of shortage. In the seventeenth century, the devastation of roaming mercenary soldiers, living off the land, had been more serious than that of plague or famine, and these men were often the harbinger of both. Now the intendant imposed strict discipline on the troops and kept them out of the villages.

Since the intendant and his subdelegate had taken over many of the seigneurie's administrative functions, contact between the village inhabitants and the seigneurie had degenerated into disputes with the estate managers and the wealthy *fermiers* (seigneurial revenue collectors) who cultivated his domain. They were outsiders whose interests clashed with those of the village. Stating that suits against the lord were contrary to their interests, they often refused to share the costs. The village argued that all who possessed communal rights or shared the use of communal properties had a stake in the outcome. In 1774 three inhabitants of St. Martin-de-la-Mer who described themselves as

79. In fact, communities had come to expect aid from the intendant. In 1786 the curé of Talant wrote to the intendant that the winegrowers in his parish were "ruined this year by harvesting the grapes at exorbitant cost and by not selling nonquality wine, which remains in the cellars. They await impatiently that the goodness of a wise and swift government come to their aid and obtain for them the means that it [the government] decides will be the best to relieve them from the misery into which they have fallen" (AD, C-15, subdelegation of Dijon, parish of Talant).

"lessees, or cultivators of the seigneur's land," along with the farmer of the lord's revenues, refused to pay the costs of the community's lawsuit against its seigneur, which the community had lost. These four claimed that they were "so completely recognized as outsiders that the community has never called them for any assembly." They added that they were "being forced to pay a portion of the fees of a lawsuit, from which they will never be able to draw any advantage and from which they will profit if the seigneur wins." The community insisted that

> It seems hard on a *fermier* to be forced to take sides against his seigneur for the sole purpose of preserving the public good; it seems equally hard on an individual to be constrained to join a lawsuit for the preservation of communal rights when his residence is only accidental and momentary. But these considerations must cease from the moment that the *fermiers* or the seigneur's representatives enjoy the same rights as the other inhabitants; everything that relates to the public good is shared with them, and it is just by virtue of their participation in the advantages that result from tenancy that they contribute to the expense of maintaining these rights. It is a charge that falls on the entire body, of which he is a part.

The four claimed that, as *"fermiers* of the seigneurie," they did not enjoy the same rights as the other inhabitants; they enjoyed only those rights belonging to the seigneur. Nine years later, the court ruled in the community's favor because determination of who should pay the *taille négotialle* for the court costs was based on the rolls for the *taille royale*. "It is necessary to order that the imposition be made in proportion to an individual's tax assessment and that it be demanded from all the individuals included on the tax rolls."[80] This decision of the court invited the four to countersue on the grounds that since they paid the *taille royale*, they should enjoy the other privileges that the community enjoyed. This case was typical. The lord's *fermier* usually did not have *incolate* rights (privileges associated with village residency) and therefore could not use communal properties. Yet the community expected him to help pay the costs of lawsuits, as did the other inhabitants. Such disputes only

---

80. AD, C-1662, Saint Martin-de-la-Mer, May 1774 to 21 June 1775, 24 Feb. 1776, 27 June 1776, 23 July 1776, 11 Jan. 1777 to 1783: Procès-verbal. A similar dispute arose in 1781 in Flagey-les-Auxonnes.

intensified the antagonism between the *fermier* and the community; they are a further indication that the community and the seigneurie were moving in opposite directions.

Considering the increase in the intendant's activities, it should be no surprise that in the late 1760s, petitions by communities to the intendant often began, "You who are the protector of communities."[81] This sentiment and expression had once been reserved for the seigneur alone. Not only had the intendant replaced the seigneur as the community's protector, but he was now the village's link with the crown; the lord no longer acted as mediator between the king and the village. It was by petitioning the intendant that a community gained access to the king's authority. The lord still belonged to a social elite headed by the king as first gentleman of gentlemen, but in the province the intendant alone represented the king's preeminent authority as sovereign.

The events after 1789 suggest that what the communities had come to expect from the intendant perhaps exceeded what the intendant could actually do for them. Help in limiting or abolishing seigneurial exactions was foremost among these expectations. In January 1770, when the new seigneur of Grenant made unprecedented demands on the community, the inhabitants wrote to the intendant, asking him to "interpose your powerful authority to make these persecutions stop and to see that justice is done."[82] Communities even criticized the intendant for supporting those seigneurial rights that remained intact. For example, in 1785 the curé of Thorey-sous-Charny wrote to the intendant protesting the seigneur's doubling of his parish's dues under *droit d'indire*. He emphasized that "we have only one resource [referring to the intendant's protection] . . . [and can

81. For example, in 1772 the inhabitants of Bligny began a letter to the intendant with "You are the protector of communities" (AD, C-906).

82. AD, C-659, Grenant, 1770: Letter from community to intendant, signed by "les habitans sachant signer [the inhabitants who know how to sign their names]." The document seems to have been sent door to door and signed secretly. It was not the result of an assembly meeting, since the new seigneur did not allow the village assembly to meet; he hoped in this way to block resistance to his program of reinforcing the collection of seigneurial dues. The subdelegate explained the inhabitants' plight to the intendant: "They could not oppose him as a community because they were forbidden to assemble, and . . . to discuss anything would continually expose each of them to the threat of lawsuits, which would ruin them to the point that they would have to leave the area."

make only] one last effort against tyranny." The curé was disturbed because the intendant had not seemed eager for the community to seek redress in the courts; he expected that in the name of justice the intendant would intervene on the community's behalf. By not doing so, he warned, "the protector of communities is made out to be the oppressor."[83] The implication here was that if the intendant failed to aid communities, he was supporting seigneurial rights.

CONCLUSION

Between 1750 and 1770, the relationship between the village and the seigneurie was altered. According to legal theory, which was based on conditions that had long ceased to exist, lord and peasants were bound by mutual obligations; the peasants paid dues and rendered services in exchange for the lord's protection and administration. By midcentury, however, the king's bureaucracy had taken over most of the seigneur's functions that might have justified his collection of dues. With the seigneur's political, administrative, and judicial functions steadily decreasing, all that continued to bind peasants to their lord was a system of feudal dues. The seigneur was no longer the leader but a mere landed proprietor; the seigneurie was but a business. Nowhere is the communities' changed perception of the seigneurie clearer than in the disputes over *guet et garde*. The seigneurial residences of the eighteenth century, surrounded by parks that separated them from the village, reminded the inhabitants that the châteaux no longer symbolized the lords' leadership and protection but rather represented their wealth as private citizens. The château walls that had once bound the community to the seigneurie now represented what divided them.

The village had also changed. The state bureaucrats had codified and standardized village procedures so that villages could be easily controlled from a distance. The reconstructed villages were then better able to function and to regulate themselves. In addition to increasing the village's capacity for self-government, the bureaucracy's more efficient supervision had the effect of

83. AD, C-1709, Thorey-sous-Charny, 25 Nov. 1785: Curé to intendant.

changing the community's perception of the seigneurie. Peasants were no longer dependent on the lord for protection or administration and began to see seigneurial dues as vestiges of days when the king was not yet strong enough to protect the village from violence and oppression by the nobility. According to this new interpretation, lordship had originated in violence and was being maintained by force.

To contemporaries, it was this new interpretation of feudal rights, not the frequency of the court cases between lord and peasants, that was most alarming. Peasants were not limiting their attacks to specific traditional rights but were going much further and challenging conditions communities had never before questioned and finding them intolerable. Historians of Burgundy and of France have overlooked this aspect of the legal disputes and have generally argued that displays of antiseigneurialism were a response to new estate management policies. Their interpretation of peasant contention on the eve of the Revolution needs to be reevaluated, for there is little evidence that the feudal levies increased in the twenty years before 1789; therefore, the innovation of and aggression by the seigneurs did not coincide with this spate of court cases. In fact, when Burgundian historian Saint-Jacob wrote of reaction, he was referring to the years between 1730 and 1740. If ever there was an increase in feudal dues, it was in the seventeenth century. That increase was certainly greater than any the eighteenth century witnessed, yet it occurred without the opposition that was aroused by the comparatively smaller increase of the eighteenth century.

The view that the increase in feudal levies alone accounts for the tensions and the litigation is inadequate because it does not explain the most interesting and problematic new legal developments: the expanding scope of the litigation and the radical transformation of the legal discourse. To say that this legal challenge by communities was prompted solely by the changed economic policies of the seigneurs misses the point; such an interpretation neither anticipates nor explains the changing language and strategy used in the court cases. Yet, it was just those changes in language and strategy that most alarmed contemporaries. In this chapter I have argued that the devastating attack launched by lawyers and peasant communities on the historical and moral foundations of seigneurial authority can be traced to the changing aspirations and self-definition of communities. In this analysis, the rise of the bureaucratic state, not innovative ways of collecting feudal dues, was the critical destabilizing force. The absorption of the village into the bureaucratic structure of the absolutist state gave communities a new self-image.

Six

The Limits of Reform

Believing common rights to be harmful to agriculture, the central government issued edicts beginning in the 1760s that allowed landowners to challenge these rights. Liberal historians of the French Revolution cite the edicts to argue that the state was an agent of modernization and liberal reform. Historians with a socialist orientation cite the same edicts to demonstrate that the state was collaborating with wealthy peasants and aristocrats to promote capitalism by crushing the old peasant communities. Both of these groups link increased state power with the forces of historical progress, modernization, and capitalist expansion. In focusing on what the state hoped to accomplish via royal legislation, both liberal and socialist historians have ignored a very important point.

Far from enforcing the edicts, the royal representatives in the provinces—the intendants—actually aided communities in preserving communal rights. The intendants restricted the sale of communal properties, discouraged communities from attempting enclosure, and regularly found reasons to prevent the partitioning of common lands. The bureaucrats also intervened to defend the equal distribution of firewood from village forests. When orders were issued from Paris requiring that communal firewood be distributed according to tax payments, the bureaucracy instead helped communities maintain the allotment of equal portions. Likewise, while the King's Council was calling for the curtailment of gleaning rights, the king's provincial administrators protected the right of the poor to collect the stubble on the harvested fields. Yet these administrators were not representatives of local interests who had drifted away from royal control; they were members of the same King's Council that issued the orders for restructuring agriculture. The intendants had been sent to the provinces to represent the king and were responsible to him alone.

CONSTRAINTS IMPOSED BY MEDIEVAL STATE BUILDING

First we will analyze the process by which the kings of France tried to transform a mosaic French state into a uniform nation to understand why, in the eighteenth century, policy set in Paris had come to be very different from that implemented in the provinces. The politics of early state building led the crown into institutional commitments that were to restrict the choices available in the eighteenth century. We will see that in attempting to establish a relationship with the village, the crown was responding to political imperatives that had arisen quite independently of the pressures for agrarian individualism. The crown's first efforts to establish a relationship with the communities were part of the efforts of the Capetian monarchs to overcome the fragmentation of political power and to unify the nation. The crown called upon the communities to assist it in building a centralized state. In the long run, the king needed to link up with a local body in order to bypass the jurisdiction of the lords. The crown's initial gains were in the areas of justice and finance, which became the pillars of the early modern state.

To win the loyalty of their peasant subjects, the kings of France during the Middle Ages began to establish a system of royal courts that would be superior to the local seigneurial courts. The royal courts took over many areas of jurisdiction where seigneurial courts had not been effective. Next, the monarchy developed special procedures by which litigants could bypass the seigneurial courts and go directly to a royal court. The dictum that all rights of justice originated as a grant from or a confirmation by the king provided the royal courts with a justification for taking precedence over all other courts in the realm.

The royal courts gradually recognized the communities as proper litigants and thus conferred a legal identity upon them. In the jurisprudence of these courts, village assemblies could make a contract, authorize expenditures, and even sue the local seigneur. The assemblies were also authorized to engage in common business transactions and to initiate lawsuits in defending those transactions. The courts recognized that villages could own property collectively, as corporations, and could elect representatives if the *plus saine et majeure partie* participated, that is, by majority decision. Collective ownership of property was permitted to all bodies defined as *universitates*, which included monasteries, religious orders, and guilds as well as villages. The definition of the term *universitas* was suitably loose[1]—it is unlikely that royal authorities wanted it to have too precise a meaning. The vagueness permitted individual officials to apply it as they saw fit. By the fourteenth century, communities were legally defined as corporations and entered the mainstream of administrative law. In acknowledging the communities' corporate identity, the crown may have done nothing more than officially recognize the relationships and procedures that already had a de facto local significance, for they had been established in the community's relationship with the seigneur.

To justify extending fiscal authority over the peasantry, the crown again asserted its supremacy in the feudal chain of command by claiming that the right of lords to collect various dues or *banalités* was a privilege granted by the monarchy. According to this view, seigneurs were collecting funds as the king's surrogates. But it was not until the end of the Hundred Years' War that the Estates General confirmed that the crown could tax the peasantry directly, at least until the English were driven from French soil. The crown never surrendered that prerogative.

The king did not develop mechanisms to tax peasants as individuals, however. Such mechanisms would have required the establishment and maintenance of a large body of accountable officials at the local level, which was too expensive. Moreover, it was

1. Pierre Michaud-Quantin, *Universitas: Expressions du mouvement communautaire dans le moyen âge latin* (Paris, 1970).

easier to assess the peasant community and to hold it collectively responsible for its individual members, especially since the habits of collective responsibility had already been formed. Seigneurs had earlier found it more convenient to hold the community responsible for the sums owed by its individual members. Should the community refuse to honor its obligations, the property of the wealthiest members of that community could be impounded by the seigneur. The wealthy inhabitants would then have to find some way of recovering their losses from the community. The seigneur's agent had enforced this practice, called *contrainte soli- daire,* to ensure that the seigneur's dues were paid.

Asserting the priority of the king's fiscal prerogatives, his officials insisted on the community's freedom from seigneurial supervision in matters concerning royal taxation. Theoretically, communities could assemble without the lord's permission to discuss such matters. However, it is probable that meetings of the village assembly, for whatever purpose, were supervised by seigneurial agents. The crown's assertion of the village's independence in fiscal matters may at first have been no more than a claim, but its significance was that later, the crown could assert the village's fiscal independence of the seigneurie to justify extending royal authority over the village.

Thus, the medieval kings of France took some important steps toward asserting the crown's authority over matters pertaining to both national and local policymaking. However, during the Middle Ages the local authority of the king's officials never infringed on the lord's jurisdiction over communities. Seigneurial agents continued to audit all details of village administration, and this function remained the basis of seigneurial authority. Although the central authority had made much progress in the areas of finance and justice, not until the late seventeenth century did the crown begin to compete with the lord for administrative leadership of the communities.

ABSOLUTISM AND STATE FINANCE
DURING THE REIGN OF LOUIS XIV

The seventeenth and eighteenth centuries saw the rapid extension of royal authority throughout France. The corporate rights and responsibilities of villages (such as ownership of common lands, common-use rights with regard to private lands, and collective responsibility for taxes) also received their most complete elaboration in royal jurisprudence during this period. Citing medieval precedents, royal policymakers designed a complex legal and administrative system to ensure that the village's corporate responsibilities and properties would come under direct royal supervision. The impetus for increasing supervision over taxpayers was changing military technology: the need to create, discipline, and maintain standing armies had greatly increased the costs of war to the state.[2] By taxing the resources of its citizens, French kings could finance and field the largest army in Europe. The key to that power lay in state finance, which Louis XIV spoke of in his *mémoires* as "that which moves and activates the whole great body of the monarchy." In 1661, however, when Louis began his personal reign, that "great body" was moribund; the crown was on the verge of bankruptcy. Many advised against raising the taxes levied on the peasants on the grounds that, thanks to Louis's predecessors, they were already paying enough. The tax increases imposed by Richelieu and Mazarin had often unleashed rebellions so severe that, despite social divisions, entire provinces had united against the king. Wishing to avoid a renewal of such opposition, Louis embarked on another course. By offering lower interest rates on future

2. One solution was to raise revenues to pay for mercenary troops and supplies. This could be done in Western Europe but not in Eastern Europe. In the absence of mobile urban wealth and lacking an internally developed market economy that could generate substantial funds for the state, rulers in Eastern Europe could not expand their fiscal capabilities sufficiently. Therefore, they redefined the social and economic obligations of their subjects. Consider the two states that were to become the great powers of the East: the Russian and Prussian states. Both increased the services required of the nobility and the peasantry. The lords were committed to state service and peasants were tied to the land. The nobility was thus militarized and peasant serfdom was reinforced. Unpaid military service was demanded of each peasant, in addition to laboring on the lord's estate. The lords acted as both estate managers and military chiefs. Unlike the states of Eastern Europe, France had other options. Neither lords nor peasants had to be compelled to serve in the military, for the French state could raise funds for an army by drawing on the kingdom's abundant mercantile and urban wealth. The highly developed market economy had put a great deal of that wealth into circulation. Even the peasants were governed by the market, where they bought and sold food and labor services. See George Clark, *The Seventeenth Century*, 2d ed. (Oxford, 1947; reprint 1970), p. 98. See also Michael Roberts, "The Military Revolution, 1560–1660," in *Essays in Swedish History* (London, 1967), pp. 195–226; and David Bien, "Uselessness, Survival, and the State: A Problem in Comparative Perspective" (manuscript).

loans and restructuring the tax farms, the crown achieved substantial savings. The king even repudiated part of the existing
debt by reducing interest rates on loans already contracted.

The most important action to increase royal revenues was
carried out not in Paris but at the level of the village. Louis XIV
appointed commissioners—the intendants—to regulate village
finance and to ensure that the crown received a larger portion of
what the village produced. He also attempted to diminish those
charges on the village whose effect was to divert surplus from
the land to creditors other than the state. During the preceding
century, villages had contracted extensive debts to private creditors. This made tax collection more difficult, and it meant that
the king was getting a smaller portion of the village's surplus
income. The problem was particularly evident in Burgundy. A
century of warfare (1550–1650) and pillage by mercenary armies
that lived off the land had left Burgundian communities deep in
debt, their communal properties sold or mortgaged, and their
finances in disorder. The loss of communal properties that could
be used as collateral made it more difficult for communities to
borrow funds to meet internal village expenses. Consequently,
villages had to levy taxes to defray those expenses, with the
result that less was left for the royal tax collectors.

By 1672, the king's foreign adventures were requiring additional
funds. Because the crown was determined not to increase direct
taxes on the peasantry, and because seigneurs and townspeople
were exempt from taxes, borrowing and higher indirect taxes were
necessary. Taxing the nobility or the merchants as individuals
without making political concessions would have fomented revolts by those groups. Since these men of wealth could not be taxed
directly, their resources were borrowed instead. The increased borrowing had important implications for communities, for to attract
investors the crown had to provide guarantees that villages would
be solvent. The financiers (especially the *receveurs généraux*)[3] who
collected the direct taxes needed assurances of village solvency to
raise credit from their network of investors. Moreover, the crown
depended on taxes from the villages to pay the interest on the

3. See Daniel Dessert, "Finances et société au XVIIe siècle: A propos de la
Chambre de Justice de 1661," *Annales E.S.C.* 29 (July–Aug. 1974):847–81.

growing state debt. After the 1670s, then, protecting village resources was no longer simply a question of efficient tax collection.
Village solvency became the basis of royal credit.

The credit arrangements that were necessary for the crown to
keep its financial commitments and that made France's bid for
European hegemony possible required extending the authority of
the king's ministers into areas that had never before fallen under
royal control. These extensions of bureaucratic authority were
to have dramatic long-term consequences, many of which could
not have been foreseen. The measures that increased the intendant's supervision over village finance were developed on an ad
hoc basis as required by the financial needs of the state. When
the nation's survival depended on its ability to field an army or
secure the frontier for the next war, rulers could not pause to
consider theories or systems for transforming the society, nor to
ponder whether emergency measures taken to secure needed
troops, supplies, and administrative personnel might turn out to
be fundamental reforms.[4]

Thus, historians of the reign of Louis XIV who have claimed
that he had a deliberate, rational, systematic, and long-term plan
for restructuring society might be mistaken. Hindsight leads one
to conclude that there was a consistency to the Ludovican re-

4. Even though France was the most populous, the wealthiest, and the most
geographically compact of the Continental powers, it was not free from the
pressures felt by all other European states. France, it must be remembered, had
been a battlefield during the previous century, and maintenance of French military leadership was necessary to keep European wars from being fought on
French soil. Furthermore, in any full-scale European war, France would have to
fight on several fronts at once. Consequently, France had to be as strong as all
the rest of Europe combined. Even when national survival was not being threatened, invasion was to be avoided at all costs. On this point Louis XIV wrote in
his memoirs: "The smallest army that might invade our lands takes more from
us in one day than it would have cost us to maintain favorable diplomatic
contact for ten years, and the reckless administrators who do not understand
these maxims sooner or later find punishment for their miserly behavior in the
devastation of their treasures, the desertion of their allies, the scorn and aversion
of their people." A devastated countryside could not pay taxes. Louis XIV,
Mémoires de Louis XIV, ed. Jean Lognon (Paris, 1927), p. 181. Louis XIV expressed his concern with keeping enemy troops off French soil in the negotia-
tions during the Nine Years' War, when it was suggested that he should give up
the gains of the Treaty of Westphalia. "What!!" Louis exclaimed. "Am I to
sacrifice the work of thirty years —I who have struggled so hard lest my enemies
shall come into my house? Rather war for ten years more." Srbik, *Wien und
Versailles*, pp. 105, 204. Cited in R. M. Hatton, "Louis XIV and His Fellow
Monarchs," in R. M. Hatton, ed., *Louis XIV and Europe* (Columbus, Ohio, 1976).

forms. Those reforms that were issued as laws in the form of edicts appear to have been particularly deliberate. Edicts required elaborate justification and were headed by lengthy preambles. Once they had been registered by parlement (a complex and sometimes lengthy process), the edicts became part of the permanent body of royal jurisprudence. An edict of the seventeenth century could be cited in litigation of the late eighteenth century. When financial matters were at issue, the crown used edicts; they had credibility because they gave the impression of having provincial consent. Fiscal edicts constituted the juridical authority for the new tax contracts. Registration of such edicts could mitigate public disquiet, making it easier to collect the new tax. Because Colbert's reforms were issued as edicts, they seem more rational and systematic than they in fact were. The quest for strategic advantage in the international arena often prompted the measures and explain their timing. Neither Colbert nor Louis foresaw the far-reaching importance their reforms would have for France's subsequent social and economic development.

Let us consider how the new fiscal arrangements influenced the relationship between lords and peasants. Although the intendant's legal authority over the village was essentially that of a fiscal agent, there was no real limitation since almost every decision made by the village government (with the exclusion of harvest regulation) concerned finance. Even nominating a village *syndic* was deemed a financial matter, since he maintained village accounts. Matters as routine as hiring a village shepherd or schoolteacher, acquiring or maintaining a bull for the village herd, and repairing fountains or church walls involved finance and hence came under the intendant's supervision. Eventually the intendant's jurisdiction became so extensive that the seigneur's traditional role of village leader was challenged.

It is unlikely that Louis XIV hoped that village insolvency would provide royal administrators with the opportunity and the justification to replace the seigneur in his administrative leadership of the village. The king probably considered the seigneur's control over the village necessary for maintaining social order. Far from seeking to undermine that order, he wished to impress tax farmers with his state's competence and resolve. In the eigh-

teenth century, however, the situation changed as the intendants became more expert in implementing the functions assigned by the Ludovican edicts. One hundred years after the
issuance of the edicts, and only then, were intendants able to
challenge seigneurial administration. The most important new
piece in the machinery that made it possible to mount this challenge was the expanding system of subdelegates. Even though
the crown did not issue new edicts that explicitly extended the
intendant's authority, the seigneurs found their own authority
being gradually eroded and were ultimately forced to abandon
many of their long-held administrative rights over the village.
The turning point occurred in the 1750s, when seigneurs were
replaced by subdelegates in presiding over meetings of the
village assembly. This contributed to tensions between lord and
peasant.

The continual erosion of their administrative functions meant
that the feudal lords were being reduced to the status of private
individuals. Nevertheless, seigneurial dues remained intact.
Peasants, though subject to increased royal taxation and surveillance, did not receive relief from feudal obligations. Royal administrators might not have perceived the dangers implicit in
the fact that feudal dues had survived whereas the seigneur's
governing functions were disappearing. The crown's officials encouraged communities to challenge and to verify seigneurial
dues and exactions that competed with royal taxes, thus inviting
peasant litigation against the seigneurs. But the communities'
lack of success in such litigation heightened peasant frustrations
and united communities in opposition to the lords.

The bureaucrats were disrupting the traditional relationships
between lord and peasant, but intendants cannot be accurately
described as having modernizing or revolutionary aims, for they
often protected and preserved age-old habits and routines. We
have seen how they insisted on full participation in village assemblies, attempted to protect collective agriculture, and supported common grazing and gleaning rights; all were conservative positions in the eighteenth century. They insisted, as well,
that the practice of *contrainte solidaire* be continued in order to
guarantee the payment of royal taxes. The intendants even renewed many of the ties and reconstructed many of the struc-

tures that had earlier characterized the communities' relationship with the seigneurie. In this sense, the bureaucrats, and not the seigneur, can be described as the conservers of traditional forms and practices in the eighteenth century.

THE OBSTACLES TO AGRICULTURAL EXPANSION

The crown's administrative *tutelle* over communities was to have long-term economic implications as dramatic as the political consequences just discussed. Louis's seventeenth-century administrative policies retarded developments that seemed to have been on the verge of transforming the social and economic structure of the village.

In 1786 the intendant sent printed questionnaires on agricultural conditions to the parish priests of Burgundy. The 126 surviving responses indicate that new methods and crops had made little progress.[5] In the southeast and in Bresse, some farmers had experimented with American corn. Onions were introduced in the area around Auxonne, and in the Morvan some innovative farmers were growing potatoes. Attempts to find new ways to support livestock without utilizing the arable land were unsuccessful, however. A significant breakthrough would have been the planting of turnips or grasses on the fallow land that would enrich the soil and feed livestock. However, such methods were not discussed. The responses with regard to capital improvements were also disappointing. Capital improvements such as enclosure, drainage, and artificial meadows were not mentioned in the reports.[6]

Arthur Young, an English agronomist, observed that agriculture in France had not changed since the tenth century. Contemporaries would have agreed; they believed that the peasantry's

---

5. AD, C-15: "Dépêche de M. de Calonne qui l'accompagne, et réponses faites par les curés de 126 paroisses de la généralité au questionnaire qui leur avait été envoyé sur la situation de l'agriculture dans leurs contrées."

6. Ibid. Perhaps the curés were the wrong people to ask for general comments; they seemed more concerned with preserving the sanctity of the village cemetery. If it were not enclosed, village livestock would be free "to soil the souls of the dead." The curés had been asked to report on agriculture, but it was in discussing the drinking habits of their parishioners that they waxed eloquent.

unwillingness to innovate was rooted in their stubborn and irra-
tional nature. Historians since then have generally focused on
the ethos of the ruling elites. According to this interpretation,
seigneurs thought not of capital investments but of squeezing as
much as possible from their estates, so that they could live a life
of luxury in the towns. The seigneurs, we are told, were constantly seeking ways to minimize expenses and maximize income. This meant strict estate management and forceful assertion of seigneurial rights. Why bother with capital investments
when rents had increased during most of the century and, because of the hunger for land, could be expected to continue rising? By midcentury, as the land shortage spread, it was uncom-
mon to find calamity insurance for tenants, whereas earlier they
could at least count on rent reductions. Instead of offering tenants inducements to improve (such as rebates or conditions for
sharing the costs of improvements), it seemed to make sense to
"squeeze" them for all they were worth. The leases of the late
eighteenth century attest to this apparent lack of seigneurial
interest in capital improvements. From this evidence, historians
have concluded that landlords did not care enough to protect
even their most enterprising tenants. Such tenants were fleeced
since others could easily be found to take their place.

But to attribute this failure to encourage agricultural improvements to peasant mentality or to seigneurial life-styles is to
ignore what the contemporary spokesmen for agricultural reform were saying. Agronomists, estates, and parlements all insisted that capital improvements would not occur until common
rights to the land were abolished. Holders of capital needed
greater incentives, including the guarantee of reaping benefits, if
they were to risk investments. In other words, agricultural reformers were attacking communal grazing rights, not the attitudes of seigneurs. Behavior would not change until the laws,
the customs, and the institutional framework of agriculture
were altered. Actually, there was no lack of interest in agricultural improvements among the elites. The subject of how to
improve agriculture was discussed both in Paris and in the provinces. Even such literary societies as the Academy of Dijon were
offering prizes for essays on agriculture. But ideas for reform
were not put into practice, because practice, it was held, was

governed by the medieval regulations of open-field agriculture. Neither learned treatises nor royal legislation could overcome the inertia caused by communal traditions.

In the long run, the failure of the crown's edicts to reform agriculture can be attributed to the success of earlier royal policies encouraging the preservation of communal rights and properties. Although the documents reveal few examples of communities actually recovering the lands they had lost, the monarchy's seventeenth-century campaign to liquidate communal debts and to preserve communal property had a tremendous impact on rural society. Few examples can be found of villages losing communal properties to creditors after 1670. By preventing communities from using their properties as collateral for loans, the king's policies terminated a process of communal indebtedness, bankruptcy, and foreclosure. But for the crown's intervention, rural society might have been transformed; in a few more generations an entire social group that depended on communal rights for its survival might have been eliminated.

This group, the smallholders, was most threatened by the loss of the commons, although it benefited least from their preservation. That is why smallholders generally supported dividing the commons equally among the inhabitants. But the intendants feared that insolvent smallholders would eventually lose the partitioned parcels to wealthy inhabitants and that the well-to-do would benefit in the long term from partition. To discourage partition, the intendants argued that the preservation of communal rights and practices enabled smallholders to pasture a few cows or sheep on the commons and thus gain the extra capital needed to rent land or to pay taxes. Without the commons, this group would have been forced to join the ranks of the rural proletariat and to earn their living by working for wealthier neighbors. Worse, bankruptcy might have forced many to leave the village and to become itinerant laborers.

The crown took another step to preserve traditional agriculture by helping smallholders. Louis XIV declared it illegal for creditors to seize peasant livestock in payment for debt. In the late seventeenth century, the lifetime savings of a day laborer may not have been enough to purchase a single cow. Since smallholders could

not easily replace livestock once lost, the royal legislation provided them with a critical threshold of security.

As noted, the elimination of smallholders would not have led
to the transformation of agriculture the agronomists were seeking because the end of collective grazing and the elimination of
the fallow land would not have been achieved by the decline of
the small holding. Both rich and poor strove to preserve common rights and properties, though for different reasons. The poor
were more interested than the wealthy in partitioning the common lands, which was permitted by royal edicts. But the poor
were not motivated by a desire to enclose and to improve the
land; rather, they wanted to occupy land, any kind of land, in
any possible way. Moreover, the poor often supported partitioning the commons to defend them from being usurped by the
wealthy. Even if the commons were partitioned, the poor did not
have the capital to build fences or hedges. The wealthy, on the
other hand, did not favor partitioning, since they already dominated the commons with their larger herds. For the same reason,
they did not favor curtailment of collective grazing rights (from
which they benefited most) or enclosing their properties, since
they did not pay for these rights. Nor did the wealthy envision
that, by eliminating common rights and properties, they could
eliminate the smallholders, whose continued existence was an
obstacle to improvement and to the development of capital-
intensive agriculture.

In ways the crown did not foresee, its fiscal policies prevented
the alignment of forces in the village that might have led to
improvements in agrarian organization and techniques. Instead,
the royal policies gave the village an enemy against whom it had
to struggle to protect its heritage of communal rights and properties. The community was most concerned with preventing the
seigneur from usurping communal lands. This threat united the
village in defense of its open-field tradition.[7]

---

7. One region in Burgundy where pressures for enclosure were developing
was the Brionnais, whose soil was poor and best suited for grazing. Proximity to
the Lyon market meant that even poor inhabitants might be able to live by
specializing in livestock husbandry. Some progress was made toward enclosure
and improved husbandry in this region during the eighteenth century.

In short, it was because of the policies initiated by Louis XIV that Burgundy remained a province of free peasant smallholders who owned much of the land and who, on account of collective grazing rights, controlled the use of lands they did not own individually. The crown's seventeenth-century policies, which preserved common lands and rights, contributed to a continuation of the subdivision of holdings and the open-field system. Agricultural change did not occur because, in protecting communal properties, the crown had arrested the forces that would have weakened the communal system.

Although royal policies reconciled common rights with commercial farming, the persistence of those rights prevented the application of more productive techniques. Capital accumulation occurred within the framework of communal agriculture; yet agriculture did not achieve its peak output. Wealthy inhabitants used the communal system to increase personal fortunes without making technological changes that would increase overall productivity. Common-field agriculture did serve to redistribute income but in a way that did not necessarily serve the interests of the poor.

The stagnation of agriculture in Burgundy is an example of what happens when fiscal policies determine social and economic development. Since the community's capacity to meet its fiscal obligations depended upon its possession of common fields and rights, the maintenance of the traditional communal agricultural system was consistent with the state's fiscal and administrative aims. Agricultural technology in Burgundy stagnated because of the way the peasant community was fiscally and politically integrated into the structure of the absolutist state.

WHY LOUIS XIV'S REFORMS WERE
SO DIFFICULT TO OVERCOME

Louis XIV's fiscal reforms not only determined the course of economic development but fixed the style and defined the scope of bureaucratic authority. The necessity of financing the king's wars had been the principal stimulus and justification for the expansion of central authority. The institutions of central authority developed as a result of the crown's efforts to increase its fiscal prerogatives in order to ensure the state's financial stability and access to credit. The *contrôleur général* became the king's principal minister and assumed authority over many other branches of government. The intendants were above all fiscal agents; they reported to the *contrôleur général*.[8] The establishment in the seventeenth century of a strong central government with emphasis on the Ministry of Finance was the cause of the state's failure in the eighteenth century to restructure society and to transform the economy.

The development of administrative structures and law that stabilized and coordinated state finance was one of the strengths of the Ludovican state. Coordination of fiscal and bureaucratic procedures provided the monarchy with the financial resources to make its bid for European hegemony without changing the kingdom's political structure. Unlike Frederick in Prussia or Peter in Russia, Louis XIV did not have to impose mandatory state or military service on the nobility, or forced labor on the peasantry. Moreover, Louis XIV did not have to consult with a national representative body to increase royal revenues; therefore, such an increase did not raise constitutional issues as it did in England. The French king was more fortunate than most other European monarchs; he could finance the new military and administrative structures without fomenting revolution from above or, so it seemed, from below. He could fortify France's vast frontiers and develop an elaborate system of military supplies around Vauban's fortifications by making traditional corporate groups such as guilds and villages pay the state to protect their privileges.

The reforms of Louis XIV, unlike those of the Prussian rulers or Peter the Great, preserved many traditional liberties. The implementation of royal policy depended upon accommodating local groups, even though the monarchy continually came into conflict with pluralistic sources of provincial authority, such as the parlements. Unlike the autocrats of the East, the French king could tap local resources only by negotiating with, and recognizing the prerogatives of, these intermediary bodies. They

---

8. In the late eighteenth century, the intendants still defined themselves as "commissaires députés par sa Majesté pour la vérification des dettes et affaires des communautés en Bourgogne."

were perhaps less independent than they had been, but they were not eliminated. In some ways, such groups as the guilds, the communities, and perhaps even the provincial estates may have actually become stronger as a result of Louis XIV's reforms. The Old Regime state in France was "absolute" in only one sense: The state's most important representatives were empowered by orders issued by the crown that were not subject to provincial custom or law. These orders, called *arrêts*, reflect another basic characteristic of the early modern state—its military orientation. The powers accorded to the intendants were similar to those accorded the military commissioners who, under the pressures of wartime, took over the functions of civil government.[9] In this sense, French "absolutism" was the extension of wartime practices to peacetime.

By 1750, both the domestic and the international situations were changing, and the policies that had made Louis XIV's France the pacesetter in Europe were encountering opposition by groups that wanted greater economic individualism and political liberty. France's competition with England for a share of the world empire meant that, given France's traditional desire to maintain the Continental supremacy of its armies, its fiscal resources were strained. By 1763 England had in effect defeated France in the Seven Years' War. The defeat by a nation that enjoyed both parliamentary government and agricultural reform raised doubts about the monarchy's administrative traditions and strengthened those voices in France demanding political and economic liberty. The call for such reforms was not prompted by a desire to imitate England, for similar ideas had long circulated in France and had precedents in French traditions.

By the late 1760s, policymakers within the King's Council were seeking ways to legislate those demands for greater freedom. There were several reasons for their attempts. The ideas were popular, and the crown feared that an ideological front might develop uniting the kingdom's discontented elites in opposition to the bureaucracy's support of corporate traditions. The crown feared, as well, that the circulation of ideas encour-

---

9. See Gabriel Hanotaux, "Etat et commissaires: Recherches sur la création des intendants des provinces, de 1635 à 1648," in *Forschungen zu Staat und Verfassung: Festgabe für Fritz Hartung* (Berlin, 1956).

aging the abolition of guilds, of collective rights in agriculture, and of controlled grain prices might give a common purpose to groups with basically divergent outlooks and interests.

The policymakers also believed that greater economic freedom, and the encouragement of individual wealth, might create a stronger state. Many members of the King's Council shared the idea of those outside the government that producers needed incentives based on self-interest. By embracing economic individualism, and by collaborating with capitalist entrepreneurs, royal policymakers sought to encourage private citizens to finance industrial and agricultural development on the basis of self-interest. In attempting to coordinate public policy with private interests, policymakers hoped that as private wealth grew, so would total tax receipts. There is no reason to assume that in thinking more about economic growth, the ministers of Louis XV thought less than their seventeenth-century counterparts had about military victory or global hegemony. On the contrary, increasing the gross national product seemed a way to increase the tax base and thus to achieve France's military and colonial goals.

Finally, espousing the liberal policies was one way for the government to win the support of the parlements and the estates, both of which were among the prime movers for liberal programs. Both groups were essential to the functioning of the state's financial system. The support of the parlements was needed to register the loans and other fiscal devices. Creditors were more likely to loan once a measure had received parlementary approval. The estates' role, on the other hand, was primary. They were needed both for ordinary tax collection and assessment, and for credit operations such as floating loans. Both petitioned the crown for legislation that would permit agrarian individualism and terminate *contrainte solidaire*. Many of the edicts of reform that were finally issued by the monarchy utilized the same language found in petitions from those two bodies.

Not all ministers in the king's service supported the reform legislation, however. *Contrainte solidaire* was one of the issues over which policymakers in the King's Council clashed with the Burgundian intendants. In 1775 the controller general, Turgot, issued an *arrêt* abolishing *contrainte solidaire*. Turgot wrote to the Burgundian intendant, Dupleix, explaining his position. "It is not possible to conceal from oneself the injustice and the inconveniences that result from these *contraintes solidaires*," he said. "Certainly you are, more than anyone else, in a better position to appreciate the advantages that the taxpayers must expect from abolishing this kind of prosecution." Interestingly, Turgot argued that the practice "spreads alarm in the communities and brings about disruption and disorder in the affairs of those taxpayers who merit most, by their good behavior, the protection of the government." He was referring to the *principaux contribuables*, those inhabitants who were the most common victims of *contrainte solidaire*. Turgot wanted to protect the prosperous larger landowners because he considered them the most important source of wealth and industry in the kingdom. In the long run, he argued, abolition of *contrainte solidaire*, by encouraging the increased productivity of the wealthier peasants, would result in higher tax yields. In general, Turgot believed that successful producers should be given incentives to produce more. His ideas clearly represented what historians identify as the most liberal and progressive intellectual tendencies of his era.

Intendant Dupleix was sympathetic. He wrote to Turgot that "at first glance, nothing seems more just than the suppression of these prosecutions against the principal taxpayers." Referring to his experience as intendant of Burgundy and to that of his predecessors, Dupleix said that he found Turgot's program impractical, however, because as intendant, he was concerned with the day-to-day problems of collecting the *taille*, maintaining communal financial stability, and ensuring that communal legal expenses were paid. Since the community's most important financial obligations were collective, some corporate mechanism of coercion was necessary. In his experience, the intendant had found that the mere threat of applying *contrainte solidaire* was often sufficient. The alternative (liability of each individual to creditors or to tax collectors) seemed impractical—a goal, perhaps, for the future. Moreover, Dupleix did not want communities to fall back upon the mortgaging or selling of communal properties. To ensure the community's access to credit, the intendant could propose nothing more effective than *contrainte solidaire.* These were the practical reasons that led Dupleix to oppose Turgot: "All that is odious about this kind of prosecution disappears; one sees only an efficient means of preventing most of the taxpayers from being overwhelmed by considerable charges from one year to another."[10] Dupleix was not alone in believing that abolishing *contrainte solidaire* would weaken the foundations of bureaucratic power; no Burgundian intendant complied with the order to abolish *contrainte solidaire.* In the decade before the Revolution, both the Parlement of Dijon and the Estates of Burgundy sent petitions to the king stating their regret that the intendant and his agents still regularly employed *contrainte solidaire.*[11]

Turgot wanted to abolish *contrainte solidaire* for the same reason that he wanted to free the grain trade from consumer-oriented government regulation: to permit the enclosure of private property and to partition common lands. In his view, these moves would stimulate economic and social development by encouraging individual initiative. He was ready to sacrifice the peasants' common rights to the farmers' private interests in order to increase agrarian productivity. The intendant's correspondence suggests that he, too, supported the goal of increasing the gross national product. He expressed no doubts that the reforms were necessary to achieve long-term growth. But his primary concern was that the province pay its annual taxes. *Contrainte solidaire* was only one economic issue over which the intendant and King's Council clashed. Intendants helped peasants evade royal legislation that authorized enclosures and partitions, and also helped the communities preserve the custom of equal division of timber from communal woods. Moreover, they supported the preservation of gleaning rights, which the King's Council, along with the estates and the parlement, wanted to curtail. In addition to resisting these pressures from on high, the intendants opposed requests from the local level;

10. AD, C-5085: Correspondence between Contrôleur Général Turgot and Intendant Dupleix, 22 Nov. 1775.

11. AD, C-3335: Cahier des remontrances of 1785 of the Estates of Burgundy. Mention is made of the parlement's earlier remontrances against *contrainte solidaire.* The Elus, like the intendant, wanted to continue *contrainte solidaire.*

wealthy peasants were petitioning for the abolition of the age-old village assemblies.[12]

The intendant's opposition to abolishing *contrainte solidaire* and the various collective agricultural practices of communities reflects his concern that the reforms would make taxes harder to collect. Reforms of the village's corporate institutions would cause communal financial instability, thus making it more difficult for the *receveurs généraux* to collect the direct taxes and also to get the credits and investments they needed from their networks of investors.

With the exception of the period 1735–1740, state expenditures exceeded revenues during the eighteenth century—especially after 1760. Toward the end of the eighteenth century, servicing the debt consumed nearly 60 percent of the yearly intake.[13] After 1770, it was harder for the peasants to pay their taxes because of an economic recession. In view of such pressures, the intendants thought it better to utilize known methods than to experiment with untried ones. Their loyalty to established routine was more a matter of convenience than of ideology. The intendants, as the link between the village and the world of high finance, were caught up in the reality of tax collection. The agrarian reformers and the parlementaires were free to absorb and to promote the new ideas. They did not consider that abolishing the corporate institutions of the village would disrupt the routines of tax collection upon which the state's credit rested; they thought that the agricultural system could be changed only by risking the loss of short-term tax revenues. Those closer to state finance knew this and knew as well that the state was living a hand-to-mouth existence. The king's officials did not want to risk the loss of short-term revenues for long-term gains in productivity that might, in the future, increase tax yields. A national financial setback could lead

12. The position of the King's Council on abolishing Burgundy's village assemblies in favor of councils is not clear, but the crown encouraged the creation of such councils in neighboring Champagne. The municipal reform bill of 1787 created Councils of Notables in many of the provinces. However, for reasons discussed in Chapter 3, Burgundy was excluded.

13. M. Morineau, "Budgets de l'Etat et gestion des finances royales en France au dix-huitième siècle," *Revue historique* 239 (Oct.–Dec. 1980), pp. 289–337.

to bankruptcy, defeat of French troops in the American Revolution, and humiliation at home and abroad.

In summary, the intendants blocked the reforms of the village's corporate institutions because they did not want to risk losing the yearly revenues from the village. They knew that the entire system of credit depended on village solvency, since interest on the debt could be paid only from the proceeds of the taxes. In the 1780s just as in the 1680s, the crown needed to guarantee the solvency of the village to secure advances from financiers. The Ludovican reforms became permanent because the deficit became permanent. The community and its corporate traditions survived because of the way the crown managed to meet the financial needs of the seventeenth-century military revolution. The crown's financiers unwittingly underwrote the survival of the corporate village and its collective system of agriculture. High finance, ironically, kept medieval corporate forms alive.

The Burgundian intendants, usually viewed as the agents of modernization, did all within their power to block the implementation of programs that were inspired by the ideals of individual liberty. Even though the intellectual and social evolution of the eighteenth century repudiated the corporate traditions upon which bureaucratic powers depended, Burgundian intendants refused to yield. Their most important administrative and political powers derived from their role as guardians of the communities' collective identity. The abolition of corporate institutions would have hampered the bureaucracy's performance of routine functions such as collecting taxes. As political functionaries, their authority had come to depend on the preservation of the community's corporate identity. To maintain their authority, they preserved the traditional communal institutions, and blocked agricultural reform.

THE STATE AND CAPITALISM

The central government's relationship to Burgundian communities raises serious doubts about the crown's commitment to capitalist expansion. It suggests instead that the bureaucracy's victory over the seigneurie for control of the village set into motion a political process that allowed communities to defend corporate rights and properties.

Integration into the administrative structure of the absolutist state provided communities with a windfall of political benefits. Foremost among them was a village assembly that was more politically effective. The king's officials could not maintain a constant local presence after seigneurial control had been replaced by royal tutelage of the village. Therefore, they provided the province's more than one thousand villages with rules that were uniform throughout the province. This included standardizing assembly procedures so that each village followed the same formalities when leasing collective properties, contracting public works, or electing village officials. Although it may not have been the bureaucracy's intention, the village could then more effectively pursue interests that had separated it from the seigneurie.

In addition to introducing policies that made village assemblies more capable of independent action, intendants strengthened such legal mechanisms as *contrainte solidaire*, which held all inhabitants personally responsible for decisions made by the assembly. The advantage to the crown was that a village would have to answer to the intendant directly when it reneged on an obligation. With enforcement of *contrainte solidaire*, village financial commitments gained credibility. If the village failed to honor a contract, a creditor could turn to the intendant who, if all else failed, could seize the property of the wealthiest inhabitants as payment. The intendants could apply administrative law to settle disputes that arose between the village and its creditors, thus entirely circumventing the slow process of parlementary law. In this way, the administration could more firmly guarantee that a village would live up to its obligations. An additional reason for insisting on collective liability was that transacting business with the community was less expensive than with the peasants as individuals. Courts, creditors, or building contractors could find information about communities more cheaply than they could about individual peasants. The crown gained from these policies, but there were also long-term, if less obvious, advantages for the community. Because the will of the assembly was recognized by administrative law, communities could conduct collective business more effectively than before. Since it was less of a credit risk, the village could more easily summon the necessary resources when it wanted to sue. Therefore, the policies that intensified collective restraints strengthened communities.

Peasants who wanted to preserve their traditional communal rights of fishing, pasturing, and wood gathering found that they had an ally in the intendant. They counted on him to hear, and to approve, statements of village efforts to maintain common rights. He also alerted communities to possible violations of their rights and assisted the inhabitants in formulating their grievances. In court, the peasants did not always succeed in preventing seigneurs from seizing forests, usurping common lands, enclosing fields, or depriving the village of its rights to use the common lands. Nevertheless, the increase in litigation had a fundamental impact on the protocol of popular resistance. Instead of expressing their discontent in cathartic and dramatic outbursts that included rioting and looting, peasants took their grievances to court, hiring lawyers to hammer away at the theoretical presuppositions of feudal rights. The increase in communal litigation marked a distinct stage in the history of peasant contention. The disputes fostered a legal discourse whose concepts would be used during the Revolution to dismantle feudal property.

The increased effectiveness of assemblies also had significant economic consequences because those institutions controlled local agricultural production. The assembly regulated crop rotations and the timing of postharvest grazing on the stubble; it also governed the use of fallow land. Spokesmen for agrarian interests had hoped that abolishing the assemblies and permitting wealthy inhabitants to form village councils would be a way to overcome collective control. They anticipated that the wealthy council members would behave rationally and would recognize that their long-term interests would best be served by the elimination of collective practices. But the intendants in Burgundy blocked all efforts by the village notables to create such councils. Instead, the bureaucracy insisted that all the villagers attend and participate in the assemblies and fined inhabitants who did not. The control exercised by this bedrock unit of local administration generally discouraged private initiative. In full meetings of the village assembly, the protection of most common-use rights was usually a foregone conclusion. The continued authority of the village assemblies to allocate communal grazing rights created a disincentive to invest in the costly surveys, new roads, fencing, walls, and drainage systems often required by enclosure.

State making strengthened communal rights in yet another way. Government policies did not separate the interests of potential rural leaders—the wealthy farmers—from those of the community. The crown's policies, by giving wealthy peasant elites advantageous access to communal rights, in effect made them defenders of communal properties. Corporate rights had powerful support within the village and were defended by the village precisely because the wealthy peasants profited most from their preservation. The social inequality existing in the village worked to protect common fields, wastelands, pasture, and meadows. The poor often wanted to partition those properties equally but were opposed by the rich, who monopolized the commons without paying for their use. This monopoly also gave wealthy peasants a reason to commit resources and energy to defending communal fields and rights from landlords, *feudistes*, *fermiers*, notaries, and townspeople.

The monarchy, then, cannot be held responsible for providing the prerequisites of capitalist expansion. By reinforcing communal agricultural practices, royal officials drove the moneyed classes to become involved in state finance, where quick, short-term profits were available. The physiocrats eloquently insisted that investments aimed at eliminating the state's debts siphoned off the funds needed for the regeneration of the agrarian economy. Such investments, they warned, were made at the expense of capital improvements in agriculture. For the physiocrats, the notion of fiscal capitalism was a contradiction in terms.

A number of historians have argued that the absolutist state collaborated with the kingdom's elites by sharing the spoils of surplus peasant production. According to this interpretation, absolutism was a system of centralized surplus extraction in which political exploitation substituted for direct economic extraction. Absolutism permitted surplus extraction by means of political exploitation and allowed the French ruling class to re-

compose on a stronger basis. The spoils of class exploitation
were redistributed to the elites in the form of offices and interest
payments. In support of this view, Pierre Goubert has written
that the elites' involvement in state finance allowed them "to
participate in the general pillage of the kingdom."[14]

The present study suggests that those investments in state
finance raised issues concerning political participation that ultimately led to the fall of the monarchy. The elites invested in a
state they could not control—a state that had a history of fiscal
and monetary expediencies designed to minimize debts. Attacks
by the controller generals—Terray, Turgot, and Necker—on the
financiers recalled the early reign of Louis XIV, when the crown
ordered the Chambers of Justice to cancel debts and to forcibly
recover sums from the financiers. But now the financiers had
more leverage. Because their operations had become national
and highly centralized, they knew the king could not declare
bankruptcy and hope to find an alternative source of funds. The
financiers were able to force the king to remove reformers before
their policies could be implemented. Whereas these financiers
were able to influence royal policy through personal intrigue,
English aristocrats in Parliament consulted openly on fiscal policy. Like their English counterparts, however, the French elites
wanted to exercise control over and guarantee elimination of the
government debt, but the French king would not even discuss
the creation of mechanisms that would bind the crown to policies protective of investors. Instead, the crown persisted in con-
ducting its financial activities under a cloak of secrecy, even
refusing to disclose its budget. While refusing accountability to
its investors, the crown continued a foreign policy that required
additional borrowing and that jeopardized its ability to support
the debts it had already contracted. The state's intransigence
was costly: due to its creditors' lack of confidence, the crown
found it more difficult to borrow, and interest rates soared. But
it also paid a political price; its intransigence contributed to
mounting dissatisfaction among the elite upon whom it de-

14. See Pierre Goubert, introduction to Daniel Dessert, "Finances et société
au XVIIe siècle: A propos de la Chambre de Justice de 1661," *Annales E.S.C.* 29
(July–Aug. 1974):847. An argument similar to Goubert's is elaborated by Robert
Brenner in "The Agrarian Roots of European Capitalism," *Past and Present* 97
(Nov. 1982):16–113.

pended for financial support. The increasing opposition led, eventually, to revolution.

In sum, neither the political events that precipitated the Revolution, nor the institutional structures of the prerevolutionary state, suggest a class alignment of state and capitalist landlords against the peasantry in Burgundy. The crown's officials had created a legal and political environment favorable to communal rights in which communities were better protected from the potentially disruptive elements of a free market economy than they had been in the seventeenth century. The commitment of the king's officials to independent village assemblies provided communities with a means by which to defend collective rights and properties. The policy of insisting on corporate responsibility for taxes penalized enterprising producers. The royal bureaucracy also blocked the program of social transformation advocated by the physiocrats. To prevent the transformation of small producers into a rural proletariat, bureaucrats protected the communal pasture rights that were a prerequisite for the survival of the peasant smallholder. In implementing all these policies, the bureaucracy was using state power to shore up existing agrarian structures.

This was not a reforming state, nor was it a state aligned with the interests of the propertied elite. Property holders would have been better served, economically, by policies that stimulated productive investments in agriculture, and politically, by broader participation in national policymaking. Instead, the state pursued its own particular interests. How did its policies influence the balance of forces among classes? The state is most accurately depicted as an independent interest, for its long-term imperatives had become relatively autonomous. The state's relation to the means of production was distinct from that of any particular group or class.

OF POLITICAL BONDAGE: STATE POWER AND THE PERSISTENCE OF COMMUNAL INSTITUTIONS

Social theorists often look back nostalgically to the old rural communities. An extensive literature exists in which communities are described as precursors of socialist traditions, cells of a primitive communism, whose independence is perhaps reminiscent of the autonomy of the tribe before the conquest of the seigneurie. This interpretation of communal origins has strong appeal because of its relevance to contemporary politics: it can provide a pedigree and a historical justification for socialism. The community existed before the seigneurie and before the state. It, not private individuals, originally owned the earth. The triumph of individualism is an aberration made possible by the relatively recent rise to power of the capitalist class. By usurping state power in the eighteenth century, that class was able to overturn the age-old traditions of collective control.

We are told that in the precapitalist state, the government regulated the economy to protect the local community from the disruptive effects of the free market. Charles Tilly provides a compelling explanation of the precapitalist ideology that rationalized state control. Borrowing E. P. Thompson's suggestive terminology, Tilly describes the state as committed to upholding a "moral economy" in which "the residents of a local community had a prior right to the resources produced by or contained within; the community as such had a prior obligation to aid its weak and resourceless members. The right and the obligation to aid [took] priority over the interests of any particular individual and over any interests outside the community. It even [took] priority over the interests of the Crown, or of the country as a whole."[15] Tilly asserts that in the eighteenth century, however, the state departed from this tradition of protection; by promoting a rival morality of possessive individualism, it hastened the destruction of the old communities.

The literature on the peasantry and the French Revolution almost uniformly confirms the view that by promoting capitalism, the state brought about the demise of the communities. Furthermore, it generally supports the view that because peasants preferred subsistence and mistrusted the market, state power was essential to compel them into the market. This study suggests a different sequence of events and a different interpretation of the preindustrial peasant mentality. The communities rushed to their demise not when the state was strong, but in the

15. Charles Tilly, *From Mobilization to Revolution* (Reading, Mass., 1978), pp. 3–4.

sixteenth and early seventeenth centuries when it was weak. If villages had been left on their own, individualism might have triumphed without any help from the state. Had the state not intervened to strengthen communal institutions in order to halt their progressive disintegration, communities might have entered the eighteenth century divested of their communal lands, and most certainly the village assembly would have been superseded by Councils of Notables. The rise of the absolutist state prevented both developments from occurring.

The protection and promotion of communal property rights was essential to the crown's fiscal programs; the king's finances depended on village solvency. The intendant defended the communities' patrimony of rights and properties to maintain the financial ties that bound the rural villages to the national financial network. Thus, creation of the national credit network and the promotion of capitalist hegemony were not related. It is when we consider the fate of communal property that the needs of state finance and those of capitalist development seem clearly incompatible. State finance depended on communal property; capitalist development required its elimination. Therefore, the growth of state finance in the eighteenth century should not be viewed as an example of capitalist expansion.

The preservation of communal institutions also served to strengthen the crown's control over rural areas; such institutions suited the needs of bureaucratic surveillance. With its limited administrative capabilities the French state could not supervise individuals; it lacked an elaborate bureaucratic machine and could not afford the costs of direct local administration. Another problem was that it could not find reliable independent collaborators within the local community. Unlike the English monarch, the French king could not trust the local nobility. In fact, the French king had established his local authority by supplanting that of the local seigneur. How much easier it would have been if he could have depended on an unpaid local gentry to perform the tasks of local government and to link nation and village. Not having that option, the French state found collective restraints to be the cheapest and most effective way to supervise the peasantry.

Thus, communal rights and properties and collective responsibility for tax collection were not spontaneous expressions of peasant culture. Both were measures imposed from above to ensure political domination of the agrarian population and to facilitate resource extraction.[16] This program for political control had economic consequences, however, for it guaranteed the continuation of open-field agriculture.

16. The most complete statement of the reasons why states create communal institutions can be found in Samuel L. Popkin's pathbreaking study, *The Rational Peasant: The Political Economy of Rural Society in Vietnam* (Berkeley and Los Angeles, 1979).

Seven

Seven

Financing the French Revolution

The French Revolution promised the liberty of the individual and the expansion of private property and thus heralded a new age of prosperity. In formulating their commitment to these two principles, the leaders of the Revolution drew upon several generations of thought that linked personal freedom and private property with economic growth. By legislating the principles of economic liberty, the Revolutionary government expected dramatic progress to be made in agriculture. Like the monarchy, the Revolutionary leaders called for new agrarian institutions that would harness individual initiative. Property owners, they insisted, needed incentives to invest in land improvement if they were to surmount the technical conservatism of traditional agriculture. To encourage a spirit of enterprise among farmers, the Revolutionary government intended to abolish communal institutions that subjected land to practices benefiting the community instead of individual owners, such as forced crop rotation, mandatory fallow land, common pasture and meadowland, and common pasture rights. By abolishing collective rights in agriculture, lawmakers hoped to overcome, once and for all, the low productivity and technical rigidity of common-field farming.

The debates of the Constituent Assembly seem to indicate that most delegates to the Revolutionary assemblies agreed that communal properties and rights stood in the way of agricultural progress. But what would be the best way to abolish common fields—to sell them off or to divide them among individual inhabitants? In 1790 the government issued a questionnaire soliciting the opinion of all local officials.

The response of local officials in Burgundy anticipated the legislation that was later adopted by the Revolutionary government. The Burgundians were emphatic about the relationship between personal freedom and the sacredness of private property; a revolution that provided only one was inadequate. If individuals were to be truly free, property also had to be free. The first step should be to eliminate communal properties, because they breed vice and sloth. "The inhabitants where common lands are extensive are usually lazy; they pass their lives in sloth, leading thin, undernourished herds. They live and die poor and because of laziness, they turn nothing to profit. Their children imitate this pernicious example and become a race of lazy good-for-nothings; the bane of the society." In contrast, the Burgundian officials reported that "where common lands were already divided, necessity, the mother of industry, compelled the peasants to work and to seek a way out of poverty. Freedom increases the sphere of speculation, and the assembly, by investing property with a sacred character, will inspire those citizens who lack it with the desire to seek it." Even the most ungrateful and sterile lands could be put into cultivation by farmers who were motivated to increase their personal wealth. "If the Revolution is to free the French people, it must also free agriculture and the proprietor. England owes its flourishing condition to its agriculture. The revolution that freed the English people also allowed the division of all communal land. There, because the laws protected the industrious and because the English have been completely freed from communal obligations, their fields are covered with livestock. This, too, could happen in France if only the government would set up similar laws that protected the industrious."[1]

1. AD, L-640/32: "Rapport sur le Partage des Communaux fait au nom du Comité d'Agriculture à l'Assemblée Administrative du Département de la Côte-d'Or." Voted by the assembly of the district on 4 Nov. 1791. Signed by the secretary of the department on 20 Nov. 1791; on 11 Feb. 1792, the director addressed the report to the national legislature's Committee on Agriculture.

Even before legislation to abolish communal lands was written, the officials of the Revolutionary government had done much to limit communal properties simply by ignoring the pre-Revolutionary restrictions on their sale. Since the 1660s, the monarchy had not permitted villages to alienate collectively owned properties. The officials of the Revolutionary government allowed communities that were short of funds to sell communal lands to individuals, however. Believing that "the best method to make land productive was to confine its usage to individual proprietors," one Burgundian official proposed to his superiors in Paris that the best way to advance agriculture was to sell communal properties to large landowners who were solvent. Partitioning the properties among all inhabitants, he noted, would create inefficient small parcels. Besides, partitions would deprive the community of an important potential source of collective revenue.[2]

Most of the major reforms enacted by the new government were aimed at liberating property owners from collective restraints. On June 5, 1791, mandatory crop rotations determined by the community were abolished by a law that permitted property owners to follow the rotations of their choice. Another essential agrarian reform, codified on September 28, 1792, declared that the right to enclose was essential to the right of property and could not be contested. A law of August 10, 1792, legalized the alienation or sale of communal properties and ordered indebted communities to sell communal properties. On August 14, 1792, the first of two laws was issued ordering communities to divide communal properties among the inhabitants. By declaring partitions obligatory without establishing regulations or procedures, this law raised expectations without providing solutions. Nevertheless, it encouraged local officials to accept the partitions proposed by communities.[3]

On June 10, 1793, the National Convention issued a complete code that specified and regulated all stages of the partition pro-

---

2. AN, F10/333: Report from Arnoult, the procureur général–syndic et député des communes du bailliage de Dijon, to the Committee on Agriculture in Paris. The director of the national legislature's committee informed the Conseil Général of the Côte-d'Or that Arnoult's report contained several points "contrary to justice."

3. The laws are collected in AD, L-1-11, Lois et décrets, 1789–an VIII.

cess, including voting and assigning the costs; it also included guidelines for settling disputes. This law declared all previous partitions null and void. Indebted communities could not divide their lands until their debts were paid off, however.[4] Because most communities had accrued debts in supporting the Revolution, this stipulation marked a significant change in the Revolutionary government's commitment to agrarian individualism.[5] From that point on, the government's fiscal concerns took priority over agricultural expansion.

An action taken by the government in the following month severely restricted the course of agrarian reform. On August 24, 1793, finance minister Cambon declared that the debts acquired by communities in supporting the Revolution would become national debts. Communal assets became national properties up to the amount of debts, even though the debts were owed to private creditors. In other words, communal properties, like communal debts, were nationalized. This financial reform made it much more difficult for communities to get permission to alienate communal properties because state officials could and did use the reform to block such sales.[6]

In explaining this drastic measure, Cambon expressed the need to "seize with alacrity the occasion to give hope and consolation to the crowds of creditors who have waited and solicited their payment without success."[7] The Revolutionary government was at war and depended on private investors to advance funds to the state, provide loans, and buy nationalized lands, but

4. Ibid.
5. The law of 10 Aug. 1791, which contained a similar stipulation against partitions by communities with debts, was often ignored. By contrast, after June 1793 officials investigated much more rigorously the financial state of villages before authorizing partitions. The list of communities that were denied permission on account of debts is extensive.
6. AD, L-1724. It was not long before the implications of Cambon's reform to prevent the alienation of communal properties became clear. Echirey was authorized on 17 Aug. 1793 to sell communal properties in accord with the law of 10 Aug. 1792, which ordered communities to sell communal property to pay debts. However, on 8 Sept. 1793, that authorization was revoked. Citing the legislation of 24 Aug. 1793, the officials explained that Echirey could no longer sell its communal properties; they became national property up to the amount of Echirey's debts.
7. AD, L-1723. "Le directeur général provisoire de la liquidation, au Directoire du district de Dijon." Cambon used the phrase "une foule de créanciers" possibly to denote his concern for even the most humble of the nation's investors.

because of the declining value of the *assignat* and the difficulty of collecting taxes, potential investors were turning their backs on the Revolution. Why, then, was the protection of communal properties included in a plan to restore confidence in state finance? The answer lies in the connection between communal property and the village's ability to pay taxes. The village was integrated into the financial structure of the nation in ways that were unfamiliar to the economic reformers and the men of law who dominated the Revolutionary assemblies.

The connection between communal properties and the fiscal solvency of communities was, however, becoming clear to local tax officials. In a letter dated May 23, 1793, to his superiors in Paris, the conseil général of the Côte-d'Or was explicit about the relationship. Referring to the chronic difficulty of collecting taxes from the villages, he said he was "convinced by the experience of the previous year that the lateness of municipalities that do not have communal revenues to acquit their local charges must be placed high among the causes which prevented the return of contributions in 1791."[8] Preventing the collection of local taxes from interfering with the collection of national taxes had become a major concern.[9] District officials reported that communities without some form of collective revenue had great difficulty meeting emergency village expenses. Communities with communal properties had a distinct advantage since they could lease those properties to defray municipal expenses. When faced with emergency expenses, they did not have to resort to heavy internal taxes that left little for the national tax collectors. The deputy of the *bailliage* of Dijon expressed similar concerns in a letter to his supervisors in Paris about the risks of partitioning communal lands. He acknowledged "the justice and perhaps the necessity of the laws that during the Old Regime forbade the alienation of communal properties." The reason for those restrictions, he insisted, was that the revenues from communal properties "were needed to pay the costs of public works

8. AD, L-1284, 23 May 1793: Letter from the Conseil Général de la Côte-d'Or.
9. AD, L-643. Contains much correspondence between local administrators and Parisian officials on the subjects of local expenditures and tax collection. The concern that local expenses be prevented from interfering with the collection of national taxes is especially evident in nos. 9, 15, 16, 40–42, 44–46, 49.

such as repairing public buildings, constructing canals, controlling floods, improving roads, etc." Communities without communal resources had trouble dealing with these expenses, which "could arise with little warning."[10] The officials of the Revolutionary government soon realized what officials of the Old Regime state had long known: Village solvency depended on the preservation of communal properties. Because they were better able to pay local taxes, communities with communal properties could more easily make their contributions to the state.

The nationalization of communal debts marked the turning point in the Revolutionary government's commitment to the elimination of communal property. Legislation to continue the abolition of communal agriculture was never released; therefore, the intention of the laws of 1791 and 1792 was never realized. For example, the Revolutionary government never suppressed the community's right to common pasture and as a result, the arable land of all villages was still open to the communal herd after the harvest. The government never ordered villagewide enclosures, even though without such a measure the legislation it did issue was useless. Partitions did not occur with great regularity because few villages were free of all debts. Nor did the government succeed in producing a rural code that abolished gleaning rights or mandatory rotations. Reform failed during and after the Revolution for the same reasons that the monarchy failed to restructure agriculture in the late eighteenth century.[11]

By 1796, the commitment of the Revolutionary government to agrarian individualism had come full circle. The law of June 10, 1793 (the code for partitions), was rescinded on June 9, 1796, and all legal procedures and court cases that had resulted from that law were suspended. Communities could no longer even consider partitioning their properties; many were forced to reassemble lands that had already been divided. A law of May 21, 1797, divested communities of the right to alienate or to exchange their communally owned properties. There was no longer any question of selling communal properties; many communities were ordered to reconstitute the common lands they

10. Ibid. Letter of Député Arnoult.
11. Not until promulgation of the Rural Code of 1814 were such extensive reforms enacted.

might have sold.[12] The Revolutionary government, like the monarchy it had replaced, had become the protector of village properties and rights.

Had the Revolutionary government turned its back on individualism and liberty? Far from it. The same government that declared the alienation of communal properties illegal had in fact restored the freedom of the grain trade and had gone so far as to order six-month prison sentences for anyone who publicly opposed the free marketing of grain. It was not a commitment to liberalism that was lacking. Rather, the links between village solvency, common fields, and state finance had motivated the government to reverse its agricultural policies. As the government's financial problems began to become insurmountable, budgetary concerns took priority over agricultural reform. The inclusion of measures aimed at protection of village properties in the program to nationalize the debt was in part an acknowledgment of the importance of those properties to the nation's fiscal structure.

CONCLUSION

In the philosophy of eighteenth-century liberalism, the communities were considered anachronisms that stood in the way of economic and political progress. Inspired by that liberal philosophy and by the English example, the Revolutionary government set out to dismantle the corporate village. Yet despite much ideological rhetoric in support of individualism and economic liberty, the government's administrators eventually reconstructed the village they had set out to destroy.

Was the reconstruction of the corporate village a concession to peasant violence by the Revolutionary government? The letters of provincial officials reveal little concern with either peasant welfare or the threat of peasant unrest. Problems of village debt, tax collection, and provisioning the cities and the army dominate their correspondence. Even the documents pertaining to the restoration of the village commons do not reveal fear of an

---

12. Jacques Godechot, *Les institutions de la France sous la Révolution et l'Empire* (Paris, 1968), p. 518.

autonomous peasant movement. The state had compelling reasons of its own to reconstruct the corporate village.

The administrative correspondence between Paris and Dijon suggests that the Revolutionary government had to abandon its commitment to agrarian reform because of fiscal priorities rather than because of threatened peasant resistance. Administrators of the Revolutionary government were more concerned with collecting taxes and calming the fears of tax collectors and investors alike than with encouraging agrarian change. Both before and during the Revolution, the French state, preoccupied with international wars, fiscal chaos, and administrative weakness, proved incapable of promoting agricultural growth. The Revolution brought the Burgundian countryside to conditions similar to those that in 1661 had prompted Louis XIV to reinforce communal property.

Bibliography

PRIMARY SOURCES

The principal sources for this book can be found in the Archives Départementales of the Côte-d'Or in Dijon, France.

In series C, Administration of the Province (*Archives Civiles*), there are over 7,000 dossiers. The most important part of series C for this study was the archives of the intendancy, or village administration, particularly dossiers C-400 to C-1829. These are divided into twenty-nine subdelegations; within each subdelegation, villages are listed alphabetically. Under the heading *Affaires Générales* (C-1 to C-399), dossiers C-13 to C-15 on agriculture were of special interest.

Dossiers C-2071 to C-2968 of the *Archives Civiles* concern the financial administration of the province. Dossiers C-2799 to C-2815 are declarations of community properties. Under the heading *Affaires Générales*, dossiers C-2816 to C-2848 contain documents from the Bureau of Finances, pertaining to the defense of communal rights and properties and the internal administration of communities. Dossiers C-2849 to C-2881 concern the liquidation of communal debts and include letters, ordinances, and instructions to the intendants during the ministry of Colbert. Dossiers C-2882 to C-2967 contain the judgments of Intendants Bouchu (1666) through Joly de Fleury (1756). Particularly informative are the dossiers covering Bouchu's intendancy (C-2892 to C-2907). There are only a few documents, contained in two dossiers, for the period 1740–1756.

The documents of the Estates of Burgundy are also found in series C (dossiers C-2969 to C-3721). Useful for this study were: dossiers C-2999 to C-3014 (Decrees of the Estates); C-3130 to C-3243 (Resolutions of the

Elus); C-3328 to C-3335 (*Remontrances* of the Estates); C-3353 to C-3368 (Correspondence of the Elus); C-3695 to C-3716 (pertaining to agriculture).

I also consulted series E, which includes family papers, records of estate management, and archives on the subject of seigneurial justice. Series B² (Justice) was useful, especially dossiers 600–1243: *Registres de Justice, Sentences et Procès-verbaux, Registres de Jours, Registres des Messiers.*

The Burgundian documents relevant to the Revolution are part of series L. The two collections of printed *facta* in the Bibliothèque Municipale of Dijon, Fonds Saverot and Fonds Carnot, provided additional source material.

In the Archives Nationales in Paris, series H¹ 98 to 217 (Pays d'Etats, Intendancies) yielded useful information on the intendant, the Estates of Burgundy, and the controller general. Series H¹ 1462, 1486–98, 1520–21, and 1624–27 include material on agriculture throughout the kingdom. There is information on Burgundy in series G⁷ (*Contrôle Générale des Finances*), including correspondence of the controller general and of the intendant. Series F (particularly F³) was valuable for information on the Revolution in Burgundy.

PUBLISHED SOURCES AND STUDIES

Agulhon, Maurice. "La notion du village en Provence vers la fin de l'Ancien Régime." In *Actes du 90e Congrès national des sociétés savantes, Nice, 1965,* 1:277–301. Paris, 1967.

Anderson, Perry. *Lineages of the Absolute State.* London, 1974.

Antoine, M. *Le Conseil du Roi sous Louis XV.* Geneva, 1972.

———. "Les subdélégués généraux des intendances." *Revue historique de droit français et étranger* 53 (Sept. 1975):395–435.

Antonetti, G. "Le partage des forêts usagères ou communales entre les seigneurs et les communautés d'habitants." *Revue historique de droit français et étranger* (1963), pp. 238–86, 418–42, 592–634.

Appolis, E. *Les biens communaux en Languedoc à la fin du XVIIIe siècle.* Vol. 2. Commission de recherche et de publication des documents relatifs à la vie économique de la Révolution, 1939.

———. "La question de la vaine pâture en Languedoc au XVIIIe siècle." *Annales historiques de la Révolution française* (1938), pp. 97–132.

Arbassier, Charles. *L'absolutisme en Bourgogne: L'intendant Bouchu et son action financière, d'après sa correspondance inédite (1667–1671).* Paris, 1921.

Ardascheff, P. "Les intendants de province à la fin de l'Ancien Régime." *Revue d'histoire moderne et contemporaine* (1904), pp. 5–38.

———. *Les intendants de province sous Louis XVI: Etude historique principalement d'après les documents inédits.* Vol. 2 of *L'administration provinciale dans les derniers temps de l'Ancien Régime*, trans. L. Jousserondot-Dorpat. Paris, 1909.

Argenson. *Considérations sur le gouvernement ancien et présent de la France*. Paris, 1767.

Babeau, A. *La vie rurale dans l'ancienne France*. Paris, 1885.

———. *Le village sous l'Ancien Régime*. Paris, 1879.

Babeau, Henry. "Les assemblées générales des communautés d'habitants en France du XIIIe siècle à la Révolution." Doctoral thesis, Université de Paris, 1893.

Baehrel, R. *Une croissance: La Basse-Provence rurale*. Paris, 1961.

Bamford, Paul Walden. *Forests and French Sea Power, 1600–1789*. Toronto, 1956.

Bart, Jean. *La liberté ou la terre: La mainmorte en Bourgogne au siècle des Lumières*. Dijon, 1984.

Bates, Robert H. *Markets and States in Tropical Africa: The Political Basis of Agricultural Policies*. Berkeley and Los Angeles, 1981.

———. "Some Conventional Orthodoxies in the Study of Agrarian Change." *World Politics* 36 (Jan. 1984):234–54.

Behrens, C. B. A. "Nobles, Privileges, and Taxes in France at the End of the Ancien Régime." *Economic History Review*, 2d ser., 15 (1963):451–75.

Bernard, R. J. "Les communautés rurales en Gévaudan sous l'Ancien Régime." *Revue du Gévaudan* (1971), pp. 110–65.

Bertucat, C. *Les finances municipales à Dijon depuis la liquidation des dettes (1662) jusqu'à 1789*. Dijon, 1910.

Bézard, Y. *Une famille bourguignonne au XVIIIe siècle*. Paris, 1930.

Bien, David. "The Secretaires du Roi: Absolutism, Corps, and Privilege under the Ancien Regime." In E. Hinrichs, ed., *De l'Ancien Régime à la Révolution française*, pp. 153–67. Göttingen, 1978.

———. "Uselessness, Survival, and the State: A Problem in Comparative Perspective." Manuscript

Blin, Léon. "Les subsistances en Bourgogne (1709–1710)." *Annales de Bourgogne* 12 (1940):69–80; 13 (1941):308–17.

———. "Coq du village et lettre de cachet: Un 'jugement' des élus généraux de Bourgogne (1745–1747)." In *MSHDB* 31 (1972):157–65.

Blocaille, Marguerite. "Forêts, seigneurs, et communauté au dernier siècle de l'Ancien Régime." Thèse, Diplôme des Etudes Supérieures, Université de Dijon, 1973.

Bloch, Marc. *Les caractères originaux de l'histoire rurale française*. 2 vols. Paris, 1952, 1954.

———. "Les édits sur les clôtures et les enquêtes agraires au XVIIIe siècle." *Bulletin de la Société d'histoire moderne* (1926), pp. 213–16.

———. "La lutte pour l'individualisme agraire dans la France du XVIIIe siècle." *Annales d'histoire économique et sociale* 2 (1930):329–83, 511–56.

———. *Seigneurie française et manoir anglais.* Paris, 1960.

Blum, Jerome. "The Internal Structure and Polity of the European Village Community from the Fifteenth to the Nineteenth Century." *Journal of Modern History* 43 (Dec. 1971):541–76.

Bois, Paul. *Paysans de l'Ouest.* Le Mans, 1960.

Boisguillebert, P. de Pesant de. *Détail de la France.* 1695.

Boislisle, A. de. *Correspondance des contrôleurs généraux de finances avec les intendants des provinces.* 3 vols. Paris, 1874–1897.

Bonney, R. J. *The King's Debts: Finance and Politics in France, 1589–1661.* Oxford, 1981.

———. *Political Change in France under Richelieu and Mazarin, 1624–1661.* Oxford, 1978.

Bordes, Maurice. *L'administration provinciale et municipale en France au XVIIIe siècle.* Paris, 1972.

———. *D'Etigny et l'administration de l'intendance d'Auch (1751–1767).* 2 vols. Auch, 1957.

———. "Les intendants éclairés à la fin de l'Ancien Régime." *Revue d'histoire économique et sociale* (1961), pp. 57–83.

———. "Les intendants de Louis XV." *Revue historique* 223 (Jan.–March 1960):45–63.

Bosher, J. F. "French Administration and Public Finance in Their European Setting." In *The New Cambridge Modern History,* vol. 8, ed. A. Goodwin, 565–91. Cambridge, 1965.

———, ed. *French Government and Society, 1500–1850: Essays in Memory of Alfred Cobban.* London, 1973.

Bouchard, G. "Comptes borgnes et fiscalité aveugle au dix-huitième siècle." *Annales de Bourgogne* 26 (1954):6–41.

———. "Dijon au dix-huitième siècle: Les dénombrements d'habitants." *Annales de Bourgogne* 25 (1953):30–65.

Bouchard, M. *De l'humanisme à l'Encyclopédie: L'esprit public en Bourgogne sous l'Ancien Régime.* Paris, 1930.

Boucher d'Argis. *Code rural.* 3 vols. Paris, 1774.

Bouhier, J. *Coutumes générales du duché de Bourgogne.* 2 vols. Dijon, 1742, 1746.

Bourde, A. *Agronomie et agronomes en France au XVIIIe siècle.* 2 vols. Paris, 1968.

Bourgin, G. "Les communaux et la Révolution française." *Revue historique de droit français et étranger* (1908), pp. 690–751.

———. "Notes sur l'administration de l'agriculture et la législation rurale de 1788 à l'an VII." *Bulletin de la Commission de recherche et de publication des documents relatifs à la vie économique de la Révolution* (1908), pp. 248–493.

———. *Le partage des biens communaux.* Paris, 1908.

Boutier, Jean. "Jacqueries en pays croquant: Les révoltes paysannes en Aquitaine (décembre 1789–mars 1790)." *Annales E.S.C.* 34 (July–Aug. 1979):760–86.

Braudel, F., and C. E. Labrousse, eds. *Histoire économique et sociale de la France*. Vols. 1 and 2. Paris, 1970.

Brenner, Robert. "Agrarian Class Structure and Economic Development in Pre-Industrial Europe." *Past and Present* 70 (Feb. 1976):30–75.

———. "The Agrarian Roots of European Capitalism." *Past and Present* 97 (Nov. 1982):16–113.

Bretonne, Rétif de la. *La vie de mon père*. Reprint. Paris, 1924.

Canal, S. *Les origines de l'intendance de Bretagne*. Paris, 1911.

Caron, P. *Code rural ou maximes et règlements concernant les biens de campagne*. 2 vols. Paris, 1773.

Castan, N. "Révoltes populaires en Languedoc au XVIIIe siècle." In *Congrès national des sociétés savantes, Toulouse, 1971*, 2:223–36. Paris, 1976.

Castan, Yves. "Attitudes et motivations dans les conflits entre seigneurs et communautés devant le parlement de Toulouse au XVIIIe siècle." In *Villes de l'Europe méditerranéenne et de l'Europe occidentale du Moyen-Age au XIXe siècle, Actes du Colloque de Nice*, 27–28 March 1969, pp. 233–39. Paris, 1969.

———. *Honnêteté et relations sociales en Languedoc (1715–1780)*. Paris, 1974.

Chambers, J. D. "Enclosure and Labour Supply in the Industrial Revolution." *Economic History Review*, 2d ser., 5 (1952–1953):318–43.

Chambers, J. D., and G. E. Mingay. *The Agricultural Revolution, 1750–1880*, pp. 39–52. London, 1966.

Champier, L. *A la frontière des terroirs: Le problème de l'assolement à Bragny-sur-Saône à la fin du XVIIIe siècle*. Lyon, 1949.

Chevrier, G. "Le droit d'indire d'après la coutume du duché de Bourgogne." In *MSHDB* (1952), pp. 7–34.

Chiot, R. "Collecteurs de taille en Basse-Bourgogne aux XVIIe et XVIIIe siècles." *Annales de Bourgogne* 18 (1946):258–76.

Clamageron, J. J. *Histoire de l'impôt en France*. 3 vols. Paris, 1867–1876.

Clapham, John Harold. *An Economic History of Modern Britain*. Vol. 1. Cambridge, 1949.

Clément, Maurice. "Les communautés d'habitants en Berry." Thèse, Ecole des Chartes, Paris, 1890.

———. "Etude sur les communautés d'habitants dans les provinces du Berry." *Revue du centre* (1891–1893).

Clément, Pierre, ed. *Lettres, instructions, et mémoires de Colbert*. 10 vols. Paris, 1861–1883.

Clère, Jean-Jacques. "Les paysans de la Haute-Marne et la Révolution française (1780–1825): Recherches sur la communauté villageoise." Thèse, droit, Université de Dijon, 1980.

Cobban, Alfred. *The Social Interpretation of the French Revolution*. Cambridge, 1968.

Collins, James B. "Sur l'histoire fiscale du XVIIe siècle: Les impôts directs en Champagne entre 1595 et 1635." *Annales E.S.C.* 34 (Feb.–March 1979):325–48.

Colombet, A. "L'administration communale et le statut des biens communaux dans un village du pays de Montbéliard sous l'Ancien Régime." In *MSHDB* 20 (1958–1959):155–67.

———. "L'application en Bourgogne de l'édit de 1766 sur les défrichements." In *MSHDB* 14 (1952):205–12.

———. "Une justice seigneuriale à la fin de l'Ancien Régime: Vantoux." In *MSHDB* 3 (1936):195–207.

———. *Les parlementaires bourguignons à la fin du XVIIIe siècle.* Dijon, 1937.

Corvol, Andrée. "L'affouage au XVIIIe siècle: Intégration et exclusion dans les communautés d'Ancien Régime." *Annales E.S.C.* 38 (1981):390–408.

———. "Forêts et communautés en Basse-Bourgogne au XVIIIe siècle." *Revue historique* 256 (1976):15–36.

Courtépée, M. *Description générale et particulière du duché de Bourgogne.* 4 vols. Dijon, 1847. Reprint. Paris, 1967–1968.

Dakin, Douglas. "The Breakdown of the Old Regime in France." In *The New Cambridge Modern History*, vol. 8, ed. A. Goodwin, 592–617. Cambridge, 1965.

———. *Turgot and the Ancien Régime in France.* London, 1939. Reprint. New York, 1980.

d'Arbois de Jubainville, H. *L'administration des intendants d'après les archives de l'Aube.* Paris, 1880.

Davot, G., and J. Bannelier. *Traité de droit français à l'usage du duché de Bourgogne.* 9 vols. Dijon, 1751–1767.

Debard, J. M. "Le régime des forêts dans la seigneurie d'Héricourt et celle d'Etobon." In *MSHDB* 20 (1958–1959):41–57.

De Charmasse et Montarlot. *Cahiers des paroisses et communautés du bailliage d'Autun.* Autun, 1895.

Delbeke, F. *L'action politique et sociale des avocats au XVIIIe siècle.* Louvain, 1927.

Demay, C. "Cahiers des paroisses du bailliage d'Auxerre." *Bulletin de la Société scientifique de l'Yonne* (1884–1885).

Dent, J. "An Aspect of the Crisis of the Seventeenth Century: The Collapse of the Financial Administration of the French Monarchy, 1653–1661." *Economic History Review*, 2d ser., 20 (1967):24–56.

———. *Crises in Finance: Crown, Financiers, and Society in Seventeenth-Century France.* New York, 1973.

———. "The Role of *Clientèles* in the Financial Elite of France under Cardinal Mazarin." In J. F. Bosher, ed., *French Government and Society, 1500–1850: Essays in Memory of Alfred Cobban*, pp. 41–69. London, 1973.

Depping, Georges Bernhard, ed. *Correspondance administrative sous le règne de Louis XIV.* 4 vols. Paris, 1850–1855.

Dessert, Daniel. *Argent, pouvoir, et société au Grand Siècle*. Paris, 1984.

———. "Finances et société au XVIIe siècle: A propos de la Chambre de Justice de 1661." *Annales E.S.C.* 29 (July–Aug. 1974):847–81.

———. "Le 'laquais-financier' au grand siècle: Mythe ou réalité?" *Dix-septième siècle* 122 (1979):21–36.

———. "Pouvoir et finance au XVIIe siècle: Le fortune de Mazarin." *Revue d'histoire moderne et contemporaine* 23 (1976):161–81.

Dessert, Daniel, and Jean-Louis Journet. "Le lobby Colbert: Un royaume ou une affaire de famille?" *Annales E.S.C.* 30 (Nov.–Dec. 1975):1303–36.

Destray, P. "L'état économique de la Bourgogne à la veille de la Révolution d'après trois mémoires officiels." *Enquêtes sur la Révolution en Côte-d'Or* (1911), pp. 65–98.

Devèze, M. "Les forêts françaises à la veille de la Révolution." *Revue d'histoire moderne et contemporaine* 13 (1966):241–72.

———. *La grande réformation des forêts sous Colbert, 1661–1683*. Thèse, Université de Nancy, 1954.

———. *Histoire des forêts*. Paris, 1965.

Dewald, Jonathan. *The Formation of a Provincial Nobility*. Princeton, N.J., 1980.

———. *Pont-St-Pierre, 1398–1789: Lordship, Community, and Capitalism in Early Modern France*. Berkeley and Los Angeles, 1987.

Deyon, Pierre. "A propos des rapports entre la noblesse française et la monarchie absolue pendant la première moitié du XVIIe siècle." *Revue historique* 88 (April–June 1964):341–57.

Diamond, Sigmund. "Le Canada français au XVIIème siècle: Une société préfabriquée," *Annales E.S.C.* 16 (March–April 1961):317–54.

Dontenwill, S. *Une seigneurie sous l'Ancien Régime: L'étoile en Brionnais du XVIe au XVIIIe siècle—1575–1778*. Roanne, 1973.

———. "Un type social dans les campagnes brionnaises au XVIIe siècle: Le procureur fiscal fermier de seigneurie et crédirentier." *Bulletin du Centre d'histoire économique et sociale de la région lyonnaise* (1974), pp. 1–41.

D'Orgeval-Dubouchet, P. *La taille en Bourgogne au XVIIIe siècle*. Dijon, 1938.

Doyle, W. "Was There an Aristocratic Reaction in Pre-Revolutionary France?" *Past and Present* 57 (Nov. 1972):97–123.

Drouot, H. *Mayenne et la Bourgogne*. 2 vols. Paris, 1937.

———. "Un sujet: L'exode des paysans devant la taille." *Annales de Bourgogne* 24 (1952):121–23.

Drouot, H., and J. Calmette. *Histoire de Bourgogne*. Paris, 1928.

Dumont, F. "L'intendant de Dijon et le Mâconnais." In *MSHDB* 6 (1939):203–30.

Dupaquier, J. *Introduction à la démographie historique*. Paris, 1974.

————. *Paroisses et communes de France: Dictionnaire d'histoire administrative et démographique.* Paris, 1974.

————. "Des rôles de taille à l'histoire de la société rurale à la fin de l'Ancien Régime." In *Actes du 88e Congrès national des sociétés savantes, Clermont-Ferrand, 1963.*

Durand, Y. *Les fermiers généraux au dix-huitième siècle.* Paris, 1971.

Egret, Jean. *Louis XV et l'opposition parlementaire.* Paris, 1970.

————. *Le Parlement de Dauphiné et les affaires publiques dans la seconde moitié du XVIIIe siècle.* 2 vols. Grenoble-Paris, 1942.

————. *La prérévolution française.* Paris, 1962.

Emmanuelli, Fr.-X. "Pour une réhabilitation de l'histoire politique provinciale: L'exemple de l'Assemblée des communautés de Provence (1660–1786)." *Revue historique de droit français et étranger* 59 (Sept. 1981):431–50.

Esmonin, Edmond. *Etudes sur la France des dix-septième et dix-huitième siècles.* Reprint. Paris, 1964.

————. *La taille en Normandie au temps de Colbert.* Paris, 1913.

Essuile, J. F. *Traité politique et économique des communes.* Paris, 1770.

Evrard, F. "Les paysans mâconnais et les brigandages de 1789." *Annales de Bourgogne* 19 (1947):7–39, 97–121.

Festy, O. "L'agriculture pendant la Révolution: Les journaux d'agriculture et les progrès agricoles." *Revue d'histoire économique et sociale* (1950), pp. 35–53.

————. *L'agriculture pendant la Révolution: L'utilisation des jachères.* Paris, 1950.

Fleurquin, Alexandre. *L'administration du village à la fin de l'Ancien Régime.* Thèse, droit, Université de Paris, 1899.

Forbonnais, F. V. de. *Recherches et considerations sur les finances de la France.* 6 vols. Paris, 1758.

Forster, Robert. *The House of Saulx-Tavanes: Versailles and Burgundy, 1700–1830.* Baltimore, 1971.

————. *The Nobility of Toulouse in the Eighteenth Century: A Social and Economic Study.* Baltimore, 1960.

————. "Obstacles to Agricultural Growth in Eighteenth-Century France." *American Historical Review* 75 (1970):1600–1615.

————. "The 'World' between Seigneur and Peasant." In Ronald C. Rosbottom, ed., *Studies in Eighteenth-Century Culture.* Vol. 5. Madison, Wisc., 1976.

Fortunet, Françoise. *Charité ingénieuse et pauvre misère: Les baux à cheptel simple en Auxois aux XVIIIème et XIXème siècles.* Dijon, 1985.

Fortunet, Françoise, et al. *Pouvoir municipal et communauté rurale.* Publication 5. Université de Dijon, Faculté de droit et de science politique, Centre de recherches historiques. 1981.

Frèche, G. *Toulouse et la région Midi-Pyrénées au siècle des Lumières (vers 1670–1789)*. Paris, 1974.

Frèche, G., N. A. Kisliakoff, J. Phytilis, and H. Spitteri. *Questions administratives dans la France du dix-huitième siècle*. Paris, 1967.

Fréville, H. *L'intendance de Bretagne (1689–1790)*. 3 vols. Rennes, 1953.

Furet, François. *Penser la Révolution française*. Paris, 1978.

Garnier, J., and E. Champeaux. *Chartes de communes et d'affranchissements en Bourgogne*. 4 vols. Dijon, 1867.

Garreau, A. *Description du gouvernement de Bourgogne . . . avec un abrégé de l'histoire de la province et une description particulière de chaque pays, ville . . . qui dépendent de ce gouvernement*. 2d ed. Dijon, 1734.

Garreta, J. C. "Les archives du Parlement de Dijon: Etude des sources." In *MSHDB* 22 (1962):203–44.

———. "Les sources de la législation de l'Ancien Régime: Guide bibliographique." In *MSHDB* 29 (1968–1969):275–365.

Gauthier, Florence. *La voie paysanne dans la Révolution française*. Paris, 1976.

Giffard, A. *Les justices seigneuriales en Bretagne aux XVIIe et XVIIIe siècles*. Paris, 1903.

Gillot-Voisin, J. "La communauté des habitants de Givry au XVIIIe siècle." In *Etudes sur la vie rurale dans la France de l'Est*. Dijon, 1966.

Glasson, E. "Communaux et communautés dans l'ancien droit français." *Revue historique de droit français et étranger* (1891), pp. 446–79.

Goubert, Pierre. *Beauvais et le Beauvaisis au XVIIe siècle*. Paris, 1960.

Gresset, Maurice. *Gens de justice à Besançon: De la conquête par Louis XIV à la Révolution française, 1674–1789*. Paris, 1978.

———. *Le monde judiciaire à Besançon: De la conquête par Louis XIV à la Révolution française (1674–1789)*. Lille, 1975.

Gruder, Vivian R. *The Royal Provincial Intendants: A Governing Elite in Eighteenth-Century France*. Ithaca, N.Y., 1968.

Guéry, A. "Les finances de la monarchie française sous l'Ancien Régime." *Annales E.S.C.* 33 (1978):216–39.

Gutton, Jean-Pierre. *La sociabilité villageoise dans l'ancienne France*. Paris, 1979.

———. *La société et les pauvres: L'exemple de la généralité de Lyon, 1534–1789*. Paris, 1971.

———. *Villages du Lyonnais sous la monarchie (XVIe–XVIIIe siècles)*. Lyon, 1978.

Guyot, Joseph Nicholas. *Répertoire universel et raisonné de jurisprudence civile, criminelle, canonique, et bénéficiale*. 17 vols. Paris, 1784–1785.

Hanotaux, Gabriel. *Origines de l'institution des intendants de provinces*. Paris, 1884.

Hardy, G. "L'administration des paroisses au XVIIIe siècle." *Revue d'histoire moderne* 15 (1911):7–23.

Heinrichs, E., S. Eberhard, and R. Vierhous, eds. *De l'Ancien Régime à la Révolution française.* Göttingen, 1978.

Henriot, M. "Le partage des communaux en Côte-d'Or sous la Révolution: L'exemple du district d'Arnay." *Annales de Bourgogne* 19 (1947):262–73.

Higonnet, P. L.-R. *Pont-de-Montvert: Social Structure and Politics in a French Village, 1700–1914.* Cambridge, Mass., 1971.

Hoffman, Philip T. "Taxes and Agrarian Lands in Early Modern France: Land Sales, 1550–1730." *Journal of Economic History* 46 (March 1986):37–55.

Hufton, Olwen H. *The Poor of Eighteenth-Century France, 1750–1789.* Oxford, 1974.

Isambert, Jourdan, and Decrusy, eds. *Recueil général des anciennes lois françaises depuis l'an 420 jusqu'à la Révolution de 1789.* 29 vols. Paris, 1821–1833.

Jacquart, J. *La crise rurale en Ile-de-France (1550–1670).* Paris, 1974.

Janniaux, G. *Essai sur l'amodiation en Bourgogne.* Dijon, 1906.

Jones, E. L., ed. *Agriculture and Economic Growth in England, 1650–1815.* London, 1967.

Jones, P. M. *Politics and Rural Society: The Southern Massif Central, 1750–1880.* Cambridge, 1985.

Kagan, Richard L. "Law Students and Careers in Eighteenth-Century France." *Past and Present* 68 (Aug. 1975):38–72.

Kaplan, Steven L. *Bread, Politics, and Political Economy in the Reign of Louis XV.* The Hague, 1976.

———. *Provisioning Paris.* Ithaca, N.Y., 1984.

Kerridge, Eric. *Agrarian Problems in the Sixteenth Century and After.* London, 1969.

Kierstead, Raymond F., ed. *State and Society in Seventeenth-Century France.* New York, 1975.

Labrousse, C. E. *La crise de l'économie française à la fin de l'Ancien Régime et au début de la Révolution française.* Paris, 1944.

———. *Esquisse du mouvement des prix et des revenus en France au XVIIIe siècle.* Paris, 1933.

Laurent, R. *L'agriculture en Côte-d'Or pendant la première moitié du XIXe siècle.* Dijon, 1931.

———. "La lutte pour l'individualisme agraire dans la France du premier Empire." *Annales de Bourgogne* 22 (1950):81–101.

———. *Les vignerons de la Côte-d'Or au XIXe siècle.* 2 vols. Paris, 1958.

Lefebvre, Georges. *La grande peur.* Paris, 1932.

———. *Les paysans du nord pendant la Révolution française.* Reprint. Bari, 1959.

———. "La place de la Révolution dans l'histoire agraire de la France." *Annales d'histoire économique et sociale* 1 (1929):506–23.

———. *Quatre-vingt-neuf.* Paris, 1939. Reprint. Ed. A. Soboul. Paris, 1970.

———. *La Révolution française.* 3d ed. Paris, 1963.

LeGoff, T. J. A., and D. M. G. Sutherland. "The Revolution and the Rural Communities in Eighteenth-Century Brittany." *Past and Present* 62 (Feb. 1974):96–119.

Lemarchand, G. "Le XVIIe et le XVIIIe siècles en France: Bilan et perspectives de recherches." *Annales historiques de la Révolution française* 198 (1969):642–59.

———. "Le féodalisme dans la France rurale des temps modernes." *Annales historiques de la Révolution française* 195 (1969):77–138.

Le Roy Ladurie, Emmanuel. *L'âge classique des paysans, 1340–1789.* Vol. 2 of *Histoire de la France rurale.* Paris, 1975.

———. *Les paysans de Languedoc.* 2 vols. Paris, 1966.

———. "Révoltes et contestations rurales en France de 1675 à 1788." *Annales E.S.C.* 29 (Jan.–Feb. 1974):6–22.

———. *Le territoire de l'historien.* Paris, 1971.

Le Roy Ladurie, Emmanuel, and J. Goy. "Première esquisse d'une conjoncture du produit décimal et dominal: Fin du moyen-âge au XVIIIe siècle." In *Les fluctuations du produit de la dîme.* Paris, 1972.

LeTrosne, Guillaume François. *De l'administration provinciale et de la réforme de l'impôt.* Paris, 1779.

———. *La liberté du commerce des grains, toujours utile et jamais nuisible.* Paris, 1765.

Ligeron, L. "L'assolement dans la vallée moyenne de la Saône." *Annales de Bourgogne* 44 (1972):5–64.

———. "Les dettes des communautés du bailliage de Dijon au XVIIe siècle." *Annales de Bourgogne* 53 (1981):65–79.

Ligou, D. "Les élus généraux de Bourgogne et les charges municipales de 1692 à 1789." In *Actes du 90e Congrès national des sociétés savantes: Histoire moderne et contemporaine (Nice, 1965),* pp. 95–119. Paris, 1966.

———. "Les états de Bourgogne et les problèmes fiscaux à la fin du dix-huitième siècle." In *Mélanges Antonio Marengiu,* pp. 97–128. Palermo, 1967.

Livet, Georges. *L'intendance d'Alsace sous Louis XIV (1648–1715).* Strasbourg, 1956.

———. *Les intendants d'Alsace et leur oeuvre, 1648–1789.* Strasbourg, 1948.

Logette, Aline. "Quelques nouvelles sources pour l'administration des finances à la fin du XVIII siècle." *Revue historique de droit français et étranger* 47 (Sept. 1969):409–40.

Louis XIV. *Mémoires de Louis XIV.* Ed. Jean Lognon. Paris, 1927.

Loutchitsky, J. "Les classes paysannes en France au XVIIIe siècle." *Revue d'histoire moderne et contemporaine* 15 (1910):277–323; 16 (1911):5–26.

———. "De la petite propriété en France avant la Révolution et de la vente des biens nationaux." *Revue historique* 59 (1895):71–107.

———. *L'état des classes agricoles en France à la veille de la Révolution.* Paris, 1911.

———. *La propriété paysanne en France à la veille de la Révolution.* Paris, 1912.

Loyseau, Charles. *Les oeuvres de M. Charles Loyseau.* Lyon, 1701.

McCloskey, Donald. "The Economics of Enclosure: A Market Analysis." In William N. Parker and Eric L. Jones, eds., *European Peasants and Their Markets.* Princeton, N.J., 1975.

———. "The Persistence of English Common Fields." In William N. Parker and Eric L. Jones, eds., *European Peasants and Their Markets.* Princeton, N.J., 1975.

Major, J. Russell. "Henry IV and Guyenne: A Study Concerning Origins of Royal Absolutism." *French Historical Studies* 4 (1966):363–83.

———. *Representative Government in Early Modern France.* New Haven, Conn., 1980.

Marion, Marcel. *Dictionnaire des institutions de la France aux XVIIe et XVIIIe siècles.* Paris, 1923, 1968.

———. *Histoire financière de la France depuis 1715.* 6 vols. Paris, 1914–1926.

———. *Les impôts directs de l'Ancien Régime, principalement au XVIIIe siècle.* Paris, 1910.

———. *Les impôts directs sous l'Ancien Régime.* Paris, 1914.

Martin, A. *Les milices provinciales en Bourgogne (1688–1791).* Dijon, 1929.

Martin-Lorber, O. "Une communauté d'habitants dans une seigneurie de Cîteaux au XIIIe siècle." *Annales de Bourgogne* 30 (1958):7–36.

Matthews, George T. *The Royal General Farms in Eighteenth-Century France.* New York, 1958.

Mestre, J. L. *Un droit administratif à la fin de l'Ancien Régime: Le contentieux des communautés de Provence.* Paris, 1976.

Meuvret, J. *Etudes d'histoire économique: Recueil d'articles.* Paris, 1971.

———. "Histoire des prix des céréales en France dans la seconde moitié du XVIIe siècle." *Mélanges d'histoire sociale* 5 (1944):27–44.

Meyer, J. "Finances, politiques, et économies dans la seconde moitié du XVIIe siècle (Note critique)." *Annales E.S.C.* 34 (Feb.–March 1979): 355–63.

———. *La noblesse bretonne au XVIIIe siècle.* 2 vols. Paris, 1966.

Michaud-Quantin, Pierre. *Universitas: Expressions du mouvement communautaire dans le moyen âge latin.* Paris, 1970.

Moore, Barrington, Jr. *Social Origins of Dictatorship and Democracy: Lord and Peasant in the Making of the Modern World.* Boston, 1966.

Moreau, Henri. "Note sur la situation des subdélégués de l'intendant en Bourgogne au dix-huitième siècle." *Annales de Bourgogne* 26 (1954):161–64.

———. "Le rôle des subdélégués au dix-huitième siècle: Justice, police, affaires militaires." *Annales de Bourgogne* 29 (1957):225–56.

———. "Les subdélégués et l'administration des communautés: L'exemple de la subdélégation de Beaune." *Annales de Bourgogne* 31 (1959):99–109.

Morineau, M. "Budgets de l'état et gestion des finances royales en France au dix-huitième siècle." *Revue historique* 239 (Oct.–Dec. 1980), pp. 289–337.

———. *Les faux-semblants d'un démarrage économique: Agriculture et démographie en France au XVIIIe siècle.* Paris, 1971.

———. "Prix et 'révolution agricole.'" *Annales E.S.C.* 24 (March–April 1969):403–23.

———. "Y a-t-il eu une révolution agricole en France au XVIIIe siècle?" *Revue historique* 239 (1968):299–326.

Mousnier, Roland. *Fureurs paysannes.* Paris, 1967.

———. *Les institutions de la France sous la monarchie absolue, 1598–1789.* Paris, 1974.

———. *La plume, la faucille, et le marteau: Institutions et société en France de Moyen Age à la Révolution.* Paris, 1970.

Necker, J. *De l'administration des finances de la France.* 3 vols. Paris, 1784.

North, Douglass C. *Structure and Change in Economic History.* New York, 1981.

Pagès, Georges. "Essai sur l'évolution des institutions administratives en France du commencement du XVIe siècle à la fin du XVIIe." *Revue d'histoire moderne* 7 (1932):8–57.

Palmer, Robert R. *The Age of the Democratic Revolution.* 2 vols. Princeton, N.J., 1959–1964.

———. "Georges Lefebvre: The Peasants and the French Revolution." *Journal of Modern History* 31 (1959):329–42.

Parker, David. "The Social Foundation of French Absolutism, 1610–1630." *Past and Present* 53 (1971):67–89.

Poitrineau, A. *La vie rurale en Basse Auvergne au XVIIIe siècle.* 2 vols. Paris, 1965.

Poix de Freminville, Edmé de la. *La pratique universelle pour la rénovation des terriers et des droits seigneuriaux.* 2d ed. 5 vols. Paris, 1752–1757.

———. *Traité de jurisprudence sur l'origine et le gouvernement des communes ou communaux des habitants des paroisses aux seigneuries.* Paris, 1763.

———. *Traité général du gouvernement des biens et affaires des communautés et habitants des villes, bourgs, villages, et paroisses du royaume*. Paris, 1760.

Popkin, Samuel L. *The Rational Peasant: The Political Economy of Rural Society in Vietnam*. Berkeley and Los Angeles, 1979.

Porshnev, Boris. "The Legend of the Seventeenth Century in French History." *Past and Present* 8 (Nov. 1955):15–27.

———. *Les soulèvements populaires en France de 1623 à 1648*. Paris, 1963.

Posner, Richard A. "A Theory of Primitive Society, with Special Reference to Law." *Journal of Law and Economics* 23 (Oct. 1980):1–53.

Prouhet, D. "Contribution à l'étude des assemblées générales des communautés d'habitants en France sous l'Ancien Régime." *Mémoires de la société antiquaire de l'Ouest*, 2d ser., 26 (1902).

Quesnay, François. *Oeuvres*. Ed. Daire. Paris, 1846.

Ranum, Orest. *Richelieu and the Councillors of Louis XIII: A Study of the Secretaries of State and Superintendents of Finance in the Ministry of Richelieu, 1635–1642*. Oxford, 1963.

———. "Richelieu and the Great Nobility: Some Aspects of Early Modern Political Motives." *French Historical Studies* 3 (1963):184–204.

Recht, Pierre. *Les biens communaux du Namurois et leur partage à la fin du XVIIIe siècle*. Brussels, 1950.

Renouvin, M. P. *Les assemblées provinciales de 1787*. Paris, 1921.

Richard, Jean. "Les états de Bourgogne." In *Recueil de la Société Jean-Bodin: Gouvernés et gouvernants*, 3:299–324. Brussels, 1966.

———. *Histoire de la Bourgogne*. Toulouse, 1978.

Richet, D. "Croissance et blocage en France du XVe au XVIIIe siècle." *Annales E.S.C.*, 23 (July–Aug. 1968):759–87.

———. *La France moderne: L'esprit des institutions*. Paris, 1973.

Ricommard, Julien. "L'édit d'avril 1704 et l'érection en titre d'office des subdélégués des intendants." *Revue historique* 195 (1945):123–39.

———. "Les subdélégués des intendants aux dix-septième et dix-huitième siècles." *L'information historique* 24 (1962):190–95.

Roberts, Michael. "The Military Revolution, 1560–1660." In *Essays in Swedish History*, pp. 195–225. London, 1967.

Robin, R. *La société française à la veille de la Révolution: Semur-en-Auxois*. Paris, 1970.

Root, Hilton L. "Absolutism and Village Corporatism." In *Proceedings of the Ninth Annual Meeting of the Western Society for French History*, Lawrence, Kansas, 1982, pp. 110–15.

———. "En Bourgogne: L'état et la communauté rurale, 1661–1789." *Annales E.S.C.* 37 (March–April 1982):288–302.

———. "Challenging the Seigneurie: Community and Contention on the Eve of the French Revolution." *Journal of Modern History* 57 (Dec. 1985):652–81.

Roupnel, G. *Histoire de la campagne française.* Paris, 1932.

———. *La ville et la campagne au XVIIe siècle: Etude sur les populations du pays dijonnais.* Paris, 1922. 2d ed. 1955.

Rousseau, Jean-Jacques. *The Social Contract,* Trans. Maurice Cranston. New York, 1968.

Saint-Hilaire. "Mémoire sur les communaux." *Journal d'agriculture* (July 1767).

Saint-Jacob, Pierre de. "L'assolement en Bourgogne au XVIIIe siècle." *Etudes rurales* (1935), pp. 207–19.

———. "Deux textes relatifs à des fondations de villages bourguignons." *Annales de Bourgogne* 14 (1942):219–26, 314–23.

———. *Documents relatifs à la communauté villageoise en Bourgogne du XVIIe siècle à la Révolution.* Dijon, 1962.

———. "L'égalation du cens." *MSHDB* 8 (1940–1941):28–33.

———. "Etudes sur l'ancienne communauté rurale en Bourgogne." *Annales de Bourgogne* 13 (1941):169–202; 15 (1943):173–84; 18 (1946): 237–50; 25 (1953):225–40.

———. "Les grands problèmes de l'histoire des communaux en Bourgogne." *Annales de Bourgogne* 20 (1948):114–26.

———. "Histoire économique et sociale dans les archives de la jurisdiction consulaire de Dijon." *Bulletin de la Société d'histoire moderne* (Oct. 1957).

———. *Les paysans de la Bourgogne du nord au dernier siècle de l'Ancien Régime.* Dijon, 1960.

———. "La rénovation des terriers à la fin de l'Ancien Régime en Bourgogne." *MSHDB* 13 (1950–1951):302–7.

Saint-Pierre. *Projet de taille tarifée.* 1723.

Sallmann, J. M. "Les biens communaux et la 'réaction seigneuriale' en Artois." *Revue du Nord* 58 (1976): 209–25.

Sée, H. *Economic and Social Conditions in France during the Eighteenth Century.* New York, 1927.

———. "Une enquête sur la vaine pâture et le droit de parcours à la fin du règne de Louis XV." *Revue du XVIIIe siècle* (1913), pp. 265–78.

———. *Esquisse d'une histoire du régime agraire en Europe aux XVIIIe et XIXe siècles.* Paris, 1921.

———. *La France économique et sociale au XVIIIe siècle.* Paris, 1967.

———. "Le partage des biens communaux à la fin de l'Ancien Régime." *Nouvelle revue de droit français et étranger* (1923), pp. 47–81.

———. "Quelques remarques sur l'origine des biens communaux en France." *Revue historique de droit français et étranger,* 4th ser., 3 (1924):120–29.

———. "La question de la vaine pâture en France à la fin de l'Ancien Régime." *Revue d'histoire économique et sociale* (1914), pp. 3–25.

———. *La vie économique et les classes sociales au XVIIIe siècle.* Paris, 1924.

Sheppard, Thomas F. *Loumarin in the Eighteenth Century: A Study of a French Village*. Baltimore, 1971.

Skocpol, Theda. *States and Social Revolutions*. Cambridge, 1979.

Slicher van Bath, B. H. *The Agrarian History of Western Europe, A.D. 500–1850*. New York, 1963.

Soboul, Albert. "A propos d'une thèse récente sur le mouvement paysan dans la Révolution française." *Annales historiques de la Révolution française* 211 (1973):85–101.

———. *La civilisation de la Révolution française*. Vol. 1, *La crise de l'Ancien Régime*. Paris, 1970.

———. "La communauté rurale (XVIIe–XIXe siècles): Problèmes de base." *Revue de synthèse* 78 (1957):283–307.

———. *Comprendre la Révolution: Problèmes politiques de la Révolution française*. Paris, 1981.

———. "De la pratique des terriers à la veille de la Révolution." *Annales E.S.C.* 19 (Nov.–Dec. 1964):1049–65.

———. "The French Rural Community in the Eighteenth and Nineteenth Centuries." *Past and Present* 10 (Nov. 1956):78–96.

———, ed. *Contributions à l'histoire paysanne de la Révolution française*. Paris, 1977.

Taine, Hippolyte. *L'Ancien Régime*. Paris, 1875.

Taisand, Pierre. *Coutumes générales du pays et duché de Bourgogne*. Dijon, 1698.

———. *Traité des mésus à l'usage du duché de Bourgogne*. Dijon, 1772.

———. *Traité politique et économique des chetels*. Dijon, 1765.

Taylor, G. V. "Revolutionary and Nonrevolutionary Content in the Cahiers of 1789." *French Historical Studies* 7 (1972):479–502.

———. "Types of Capitalism in Eighteenth-Century France." *English Historical Review* 313 (July 1964):478–97.

Temple, Nora. "The Control and Exploitation of French Towns during the Ancien Régime." *History* 51 (Feb. 1966):16–34.

Thompson, E. P. "The Moral Economy of the English Crowd in the Eighteenth Century." *Past and Present* 50 (1971):71–136.

———. *Whigs and Hunters*. New York, 1975.

Tilly, Charles. *The Contentious French*. Cambridge, Mass., 1985.

———. *From Mobilization to Revolution*. Reading, Mass., 1978.

———. *The Vendée*. Cambridge, Mass., 1964.

———, ed. *The Formation of National States in Western Europe*. Princeton, N.J., 1975.

Tilly, L. A. "The Food Riot as a Form of Political Conflict in France." *Journal of Interdisciplinary History* 2 (1971):23–58.

Tocqueville, Alexis de. *L'Ancien Régime et la Révolution*. 2 vols. Paris, 1965.

Toutain, J. C. *Le produit de l'agriculture française de 1700 à 1958*. 2 vols. Paris, 1961.

Turgot, Anne-Robert-Jacques. *Oeuvres*. Ed. Gustave Schelle. 5 vols. Paris, 1913–1923.

Usher, Abbott Payson. *The History of the Grain Trade in France, 1400–1710*. Cambridge, 1913.

Varenne de Fenille, Philibert Charles Marie. *Observations, expériences, et mémoires sur l'agriculture*. Lyons, 1789.

Vauban, Sébastien Le Prestre de. *Projet de dîme royale*. Ed. Coornaert. Paris, 1933.

Vovelle, Michel. "Structures agraires en Provence à la fin de l'Ancien Régime." In *Communautés du Sud*, 1:233–88. Paris, 1975.

Weulersse, G. *Le mouvement physiocratique en France (1756–1770)*. Paris, 1910.

———. *Les physiocrates*. Paris, 1931.

———. *La physiocratie à la fin du règne de Louis XV (1770–1774)*. Paris, 1959.

———. *La physiocratie sous les ministères de Turgot et Necker*. Paris, 1950.

Wolf, John B. *Louis XIV*. New York, 1968.

Wolfe, Martin. "French Views on Wealth and Taxes from the Middle Ages to the Old Regime." *Journal of Economic History* 20 (1966): 466–83.

———. *The Fiscal System of Renaissance France*. New Haven, Conn., 1972.

Wordie, J. R. "The Chronology of English Enclosure, 1500–1914." *The Economic History Review*, 2d ser., 36 (Nov. 1983):483–505.

Yelling, J. A. *Common Field and Enclosure in England, 1450–1850*. London, 1977.

Young, A. *Travels in France*. Dublin, 1793.

Zeller, Gaston. *Les institutions de la France au XVIe siècle*. Paris, 1948.

Index

Absolutism, 103, 208–14; and attacks on rural democracy by revolutionary opponents, 67; local political benefits of, 226, 232; and powers of intendants in provinces, 220; vs. royal edict of 1787 on representative government, 99–100; and state finance under Louis XIV, 26, 208–14, 219; and theory on centralized extraction of peasant surplus production, 228–29; and village councils of notables, 98

Administration, local: advantages of collective tax responsibility for, 31–35; democratic procedures in, after French Revolution, 66; effect of state bureaucratic growth on, 202–3, 207–8, 213, 226–28; and elections of village officials, 64; factionalism limited in, 70–74, 78, 81–82, 85, 91, 92; governance by majority rule in, 70–73, 113, 122; hierarchy of, 98–99; and intendant supervision of village court action, 193–202; methods for effective royal supervision of, 88–97; political equality in, before French Revolution, 70–73, 75–76; and proposals for councils of notables, 227, 232; royal edict of 1787 for reform of, 98–100; seigneurial authority in, eroded by state, 45–61, 64–65;

state control of, and royal tax collection, 28–30; state dominance of, and control of communal property, 36–40; state fiscal policies, and erosion of seigneurial authority in, 211–13; and state strategies to limit political power of magnates, 25–30; and state support of peasantry in disputes with seigneurie, 45–48, 55–61; theory on increased seigneurial authority in, 61–64; and *tutelle*, 36, 214; and village political strength, 226–28. *See also* Village assemblies

Administration, royal. *See* State

Administrative archives, 11, 12

Agencourt (village), 54

Age of Democratic Revolution, The (R. R. Palmer), 66

Agrarian reform, 18–19, 105–12; vs. communal property rights, 215–18; financial policies of state vs., 217–18, 237–40, 241; intendant vs. royal policies on, 105, 113–14, 123–33; legislation on, 236–37, 239; limits on state efforts for, 205, 206, 214–18, 227–28; obstacles to, 150–54, 214–18, 227–28, 237–40, 241; and partition of communal lands, 123–33; peasant collective traditions vs., 27n5, 141–54 passim, 150–54; reasons for, 106–8; and Revolutionary

261

Compositor: Huron Valley Graphics
Text: Linotron 202 Trump Medieval
Display: Trump Medieval
Printer: Princeton University Press / Printing Div.
Binder: Princeton University Press / Printing Div.